10 0559658 7

UNIVERSITY OF NOTTINGHAM

WITHDRAWN
FROM THE

D1577099

Managing Change in the Public Services

Managing Change in the Public Services

Edited by

Mike Wallace
Michael Fertig
Eugene Schneller

University of Nottingham
Hallward Library

Blackwell
Publishing

© 2007 by Blackwell Publishing Ltd
except for editorial material and organization © 2007 by Mike Wallace, Michael Fertig, and Eugene Schneller

BLACKWELL PUBLISHING
350 Main Street, Malden, MA 02148-5020, USA
9600 Garsington Road, Oxford OX4 2DQ, UK
550 Swanston Street, Carlton, Victoria 3053, Australia

The right of Mike Wallace, Michael Fertig, and Eugene Schneller to be identified as the Authors of the Editorial Material in this Work has been asserted in accordance with the UK Copyright, Designs, and Patents Act 1988.

All rights reserved. No part of this publication may be reproduced, stored in a retrieval system, or transmitted, in any form or by any means, electronic, mechanical, photocopying, recording or otherwise, except as permitted by the UK Copyright, Designs, and Patents Act 1988, without the prior permission of the publisher.

First published 2007 by Blackwell Publishing Ltd

1   2007

Library of Congress Cataloging-in-Publication Data

Managing change in the public services / edited by Mike Wallace, Michael Fertig, Eugene Schneller.
    p. cm.
  Includes bibliographical references and index.
  ISBN-13: 978-1-4051-3548-1 (hardcover : alk. paper)
    ISBN-10: 1-4051-3548-4 (hardcover : alk. paper)   1. Organizational change—Management.
2. Public administration.   3. Educational change.   4. Health care reform.   I. Wallace, Mike, 1950–   II. Fertig, Michael, lecturer in education.   III. Schneller, Eugene Stewart.

JF1525.O73M385 2007
352.3′67—dc22

1005596587

2006012849

A catalogue record for this title is available from the British Library.

Set in 10/12.5pt Palatino
by Graphicraft Limited, Hong Kong
Printed in Singapore
by Markono Print Media Pte Ltd

The publisher's policy is to use permanent paper from mills that operate a sustainable forestry policy, and which has been manufactured from pulp processed using acid-free and elementary chlorine-free practices. Furthermore, the publisher ensures that the text paper and cover board used have met acceptable environmental accreditation standards.

For further information on
Blackwell Publishing, visit our website:
www.blackwellpublishing.com

CONTENTS

CONTRIBUTORS

Ann Casebeer, Associate Professor, Department of Community Health Sciences and Associate Director, Center for Health and Policy Studies, University of Calgary, Alberta, Canada.

Jean-Louis Denis, Professeur Titulaire, Département d'Administration de la Santé, Université de Montréal, Québec, Canada.

Michael Fertig, Lecturer in Education, University of Bath, UK.

William Firestone, Professor and Director, Center for Educational Policy Analysis, Graduate School of Education, Rutgers University, New Brunswick, USA.

Jean Hartley, Professor of Organizational Analysis, Institute of Governance and Public Management, Warwick Business School, University of Warwick, Coventry, UK (AIM Public Service Lead Fellow 2003–5).

Eric Hoyle, Emeritus Professor and Senior Fellow, Graduate School of Education, University of Bristol, UK.

Lise Lamothe, Aggregate Professeure, Département d'Administration de la Santé, Université de Montréal, Québec, Canada.

Ben Levin, Deputy Minister of Education, Ontario Ministry of Education, Canada.

Karen Seashore Louis, Rodney S. Wallace Professor of Teaching and Learning, University of Minnesota, Minneapolis, USA.

Lyndsay Rashman, Senior Research Associate, Institute of Governance and Public Management, Warwick Business School, University of Warwick, Coventry, UK.

Eugene Schneller, Professor, School of Health Management and Policy, W.P. Carey School of Business, Arizona State University, Tempe, USA.

Dorothy Shipps, Assistant Professor of Education, Teachers College, Columbia University, New York, USA.

Paul Thomas, Duff Roblin Professor of Government, St. John's College, University of Manitoba, Winnipeg, Canada.

Mike Wallace, Professor of Public Management, University of Cardiff, UK (AIM Public Service Fellow 2003–5).

MANAGING PUBLIC SERVICE CHANGE OR COPING WITH ITS COMPLEXITY?

Mike Wallace, Michael Fertig and Eugene Schneller

What makes public service change increasingly complex to manage? How do people involved in the change process cope with this new complexity? How could the management of public service change be rendered more effective? Where might practically oriented academic enquiry productively go from here? The purpose of this book is to make a start on tackling these questions in order to put complexity more firmly on the academic and policy agenda as a key aspect of change management which many frontline professionals, managers or policy-makers would readily recognize from their daily experience.

The burgeoning complexity of change affecting the public services across many countries is widely acknowledged. An issue of self-evident practical and policy significance is therefore how to maximize the capacity to deal successfully with this complexity, and where possible to keep complexity within bounds. Academic research and theory building have potential to inform the thinking of practitioners and policy-makers alike, so that their efforts to improve the management of public service change are realistic about what can and cannot be done. Accordingly, the contributors to this book bring to bear a range of theoretical orientations, literatures and experiences as researchers and change facilitators in synthesizing what is already known, opening up ideas about what needs to be investigated further, and pointing towards promising directions for improving practice.

The term 'managing change', while long established, is something of a misnomer. It still tends to carry the beguiling connotation that change is controllable, if only managers knew how. But the management of contemporary public service change means managing the relatively unmanageable. The sheer scope, pace, ambiguity and multiplicity of change outstrip the capacity of any individual or group to ensure directive control and certainty of outcomes in practice, whatever their formal position of authority or span of control in principle.

On the other hand, there is no shortage of evidence from different countries and service sectors that public service provision is changing fast. Public service change demonstrably does occur, even if the outcomes are not always what instigators envisioned. People based at different levels of public service systems do cope with the complexity of change, one way or another, despite their inherently limited capacity for control. So there must be some possibilities for managing public service change more or less effectively. Given this limited manageability, effectiveness seems likely to mean making the most of whatever modest possibilities for maximizing control do exist within these limits. Attempts to improve the manageability of public service change might profitably focus on them. But to be in a position to identify such possibilities requires a prior investment in deepening our understanding of the complexity of change and of coping strategies as a phenomenon. That is what this book is about.

The research leading directly to the present volume has its origins in Mike Wallace's work to develop an empirically grounded and social science-informed approach for understanding complex educational change. This focus has since broadened to cover public service change. The approach centres on the complexity, contradictions and unintended consequences of change, alongside its degree of coherence. Complex change consists of multiple parts, and programmatic change adds further complexity in comprising a package of planned changes. The relative unmanageability of complex and programmatic change is conceived as being rooted in the increase that the change process induces in the ambiguity (or uncertainty of meaning) that is endemic to organizational life. But effective coping implies maximizing the potential for manageability within the limits of human agency (the ability to choose between alternative courses of action). This approach is designed to provide a basis for context-sensitive practical ideas on how coping capacity might be developed across public service organizations and systems.

The initial investigation was a sizeable qualitative study (involving 235 interviews) of large-scale reorganization of schools in England during the mid-1990s. Reorganization was conceived as an instance of complex educational change (Wallace and Pocklington 2002). The research tracked two local education authority initiatives taken under central government pressure to reduce the surplus student capacity in schools within their jurisdiction. The ensuing initiatives were introduced in overlapping phases, entailing extensive local consultation and the implementation of school closures, mergers, new building and refurbishment, and development support for staff in the post-reorganization schools. These initiatives were also introduced in the context of a raft of central government education reforms and the rest of the ongoing work of normal service provision.

The central concern of that investigation lay not with reorganization and its specific context as such, but in taking the empirical case as a starting point for the relatively inductive exploration of patterns in its complexity with management implications, and of the extent and limits of its manageability. The starting point was a pluralistic theoretical orientation based on the expression of agency within broad structural limits (governing what is considered doable and even thinkable). It enabled the research to be focused from the outset on the diversity of perceptions and actions of the people at different system levels who were struggling to make sense of the reorganization process.

The approach to data collection and analysis was inductive within this guiding orientation. The aim was to identify patterns in the complexity of reorganization and how it was managed within and between system levels, but without pre-specifying what these patterns might be. Rounds of data collection and analysis were iterative, analysis feeding back into subsequent data collection in order to ascertain the characteristics of emergent patterns. They, in turn, formed the basis for the development of theoretical ideas about what makes change complex to manage and ways in which people cope with it.

This relatively inductive strategy was adopted as a conscious move away from two dominant approaches towards theorizing the complexity of change at the time. One was to acknowledge complexity but then to ignore it, basing prescriptions for practice on an unrealistically rationalistic understanding of change and of the capacity of policy-makers and managers for 'command and control'. Little account was taken of the likelihood that the increasing complexity of the change phenomenon might affect the way it was and could be managed. The other approach addressed complexity head on. But prescriptions were derived deductively by translating ideas wholesale from complexity theory being developed in mathematics and natural scientific fields of enquiry. Both approaches had neglected the intermediate inductive step of empirical research to detect patterns in the complexity of public service change and managers' coping strategies. Real-world findings could have offered a basis for assessing the applicability of their advocates' preferred theoretical frameworks, whether old or new.

Outcomes of the research into school reorganization provided the main source of ideas for an emergent conception of complex educational change embodying characteristics of complexity with management implications. A practical planning framework derived from it included themes for rendering change as manageable as possible.

Origin and Focus of the Book

Wallace was subsequently awarded a Public Services Senior Fellowship within the ESRC/EPSRC AIM (Advanced Institute of Management Research) Initiative during 2003–5 (see Hartley and Pike 2005). Fellowship activity focused on the question: how might the initial conception of complex educational change and an associated practical planning framework, derived inductively from previous research, be refined to extend their applicability to other changes in different public service settings? The intention was to contribute towards a stronger basis for future research, and towards practical guidance on developing the capacity to manage complex and programmatic change.

While the focus on complexity of change was generic, to keep the fellowship activities manageable it was decided to concentrate empirically on education and health. As the largest and most complex public services, education and health seem likely to offer the most potent insights into the complexity of change and strategies for coping with it. These two services differ in many important respects, such as the degree of technical specialization, reliance on advanced technology, and the compulsion or entitlement to take up provision. But the complexity of education and health services is broadly similar at a high level of abstraction in ways that are significant for a focus on the complexity of change. In terms of ongoing provision, parallels include the scale of their normal operation; their highly professionalized staffing; the variety of their governance arrangements; the diversity of their service providing and administrative organizations; the range of their services; and their electoral vote-winning potential as major areas of domestic policy. In terms of the complexity of change they include the magnitude and expense of government-driven reform programmes affecting service provision, the measurement of performance and accountability, service governance and involvement of the private sector, organizational management and the management of change itself; the acceleration of technological innovation and its accompanying demand on limited budgets; and the exponential rise in public expectations concerning the quality and quantity of service provision to which they should have access.

A further pragmatic decision was to explore change in these two services within Anglo-American contexts. The reasoning was to keep the range of contextual variables within manageable bounds. At the same time, plentiful scope was offered for comparison, since many of these variables are expressed differently at the level of detail because of divergence in the evolution of each country's public services. Table I.1 gives a sense of some of the contrasts (but it should be borne in mind that the entries are so condensed that they omit much of the detail and diversity in each national and service setting – see also Levin 2001; Scott 2001).

The education and healthcare systems of the USA, Canada and the UK feature the high level of sophistication made possible in wealthy western countries; they have a long history, so the accretion of past changes has a strong impact on the parameters for contemporary change; they have contrasting administrative and governance structures reflecting their different (yet partly interconnected) national heritage; these structural arrangements differentially affect the scope for reform and emergent change; the national and regional governments engage in significant mutual 'policy-borrowing', monitoring developments in each country, exchanging information and importing and adapting ideas that appear to have worked; and, partly in consequence, there is significant overlap in the content of planned changes and responses to unplanned changes featuring in each system.

The AIM fellowship made possible exchange and collaboration with academic experts from North America (all of whom are contributors to this volume) and from the UK, consultation with senior practitioners from the UK education and health services, and dialogue between academics and senior practitioners. Fellowship activities included:

Table I.1 Contextual factors affecting Anglo-American public education and health care

Contextual factor	USA	Canada	United Kingdom
Government	Federal republic, 50 states	Confederation of 10 provinces, 3 territories	2 countries, 2 principalities
Population	295 million	33 million	60 million
Education			
Primary responsibility	State government, federal policy framework	Provincial government, some federal involvement	National governments, some devolution
Local administration	Districts, extensive delegated authority	Districts, moderate delegated authority	Local education authorities, limited delegated authority
Public and private school provision	Mainly publicly funded, publicly funded autonomous charter schools, minority of private schools	Mainly publicly funded, part-publicly funded religious schools, minority of private schools	Mainly publicly funded, minority of private schools
Percentage of publicly funded school education costs	90%	92%	88%
Percentage of publicly funded tertiary education costs	34%	61%	68%
Expenditure as percentage of GDP	5%	5%	5%
Health care			
Primary responsibility	Individuals, employers, federal assistance	Provincial government, federal policy framework	National governments, some devolution
Expenditure as percentage of GDP	15%	10%	8%

Table I.1   *(Cont'd)*

Contextual factor	USA	Canada	United Kingdom
Percentage of publicly funded health care costs	44%	71%	82%
Universal system of health care	No (approx 20% uninsured)	Yes, Medicare public insurance	Yes, National Health Service (NHS)
Funding	Private insurance, Medicare public insurance for elderly and disabled, Medicaid public insurance for poor	Medicare public insurance, some private insurance	Mainly public taxation, some private insurance
Purchasing	Employers, government, insurance companies, managed care organizations, physicians	Provincial government for all 'medically necessary' services, private insurance companies	Primary care trusts commission services overseen (in England) by strategic health authorities
Provision	Self-employed physicians, private, not-for-profit and government institutions, managed care organization facilities	Self-employed physicians, private, not-for-profit institutions	Self-employed GPs, hospital trusts and private institutions

- A critical literature review of practically oriented texts employing chaos and complexity theory deductively as a basis for prescribing public service change.
- Consultation with experts through two international expert seminars bringing North American and UK-based academics in education and health management together with senior practitioners from the UK education and health services.
- Two invitation seminars (incorporated as one day of the international expert seminars) with senior practitioners responsible for managing change at different levels of the UK education and health services, to explore the practical applicability of the framework.
- Small-scale case study research assessing the application of the initial conception and planning framework to contrasting 'extreme cases' of change in different national contexts. (One focused on the emergence of the US 'hospitalist

movement', an increasingly complex change where a hospital-based physician coordinates treatment for acutely ill patients. The other focused on the programmatic but consultative 'Kindergarten-Senior 4 Agenda' for school improvement in Manitoba, Canada.)

- Consultation with the organization theorist Professor James March about a new ironic perspective (elaborated in Chapter 4) for conceptualizing the contribution of ambiguity to complex and programmatic change.
- A think-tank exercise at the Prime Minister's Delivery Unit offices at the Treasury in London, to exchange practical ideas on managing public service change.

Presenters at the first international expert seminar shared ideas from their work on public service change, while also responding to Wallace's initial conception of complex educational change and planning framework. The North American academics and Jean Hartley, AIM Public Services Lead Fellow, were invited to revise their presentations as chapters for this book. They drew on their own work and developed their ideas in the light of the dialogue during both seminars. Wallace similarly reworked his ideas to encompass health as well as educational contexts, programmatic change and emergent change that increases in complexity. Chapters also report on other aspects of his AIM fellowship activities: the critical literature review, small-scale research, and collaboration with Eric Hoyle from the University of Bristol on theorizing the role of ambiguity in the change process.

The content of the chapters gives a sense of the exploratory nature of the seminars and other activities. The dialogue reflected allegiance to contrasting theoretical perspectives, concern with different aspects of change and experience of different national and service contexts. A mark of successful exchange when scholars and senior practitioners come together to converse about a fresh focus for enquiry and to push forward thinking is the mixture of complementarity and tension reflected in this book. The spirit of enquiry was to exchange our contrasting experiences, debate ideas with a diverse intellectual heritage and engage with contemporary practice in the UK, not to seek premature closure.

The structure of the book reflects the variety of perspectives that were brought to bear on aspects of the complexity of public service change and its management. Chapters are grouped according to the area of complexity connected with public service change that they foreground. However, it should be borne in mind that most chapters also reach into other areas. The topic itself is too vast for any chapter to focus on everything, and too interconnected for any chapter to be meaningfully confined just to one area. A brief editorial introduction to each chapter indicates how it relates to the focus of Wallace's work (elaborated in Chapter 1) on the complexity of public service change and coping strategies, which framed the exchange and collaboration with other contributors. Cross-referencing in each chapter is intended to assist readers with making connections between the topics discussed by different contributors.

Part I focuses on theorizing what makes the process of changing public service practice complex, how people actually cope with it across public service systems and so contribute to this complexity, and how they might do so more or less effectively. Part II focuses on the policy-making process that generates the complex and programmatic planned changes of major public service reform efforts, and the productive relationships between policy-makers and other stakeholder groups entailed in fostering implementation across service systems. Some groups are involved in service governance and, in a democracy, are entitled to a voice on the direction of public policy. Others are responsible for implementation of reforms, and government politicians therefore depend on them.

Part III looks at the complexity of public service change, starting from the opposite end: the service and administrative organizations where sense has to be made of external pressures for change and responses undertaken, where emergent changes in practice may spread to become more complex, and where changes in practice may be proactively encouraged and externally supported at the local level. Finally, a brief overview is offered, identifying messages across the contributions from Parts I to III that suggest some tentative answers to the questions posed at the beginning of this introduction.

Contributors were also invited to highlight in their chapter conclusion the wider implications of their work for policy and practice, and to suggest ideas for an agenda for further research and theory-building. Readers interested in investigating the management of change in the public services will find plenty of scope for making an original contribution, whether through doctoral or professionally conducted research. The focus of this book on the complexity of the change process, spanning political agenda setting to sense making in service organizations, opens up a substantial area of enquiry which is of considerable social scientific and practical importance.

ACKNOWLEDGEMENTS

Mike Wallace's research on complex educational change was funded by a grant (reference number R00023 6059) from the Economic and Social Research Council (ESRC). The ESRC also funded his AIM Public Service Senior Fellowship activity to develop and assess the wider applicability of the emerging conception of complex change and planning framework (reference number RES-331-25-0011). He and Eric Hoyle benefited from the support of Professor James March, whose writings and conversations influenced the way in which ambiguity and limits to the manageability of change have been conceptualized. The thinking reflected in the content of various chapters was valuably informed by contributions from all the academics taking part in the two international expert seminars, the senior practitioners from the UK education and health services who joined them for the integral one-day invitation seminars, and the senior government officials who participated in the two 'think-tank' exercises. However, the ideas and opinions expressed by the various contributors to the book are, of course, theirs alone. They represent neither the views of others who took part in the AIM fellowship activities, nor the view of the ESRC.

REFERENCES

Abbott, A. (1988) *The System of Professions: An Essay on the Division of Labor.* Chicago: University of Chicago Press.

Hartley, J. and Pike, A. (eds) (2005) *Managing to Improve Public Services: A Report by the Advanced Institute of Management Research Public Service Fellows.* London: AIM.

Hoyle, E. and Wallace, M. (2005) *Educational Leadership: Ambiguity, Professionals and Managerialism.* London: Sage.

Levin, B. (2001) *Reforming Education: From Origins to Outcomes.* New York: RoutledgeFalmer.

Scott, C. (2001) *Public and Private Roles in Health Care Systems: Reform Experience in Seven OECD Countries.* Buckingham: Open University Press.

Wallace, M. and Pocklington, K. (2002) *Managing Complex Educational Change: Large-Scale Reorganization of Schools.* London: RoutledgeFalmer.

PART I

EXPLORING THE COMPLEXITY OF THE CHANGE PROCESS

CHAPTER 1

COPING WITH COMPLEX AND PROGRAMMATIC PUBLIC SERVICE CHANGE

Mike Wallace

This chapter sets the stage for other contributions to the book, foregrounding the process of changing. Mike Wallace puts forward a case for social science-informed and relatively inductive approaches to understanding and informing practice, suggesting that an emphasis on coping with the contemporary complexity of public service change is more realistic than attempting tight control over the change process and its outcomes. He argues that investigators' purpose for studying, or 'intellectual project', influences the research and theoretical questions they ask (and do not ask) about public service change, and so the range of answers they obtain. These answers inform, in turn, the sort of policy and practical implications they may identify. Wallace advocates a stronger emphasis on deepening understanding to broaden the variety of theoretical ideas and empirical findings that could valuably inform reflection on and decisions about policy and practice. Further, he advocates relatively inductive studies, which remain sensitive to the diverse contexts of public service change, to build practically oriented theory from patterns in what happens empirically. The research leading to his conception of the characteristics of complex and programmatic change with management implications was driven primarily by the intellectual project of deepening understanding.

Wallace sets out this conception and incorporates some of the ideas into a practical planning framework. It centres on the metaphor of 'orchestrating' change within and between service system administrative levels. The term captures the finding from his research that key players in diverse leadership positions can be conceived as a network. They interact, sometimes directly, but often through intermediaries, in attempting to steer the change process to realise their respective and sometimes incompatible interests. Orchestration was defined consciously to span the common conceptual divide between 'leadership' and 'management'. These terms tend to separate two dimensions of coping activity, which Wallace found empirically to be integrated. In their chapters, other contributors have both connected with and challenged these ideas.

Why Focus on Coping with Complexity?

Change of one kind or another seems, paradoxically, to be a constant which complicates organizational life across all contemporary public services to a greater or
lesser extent. There is no escape from the press of political, economic, social and
technological forces that may bring reform from without and stimulate innovation from within. There is no escape from evolutionary, unplanned change affecting services from time to time, which demands a planned response. And there is
no escape from coping with all this change alongside the maintenance of day-to-
day service provision. To adopt the term 'coping' as the central concept for conceptualizing the management of change in the public services may seem rather
downbeat. But it seems realistic and indeed mildly optimistic, given the limited
capacity for managerially controlling whether to address particular changes and,
if so, how to do so alongside everything else that must be coordinated to sustain
normal service provision. Coping implies that problems are inevitable, and not
necessarily a consequence of the wrong management strategy. Some problems will
never go away because they cannot be resolved, even in principle.

One relatively inductive investigation of local improvement efforts in US
urban high schools during the late 1980s proved instrumental in introducing the
idea of 'problem coping' as integral to educational change. The complexity of those
planned changes was perhaps moderate by today's standards, but they were still
complex enough to be deeply problematic. Louis and Miles (1990: 263) emphasize the importance of 'steady orchestration and coordination', on an ongoing basis,
to cope with diverse problems arising. The latter are intrinsic to their definition
of coping (272):

> Problems are pervasive, but not all problems get solved equally well. Some are pushed
> off, others are partially dealt with, and a few get thoughtfully dealt with so that they
> stay solved and do not recur. This variation in solution quality depends largely, we
> believe, on *coping* efforts.
>
>   By 'coping' we mean the pattern of behavior that appears when a problem is noticed
> or defined. The behavior is not necessarily deliberate, or planful, but it is addressed
> to – or at least stimulated by – the problem. It usually can be seen as a discernible
> pattern, a sort of strategy for dealing with the problem, ranging from procrastinating
> to exhorting to 'fixing the system'.

Thus the essence of problem coping is routinely to deploy a repertoire of strategies for dealing in different ways and levels of depth with aspects of work that
are neither straightforward nor fully controllable. These strategies may range from
the 'shallow', appropriate for small or transient problems (such as postponing
a decision), to the 'deep', necessary to confront more serious problems (such as
dealing with the withdrawal of external funding support for an improvement
effort). The capacity for deep coping includes being comfortable with complexity, ambiguity and risk taking. Louis and Miles regard the day-to-day orchestration

and coordination entailed in problem coping as one of several means for keeping an improvement initiative going by getting round difficulties that crop up from time to time. Problem coping does not set the direction for an improvement initiative or get it under way. So this conception of coping is at heart reactive, even though effective strategies are held to include habitually scanning for problems. But with problem coping, it is implementation problems that drive the coping response, not coping that drives implementation.

Later in this chapter the metaphor of 'orchestration' will be brought centre-stage as the overarching change management theme for coping with complex and programmatic change. But the conception of coping through orchestration to be adopted here has a more proactive aspect. Coping is not confined to scanning and responding to problems arising with a specific planned change which, according to its instigators' values, will bring improvement. In the more turbulent context of unrelenting complex and programmatic change, coping takes on a more substantial role, both driving and driven by the change process. Coping becomes a way of managing by living with the complexity of change, rather than expecting significantly to simplify it through managerial action; of getting by through dealing with its relative unmanageability, rather than being thrown when control attempts fail; of accepting a significant degree of ambiguity as normal, rather than attempting to impose unrealistic clarity of meaning; of taking calculated risks, rather than trying to play safe when the consequences of actions cannot be wholly predicted; and of seeking to increase control at the margins while going with the flow of change, rather than endeavouring to make a one-off implementation decision and then tightly to steer its course.

A key determinant of coping with the complexity of change is the high degree of ambiguity that is inevitably generated. Ambiguity implies confusion over what new practices mean and how they might be learned, unless or until they have been put into place and have become routine. Ideas connected with ambiguity informed the conceptual linkage to be discussed later between identifying characteristics of complexity of change, and change management themes to cope with this complexity. These ideas will be explored in depth in Chapter 4, as constituents of an ironic perspective that offers an insightful way of thinking about how to cope with the limited manageability of complex and programmatic public service change.

Foregrounding complexity so as to understand first, inform practice second

That the complexity of public service change is increasing seems scarcely in doubt. The pace and pervasiveness of change seems equally unlikely to subside in the foreseeable future. One has only to think of the 'big picture': the international drivers of change and political responses, directly or indirectly affecting political agenda setting for all public services (see Chapter 5). They include the imperative on governments, since the 1970s, to curb burgeoning public service expenditure, threatening to outstrip the economic expansion needed to sustain it (Foster and Plowden 1996). Concerns about the variable effectiveness of public service provision and providers' protection of their self-interests have brought demands for greater accountability and tighter specification of service provision and its management. Indeed, public service management has been the target of serial political intervention whose details vary somewhat between national contexts (Pollitt and Bouckaert 2000).

The US, Canada and the UK have long been subject to the ideologically fuelled political project of 'new public management', seeking efficiency gains and quality improvements through the introduction of business practices, strong accountability mechanisms, marketization and privatization (e.g. Osborne and Gaebler 1992). The reform thrust in the UK is now shifting towards 'post-new public management' (Ferlie, Hartley and Martin 2003). This phase entails 'managed markets', devolved governance networks and partnerships (Rhodes 1997; Newman 2001), national and local target setting, performance measurement and expanded choice for service users (Office of Public Service Reform 2002). Meanwhile, in these wealthy western countries, rising public expectations about service entitlement combine with technological advances and the altruistic interests of providers to create opportunities and pressures for innovation directed towards improving the quality, sophistication and availability of services. They also generate further vote-winning pressures to expand services and improve access while restraining the vote-losing public tax burden.

Political reforms thus interact, in turn, with emergent innovations originating at different administrative levels, whether stimulated by external pressure, the planned or serendipitous spread of ideas, the exigencies of local contextual circumstances, or the professional values and commitment of service providers. (Chapter 9 refers to an example of a formally structured and resourced central government initiative to promote the dissemination of identified 'best practice'.) Unplanned changes in the wider service environment frequently add to the press for a planned response, as where the changing demographic profile of service users affects demand. The passage of time alone brings inevitable staff turnover and mutual adjustment between existing and incoming organization members. So public service managers may have to cope simultaneously with everything from substantive reforms to improve service quality and efficiency, through management reforms to enhance service providers' capacity to implement the substantive reforms, through multiple innovations and other changes emerging within their organizations or local partnership, to coordinating and sustaining the quality of ongoing practice.

Arguably, such rapid evolution in the phenomenon of public service change begs for empirically grounded and practically relevant theoretical development that addresses this new level of complexity head on. Outmoded conceptions of change applied to the public services, such as re-engineering (e.g. Davies 1997), now look increasingly simplistic. The extensive scope for planning and managerial control of processes and outcomes that they imply lacks realism, as research on re-engineering in health care demonstrates (McNulty and Ferlie 2002). New ways of conceptualizing change are beginning to emerge, but their level of empirical grounding differs. One way forward is through in-depth exploration of what makes public service change complex to manage at the operational level, surfacing patterns in its complexity which have management implications and tracking how people actually cope with it. Pure induction is impossible, since any investigator is at least implicitly informed by preconceptions necessary for focusing any empirical enquiry. Social science offers a wealth of concepts derived from research into organizational change and policy implementation within and between organizations, which may productively frame relatively inductive research. The aim is to retain sensitivity to what research sites have to tell, inside parameters set by the initial theoretical orientation.

This approach reflects a particular 'intellectual project' (Wallace and Wray 2006) or scheme of enquiry to generate knowledge that will realize specific purposes. Five intellectual projects may be distinguished that are pursued within the field of public service management (Table 1.1). Each is driven by a different rationale

Table 1.1 Five intellectual projects pursued in the field of public service management

Intellectual project	Rationale	Typical mode of working	Value stance	Typical question
Knowledge-for-understanding	Understand through theory and research	Social science-based basic research and theory	Disinterested towards policy and practice	What happens and why?
Knowledge-for-critical evaluation	Evaluate through theory and research	Social science-based basic research and theory	Critical about policy and practice	What is wrong with what happens?
Knowledge-for-action	Inform policy makers through research and evaluation	Applied research, evaluation and development activity	Positive towards policy and improving practice	How effective are actions to improve practice?
Instrumentalism	Improve practice through training and consultancy	Designing and offering training and consultancy programmes	Positive towards policy and improving practice	How may this programme improve practice?
Reflexive action	Improve own practice through evaluation and action	Action research, basing practice on evidence	Critical of practice, positive about improving	How effective is my practice, how may I improve it?

and value stance towards the phenomenon under investigation, and by a different mode of operation in generating knowledge. Each predisposes researchers to ask different kinds of questions, which lead to different (and not necessarily compatible) answers.

The primary intellectual project underpinning the social science-based and relatively inductive approach advocated here is to develop 'knowledge-for-understanding'. The findings stand to inform the more directly practice-oriented pursuit of 'knowledge-for-action'. Since the pursuit of 'knowledge-for-understanding' is not driven by a normative interest in controlling the change process, it may add new ideas and insights to the stock-in-trade of those in search of 'knowledge-for-action'. The former approach harnesses a wider range of social scientific ideas to determine the parameters of what actually happens and what can happen within the limits of human agency (or capacity for choice of action) than the later typically does.

This stance was consciously developed as a move away from the prevalent 'knowledge-for-action' and 'instrumentalist' approaches whose concerns are more directly linked to practical application, co-production of knowledge and prescribing good practice and how to improve it. Their dominant focus on improvement according to particular stakeholders' values sometimes leads to premature and unrealistic prescription. Such a focus may, on occasion, under-represent important aspects of the phenomenon of change affecting practice and improvement efforts that a relatively more disinterested 'knowledge-for-understanding' enquiry can highlight. Such aspects include cultural pluralism about what counts as improvement, differential power to impose definitions of good and bad practice, ambiguity experienced by those caught up in change, the policy context surrounding public service practice and structural parameters that delimit human agency.

A consequence of giving primacy to 'knowledge-for-understanding' is to accord core importance to contingent contextual factors affecting what happens and what different stakeholders may perceive to work in particular settings. Since the context of any organization is unique in its details (see Chapter 6 for an elaboration of contextual components), informing practice means no more than offering research-backed ideas for managers and policy-makers to consider, rather than attempting to prescribe what they should or should not do. Those directly involved in the change process are therefore left to decide how far these ideas may have applicability and so may be worth adapting and applying to their own context.

The remainder of this chapter falls into four sections. First, the underlying theoretical orientation is briefly outlined and a conception of complex and programmatic change is discussed. Potentially generic characteristics of complexity with implications for coping strategies are tentatively identified at a high level of abstraction, as expressed in both individual and programmatic change. The orchestration metaphor, key to coping strategies, is distinguished from currently popular notions of leadership and management. Second, these characteristics of complexity and orchestration (as an overarching change management theme) are incorporated into a practical planning framework, together with subordinate change management themes and stages in the change process. The practical planning framework is put forward as an aide-mémoire, offering empirically grounded points for reflection. Finally, conclusions are drawn about the implications of the analysis for theory and research related to coping with complex and programmatic change in the public services.

A Pluralistic Orientation

The theoretical orientation framing the empirically derived conception of complex and programmatic change is itself multifaceted (see Wallace and Pocklington 2002: 44–73). First, pluralism implies that power is distributed, if unequally, throughout a service system of organizations, and is expressed as stakeholders concerned with a change interact as they seek to realize their diverse interests. All involved in the change process have some agency, giving them at least a restricted capacity to act in accordance with their perceived interests.

Second, the expression of agency in interaction entails attempting to channel the agency of others in the favoured direction through facilitative means, and to delimit it through inhibitory means where any action might transgress the limits of this favoured direction. Agency is expressed within broad structural limits governed by economic factors that constrain what is deemed feasible, and ideological factors which bound what is even conceivable.

Third, various conceptual tools provide focus on the operation of agency in meaning-making through the flow of interaction and related individual and collective learning that comprise the change process. A combined cultural and political perspective on interaction draws attention to cultural determinants of power and uses of power to shape culture, the choice of policies and instruments for promoting implementation, and the mediation of interaction across a loose network of stakeholders generating variable diversity of responses among implementers.

The core concept of *change* implies doing things differently, whether doing the same things in new ways, or doing new things. The process of changing practice therefore implies some degree of individual and collective learning for all involved, to the extent that a practice and its contextual features do not map directly onto what has been experienced in the past. The degree of novelty, and so the amount of learning needed, may range from trivial to profound. *Innovations* are planned changes designed to bring about improvement according to their instigators' values. Some are intended to facilitate learning to implement other changes, ranging from training initiatives, through arrangements for inter-organizational knowledge transfer (Chapter 9), to innovatory approaches to supporting the evolution of local 'communities of learning' (Chapter 10).

Change can be conceived as a single phenomenon. But the many adjectives that have been applied to organizational change demonstrate just how empirically diverse it is. Commonly a pair of adjectives is employed to create opposing categories, as in episodic or continuous (e.g. Weick and Quinn 1999), transformational or incremental (e.g. Kanter, Stein and Jick 1992), and in the present chapter, planned or emergent, simple or complex, single or programmatic. Many changes are planned interventions flowing from policies designed to improve service provision, either incrementally or through more radical reform. Others represent planned responses to emerging, unplanned changes. Focusing on the complexity of public service change implies a dimension of variation spanning everything from a simple modification of an individual's practice to a multiplicity of linked and highly experimental practices affecting an entire public service system. *Complex change* minimally implies two tiers: an overall entity and the multiple parts it contains. Many such changes are planned as innovations. Others are locally emergent. They may evolve from disparate planned changes affecting one or more service organizations to complex sets of formalized practices adopted across a public service system (see Chapter 8).

Programmatic change adds a third tier. The overall entity comprises a package of mutually reinforcing individual changes (so a programmatic change will inevitably be complex because the programme as an entity is made up of multiple parts). The constituent changes may themselves be complex and consist of a whole made up of multiple parts. The scope of programmatic change, and therefore the complexity of the overall entity, may range from a single service sector (as with Canadian health care discussed in Chapters 3, 6 and 10) to a unified strategy spanning all public services, as with public service modernization across England. Each constituent part is of some complexity and it is also likely to interact with other changes in the programme.

While the amount of prespecification in a programmatic change is variable, enough initial planning will be entailed for a package of related changes to be put forward. Minimally, proposals for a *change agenda* may be articulated, embodying scope for emergence through consultation and local innovation inside set parameters. The early implementation of the 'Kindergarten-Senior 4 Agenda' for schools in Manitoba, Canada, illustrates how a programmatic change may include user input into centrally proposed priorities and foster local development of new practices that are deemed appropriate for particular organizational circumstances (see Levin and Wiens 2003, and Chapter 7). Where there is greater prespecification (as with waves of UK modernization reforms launched after successive general elections), a *profile of innovations* may be proposed, extending to a comprehensive strategy for their phasing and implementation. Even in the latter case, the programme may evolve with implementation experience as problems arise and new ideas surface for further innovations. A programme may contain nested innovations, some of which (as mentioned above) are designed to facilitate the implementation of others. They may include initiatives to:

- improve the provision of particular services;
- identify where improvement is needed, and measure whether and how much improvement is being achieved;
- improve the leadership and management of services to create favourable conditions for direct service improvement;

- build generic capacity to implement externally initiated change, as a means of promoting the implementation of innovations in the programme.

Characteristics of complex and programmatic change

Strategies for coping with change that may be both complex and programmatic imply taking into account certain characteristics to which a pluralistic orientation draws attention. Empirically, any change may express any of these characteristics to a different extent. It should be borne in mind that these categories are impressionistic and dimensional, not all or nothing, and so they may vary in degree. A change is interpreted as more complex to the extent that all of the characteristics are expressed. But there is no clear cut-off point where simplicity ends and complexity starts. As stated in the introductory chapter, the categories were originally generated from the findings of a single empirical study, and were supplemented by engagement with senior academics and public service practitioners. They are offered as a heuristic device, one way in to discerning patterns in the complexity of public service change, which may have some potential to inform reflection on how to cope with it. (Readers may find it useful to reflect on the extent to which any characteristic applies to complex and programmatic change in their experience.)

Table 1.2 summarizes five characteristics of complexity, each broken down into two or more constituents. The left-hand column depicts characteristics relating to a single complex change which, as defined above, is two-tiered: an entity made up of multiple parts. The right-hand column depicts additional constituents of complexity that flow from the three-tier nature of programmatic change: an entity made up of multiple innovations, each comprising multiple parts.

First, complex change is *large scale*. A considerable number of stakeholders with varying specialist knowledge and priorities will probably be affected. They are likely to hold allegiance to a plurality of partially incompatible beliefs and values relating to the change, within the limits of their assumptions about their entitlement to express these beliefs and values, and constraints on alternative courses of action.

With programmatic change, the profile of stakeholders is even more differentiated, as particular groups may be affected by several or all of the innovations in the programme at any time as the programme unfolds. What they learn collectively from their cumulative experience of the earlier innovations will influence their beliefs and values, and so their range of responses to subsequent innovations.

Second, complex change is *componential*. Its content is likely to consist of a diversity of sequential and overlapping components affecting different stakeholders at particular times. A single change may contain multiple components, implemented in phases. The variety of components will dictate that a multiplicity of differentiated but interrelated management tasks must be addressed. Different stakeholders will be responsible for different tasks at different times. But each person's contribution has implications for that of others.

Table 1.2 Tentative characteristics of complexity of single and programmatic change

Complexity of a single change	Additional complexity of a programme
1. *Large-scale* • a multitude of stakeholders with an extensive range of specialist knowledge and priorities • the allegiance of stakeholders to partially incompatible beliefs and values, within limits	*Large-scale* • a continually evolving, differentiated profile of stakeholders involved with different changes in the programme • cumulative experience and collective learning of stakeholders affecting their mediation of the programme
2. *Componential* • a diversity of sequential and overlapping components affecting different stakeholders at particular times • a multiplicity of differentiated but interrelated management tasks	*Componential* • an evolving, hierarchical profile of interrelated innovations, including those to promote programme implementation • tasks may entail managing both parallel and sequential innovations within the programme
3. *Systemic* • a multidirectional flow of direct and mediated interaction within and between system levels • an unequal distribution of power between stakeholders within and between system levels who are nevertheless interdependent • the centrality of cross-level management tasks	*Systemic* • formal leaders at central and intermediate administrative levels may have cross-level responsibility for orchestrating programme implementation • multiple central and intermediate-level agencies may be responsible for training, disseminating information, monitoring and enforcing the programme
4. *Differentially impacting* • a variable shift in practice and learning required • variable congruence with perceived interests and its associated emotive force, altering with time • a variable reciprocal effect on other ongoing activities • variable awareness of the totality beyond those parts of immediate concern	*Differentially impacting* • early innovations in the programme impact cumulatively on the capacity to cope with later innovations • variable learning required to implement one, some or all innovations in the programme within single or across multiple service organizations
5. *Contextually dependent* • interaction with an evolving profile of other planned and unplanned changes • impact of the accretion of past changes affecting resource parameters • parameters for local emergence and central direction set by the configuration of political, social and economic institutions	*Contextually dependent* • interaction between the programme and other changes • variable parameters for central direction or invitation, and the capacity to respond to emergent changes stimulated by the programme

A programme may entail multiple innovations whose implementation is to be phased in different locations at different times, with each constituent innovation containing multiple components. Innovations in the programme may be hierarchically related, with some targeting service provision, while others target the management of improvement efforts, impact measurement and the generic capacity for coping with change. Consequently, management tasks may span the various components of the profile of innovations proceeding in parallel, together with those to be implemented sequentially.

Third, complex change is *systemic*. A service system-wide change process will embody a multidirectional flow of both direct interaction and interaction through intermediaries based within and between particular service system levels. The process must involve dialogue across a formal and informal network of stakeholders based at different public service administrative levels wherever a change is initiated centrally, or at a regional system level, for implementation more locally. Many interactions will occur via intermediaries who interpret the communications of stakeholders at one administrative level attempting to influence the actions of those at a different level. Such a network is pluralistic, with actors engaging in direct and mediated interaction in pursuit of possibly diverse and even irreconcilable interests. There will be an unequal distribution of power between stakeholders within and between system levels, who are nevertheless interdependent. The formal authority of stakeholders differs widely. A service may be closely regulated and fully resourced by central government, partially autonomous from government, or include private sector organizations which are formally independent of government. But the stakeholders on whom all others depend are those who actually implement the change. The centrality of management tasks across system levels follows where instigators at a more central level aspire to change public service practice at a more local level.

Additional complexity of systemic programmatic change may flow from the extra tier of responsibilities for implementing, across administrative levels, some or all the innovations in the evolving profile making up the programme. The greater scope of a programme may even include employing a multiplicity of dedicated, specialist agencies to promote the implementation of various innovations in the programme. The establishment of each agency represents an innovation in itself, designed as a means of bringing about the service innovations. But this innovation will interact with those innovations whose implementation the agency is set up to promote.

Fourth, complex change is *differentially impacting*, a key contributor to ambiguity. There will be a variable shift in practice and collective learning required of different groups, according to the novelty of their new tasks and the diverse interests they may pursue. Shifts in practice will have variable congruence with stakeholders' perceived interests and associated emotive force, which may switch (as where a change becomes accepted). Some people may perceive that change is compromising their interests, others may see change as suiting their interests well, and both groups may change their view over time. Change will have a variable reciprocal effect on other ongoing activities, each forming part of the context for the other – whether coping with other changes or carrying out ongoing work. There will be variable awareness of the totality of any change beyond those parts of immediate concern to particular individuals and groups. Grasp of a change is likely to be hierarchically distributed. Depth of local knowledge at the service organization level contrasts with superficial awareness of a complex change as a whole. Those operating at a more central level may have an overview of a change. But they will be less aware about the impact on particular organizations and their communities than people based at a more local level.

Each form of differential impact affects individual innovations within programmatic change. But the evolving profile of innovations it embodies brings a further element of complexity. How early innovations are implemented may variably affect the capacity of implementers in different organizations to cope with the next group of innovations to be phased in. This differential may become multiplied where some implementers increase their capacity to deal with a subsequent group while others fall behind. Variation in the extent and content of learning similarly increases significantly where different stakeholder groups may be involved with implementing different combinations of innovations in the programme in single or sets of related organizations.

Fifth, complex change is *contextually dependent*. The change will interact with an evolving profile of other planned and unplanned changes. The impact of the accretion of past changes affecting resource parameters for present change may be facilitative or inhibitory. Resources always have limits, and yesterday's decisions can affect the availability of resources (including money, time and expertise) for the changes of today. Fundamentally, parameters for local emergence and central direction are set by the configuration of social, political and economic institutions. The nature of service provision depends on structural factors determining the social, political and economic context of any country, setting parameters for emergent or more centrally driven change.

With programmatic change, the profile of interacting changes expresses additional complexity because it extends to the package of related innovations making up the programme. A further source of contextual variation is the extent to which the structural factors previously mentioned affect how far a programme is prespecified and centrally directed, or is more invitational and consultative and so allows for emergent changes in diverse local settings stimulated by the programme.

Orchestrating complex and programmatic change

This metaphor describes how senior leaders may cope with their role in complex and programmatic change, both inside and across particular administrative levels. The term is used figuratively, consistent with the dictionary definition 'to organize a situation or event unobtrusively so that a desired effect or outcome is achieved' (Encarta 2001: 1023). The orchestration metaphor derives from the writing of complex music, an entity comprising multiple parts. Orchestrators work largely outside the limelight, composing or arranging music for public performance by an orchestra. In performing the music, the conductor and players each possess sufficient agency to contribute to interpreting the music within the parameters set by the written orchestration. So creating orchestral music is a pluralistic endeavour. Individuals' power to shape it is unequal but nevertheless shared. A very rough parallel can be drawn between orchestrating complex music and orchestrating complex and programmatic change. Orchestrators of public service change play a key role in shaping the change process in ways that are both public and behind the scenes, and of which other stakeholders responsible for implementation have differential awareness. Yet the latter also possess sufficient agency to mediate the change to a varying degree.

Orchestration is offered as nothing more than a loose metaphor which can draw attention to what senior leaders in complex organizational systems do in working towards the implementation of a single change or programme. (Or possibly, as explored in Chapter 8, what orchestrators do to counter the threat of an unacceptable innovation originating elsewhere in the service system.) Such leaders generally have authority to allocate tasks to others in their own and other related organizations, but typically operate within parameters that are not entirely of their choosing. Orchestration is defined as:

> coordinated activity within set parameters expressed by a network of senior leaders at different administrative levels to instigate, organize, oversee and consolidate complex and programmatic change across part or all of a multi-organizational system.

As indicated earlier, the term network is employed to cover the large number of people who interact, directly or through intermediaries, to realize their often diverse interests in respect of a particular change or programme. Orchestrators steer the change process, those based at central or regional levels being distanced from implementation in service organizations. Orchestrating a single change means addressing it alongside other changes and the rest of ongoing work. Orchestrating a programmatic change agenda, or a more concretely specified profile of innovations, additionally entails coping with the implications of each change for other changes in the package. Across a service system, orchestrators form a loosely interrelated hierarchical network of mutually dependent senior leaders based at different system levels, some of whom may be unaware of others' contribution. Their knowledge of the change or programme can never be comprehensive. Collectively, they organize and maintain oversight of an intricate variety of related tasks as the change process unfolds. Steering change through orchestration is evolutionary, often unobtrusive, and includes attention to detail.

Orchestration contrasts with visionary and charismatic 'transformational' leadership (e.g. Leithwood, Jantzi and Steinbach 1999). The current emphasis on transformational leadership overplays the extent of designated leaders' agency and underplays factors that delimit what leaders can do. Where policy-makers set the direction of change and introduce associated accountability mechanisms, service leaders' capacity to choose developmental priorities is increasingly channelled in this direction. Policy-makers may actually be seeking to harness *transmissional* leadership faithfully to implement the change according to their political values (Chapter 4). But service leaders retain some capacity to choose a direction. Those who instigate change depend on the compliance and support of implementers. Visionary leadership is more a possibility for policy-makers, or for service leaders with enough leeway to instigate emergent change within their jurisdiction which expresses their personal service values. Private sector involvement in public service provision allows entrepreneurs to choose whether to offer services within regulations governing the parameters for provision.

Orchestration is also less than transformational in aspiration because, as research implies (e.g. Moore, George and Halpin 2002; Weick and Sutcliffe 2003), policy-makers and public service organizational leaders cannot predictably and reliably manipulate a service culture by shaping others' shared beliefs, values and subliminal codes of behaviour. They are much more likely to have the capability to tighten control over others' actions. Orchestration implies coping with external demands and seeking to influence actions first and foremost.

While orchestrators may be incapable of cultural manipulation, they cannot afford not to attempt to mould a service culture. More than minimal compliance is required if others are to implement change fully. Leaders are driven towards attempting to win hearts and minds as well as changing actions, despite the ambiguity flowing from their incapacity to guarantee success. A shift of emphasis away from the visionary side of leadership towards orchestration seems more realistic than ideas fostering an overoptimistic sense of leaders' ability to choose the direction of change and to control its course through cultural transformation.

Orchestration implies both more and less than leadership. The distinction between orchestration, leadership and management has two dimensions (Figure 1.1): how far activity includes deciding the direction of change, and how far activity is distributed across organizations in the public service system. Leadership is widely conceived as stimulating change in others' practice, while management implies keeping change on track, as in the definitions offered by Louis and Miles (1990: 19–20):

> Leaders set the course for the organization; managers make sure the course is followed. Leaders make strategic plans; managers design operational systems for carrying out the plans. Leaders stimulate and inspire; managers use their interpersonal influence and authority to translate that energy into productive work.

Along the first dimension of setting the direction for change, orchestration reaches further than leadership. The unobtrusive aspect of orchestration spans management through overseeing the maintenance of momentum and ensuring that the set direction is followed. Orchestration involves monitoring others' practice relating to the change, channelling their agency in the desired direction through encouragement and incentives, and even delimiting their agency through corrective action where their practice is judged unacceptable. But orchestration also reaches less far along this dimension than leadership. As Bolman and Deal (1991) appositely

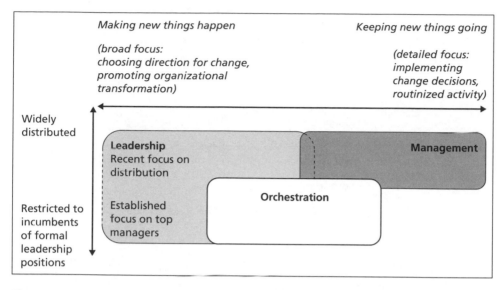

Figure 1.1 Distinguishing orchestration from change leadership and management (Based on Wallace 2004)

put it, 'things make leaders happen'. Scope for selecting the content of a change may be restricted, as with modernization in the UK where public service reforms are mandated. But the need for stimulating and steering a coherent change effort still remains.

Along the second dimension of the distribution of activity, orchestration is restricted to senior formal leaders in hierarchically ordered organizations who are in an authoritative position to shape organizational practice. It is more narrowly dispersed than distributed leadership implies. The systemic characteristic of complex and programmatic change means that orchestration involves coordination inside organizations and between them, including those at different administrative levels.

Thus the usefulness of this conception of orchestration stems from its avoidance of the distinction implied by leadership and management between making new things happen and keeping new things on track, and its avoidance of either of their extremes. Orchestration precludes some agency to select a vision implied by leadership, and is less distributive. It also excludes attendance to very specific routine maintenance tasks implied by management.

A Framework to Inform Planning to Cope with Complexity

There are three aspects to the framework: change management themes, headed by orchestration; the characteristics of complex and programmatic change; and sequential stages in the change process. (For a summary account of its application to school reorganization, see Wallace 2004.) As a planning tool, reference may be made to one or more aspects to help think through the strategy for coping with an unfolding change or programme. The framework is presented in Figure 1.2.

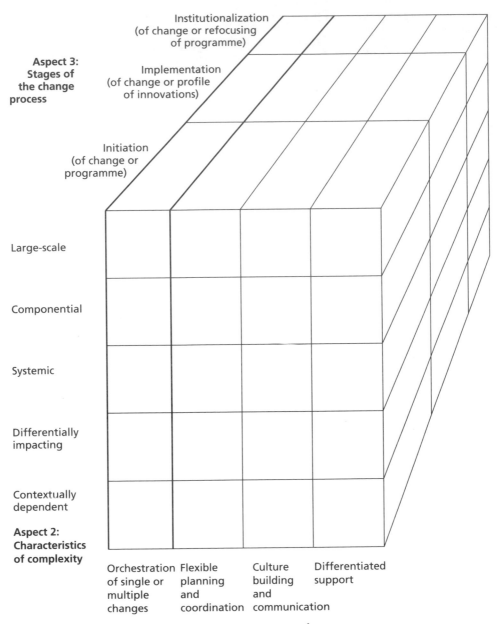

Figure 1.2 Three aspects of complex and programmatic change

Aspect 1: Orchestration and three subordinate change management themes

The framework concentrates on the process of coping with change which is complex and programmatic. An obvious limitation is that it does not extend to the policy-making process that generates public service reforms (addressed by Chapters 5–7). But the framework comes into play once a policy option is adopted. Equally, orchestration may come into play as more emergent changes arising in unconnected settings become conceived as different expressions of a single change to be managed across a service system (Chapter 8). Orchestration entails taking responsibility for task areas to deal with a complex change or a programme as a whole:

1 instigating change activity;
2 creating and sustaining favourable conditions for change to happen;
3 setting up management structures and delegating responsibilities, including those for other orchestrators, for a single change or evolving profile of innovations in a programme;
4 monitoring progress with implementing an individual change or the multiple changes in a programme and making adjustments accordingly;
5 taking corrective or adaptive action, especially in response to unanticipated interaction between changes in a programme, and in the context of other changes and ongoing work. With programmes, feedback may stimulate ameliorative policy making or a reinvention of the programme, so shifting the balance of innovations in the profile.

Orchestrators frame diverse activities that are grouped under three subordinate change management themes. They delegate responsibilities connected with these themes while overseeing the overall change effort. Many activities require specialist expertise, so may be widely distributed across administrative levels of a public service system.

First, *flexible planning and coordination* involves considering everything to be done across different administrative levels. This theme reflects ambiguity flowing from the dilemma over retaining short-term flexibility through incremental planning while also retaining coherence through sequential longer term planning cycles. Plans are coordinated for different parts of the individual change or for the profile of innovations making up a programme. They are updated through a more or less continual process of evolutionary creation, monitoring and adjustment inside the parameters set by the broad longer term direction.

Second, *culture building and communication* relates to the dependence of orchestrators on other stakeholders. The former promote a culture of support at best, and acquiescence at least, for their change or programme goals. Means include articulating and publicizing the improvement case behind change, consulting about a change agenda, or pointing towards the future benefits to be brought by a programme. Communication implies giving consistent messages and gathering feedback to assist coordination and to pre-empt resistance. For programmes, communication may include attempting to demonstrate how constituent changes interrelate to form a coherent entity.

Third, *differentiated support* means organizing the provision of whatever people need to help them implement an individual change or programme, when required. Support extends to backing up other orchestrators who are distributed across a service system. Forms of support may include information, expertise, preparatory training, time, counselling, physical resources and finance. For programmes it may extend to the innovation of establishing or restructuring multiple agencies whose role is both to meet short-term needs and to build systemic capacity to implement future innovations that may be added to the original profile.

Relating aspect 1 to aspect 2: orchestration which takes account of complexity

Each characteristic of complexity affects the task areas overseen by orchestrators. Indicatively, its *large-scale* nature implies that they may have to devise means of communicating with, gaining support from, and harnessing the expertise of a multiplicity of other stakeholders. Multiple communication channels may have to be created to establish a robust network with mutual linkages between all stakeholder groups. Orchestrators in every public service organization involved may need to work closely with their colleagues and possibly garner or sustain local community support. They may need also to inform themselves about what is happening elsewhere with relevance for the organization or organizations for which they have responsibility.

Where a change or programme is *componential*, orchestrators may have to plan for all components and the associated management tasks. Those based in service organizations may have to plan solely for those components and tasks directly affecting them. For a *systemic* change or programme, cooperation may need to be secured and supported throughout the network of orchestrators based at different system levels. Gaining support may require compromises to be struck to maximize the number of stakeholders who view the change as being in their interest. If such change is *differentially impacting* on the various stakeholders affected, orchestrators may have to take into account in their planning the likelihood that it will impact differently on different groups. Continual monitoring may be required to maintain awareness of these impacts and their unintended consequences, which could inform planning to pre-empt or to cope with problems that arise. The *contextually dependent* nature of change dictates that orchestrators take into account the legacy of past changes affecting their responsibility and resources likely to be available. They may need to be alert to the possibility that other policies and associated innovations in a programme profile may help or hinder their coping strategies. They may have to be ready to adapt incrementally as circumstances shift, always attempting to maximize the resources available to achieve their desired outcome.

Aspect 3: evolution of a single change or profile of innovations

The process of changing is often divided into a sequence of stages, while acknowledging that the transition between stages may be blurred. The *initiation* stage leads up to a decision to proceed with putting a change or programme into practice. Who makes any decision and at what point varies with the degree of local emergence or central prespecification. It may be made by central policy-makers alone where introducing a public service reform programme, with or without consultation with other stakeholders. In the case of emergent changes, orchestrators in individual service organizations may be the key decision-makers, with authority to determine the extent of consultation or participation by other stakeholders in the decision itself.

The *implementation* stage refers to the attempt to put a change or the profile of innovations in a programme into effect, possibly over a period of years. Phased implementation may affect different groups of service organizations in a specified sequence. Here orchestrators at a central or intermediate administrative level may have to deal with components of one change or the multiplicity of inno-vations in a programme which are at different stages at any time. Unintended consequences of implementation that emerge may generate a sharp learning curve, leading to adjustment or more radical rethinking of the individual change or programme, generating further change for implementers to address.

Building the change or programme into what comes to be perceived as normal practice constitutes the *institutionalization* stage. Mediation during the earlier implementation stage may result in practice varying from instigators' espoused vision. Alternative outcomes may ensue, as where implementation activity is abandoned, or is overtaken by subsequent change. This possibility is especially prevalent with programmes, where monitoring the implementation of early innovations in the profile can lead to new innovations designed to com-pensate for unintended consequences of the former. While there is a temporal order of stages, the process may not be neatly linear, particularly where com-ponents of a change or profile of innovations in a programme are at different stages at any time. The implementation period for centrally driven programmes is likely to be bounded by the duration of publicly stated commitment (often dictated by political election cycles). Institutionalization of the profile of innova-tions commonly has to occur inside the commitment period, unless it is renewed. Even then, a programme is likely to be refocused as policy-makers seek a new mandate from the electorate by promising further reform during the next political cycle.

For a single complex change, different components may be at different stages at any time during the evolution of the change process, especially where imple-mentation is phased. Similarly for a programme, constituent innovations may be initiated at different times during the implementation period of the programme as a whole. Each component of a change or innovation in the profile making up a programme may also interact with others.

Relating aspect 1 to aspect 3: orchestrating the
transition between stages

Where a complex change or programme is systemic, orchestrators at a more
central administrative level may have responsibility for working through other
orchestrators, whether based at this or a more local level. Membership of the network of orchestrators who are based at different system levels is in such cases
likely to shift stage by stage. From the outset of the *initiation* stage for a centrally
driven reform programme, government policy-makers and their senior civil servants may be orchestrators. But throughout the *implementation* stage, orchestration will become shared across system levels, with formal leaders in each
intermediate administrative organization (including implementation agencies) or
service organization. Formal leaders based at the different levels of the service
system therefore have to work together, even though they may not share the same
change goals. If and when a new practice becomes perceived as routine, at the
institutionalization stage, orchestration may become the exclusive province of
senior leaders in the organizations that are the sites of implementation.

The converse holds for an emergent change that gradually becomes more
complex. Early orchestrators may be formal leaders of individual service organizations dotted across the system and with no relationship to each other. Yet as
information about the change and its perceived value spreads, orchestrators
based at more central administrative levels may then become involved. Their jurisdiction may be regional or national.

The framework as an aide-mémoire

The framework is itself quite complex: there are multiple cells which can be explored
in relation to one, two or all three aspects. But it may be consulted selectively,
according to the practical concern of the user. Working out how to cope with a
complex change or programme might be structured by exploring the relationship
between selected categories inside any aspect that forms a cell of the framework.
Similarly, attention may be directed towards the relationship between categories
in any two, or even all three aspects. What is or should be going on may be plot-
ted by thinking though:

- For any single aspect, what a category covers or how the contents of two or
  more categories interrelate (e.g. among the change management themes what
  the key tasks of orchestration are for a change programme at hand, or how these
  tasks might connect with tasks encompassed by each subordinate theme).
- For any two aspects, how the coverage of one or more categories for one aspect
  relate to the content of categories for a second aspect (e.g. how the systemic
  characteristic of a programme impacts on who the orchestrators are, and what
  differentiated support they might need).

- For the three aspects together, how the coverage of one or more categories for one aspect relates to the content of categories embodied in both the other aspects (e.g. how the systemic characteristic of a programme affects the tasks of orchestrating each innovation in the profile during its implementation stage).

Getting Better at Understanding to Inform Coping with the Complexity of Change

If the complexity of public service change is inescapable, and if managing this complexity means coping rather than grossly simplifying it through strong control, then developing system-wide coping capacity becomes imperative for improving service provision. But how might research and theory building inform the future development of coping capacity? The thrust of this chapter has been that we need to get better at understanding the complexity of change by engaging with what makes it complex to manage and how people cope with it on the ground.

First, we need to find out more empirically about the nature of this new complexity, how people cope with it, and with what consequences. This is where relatively inductive research has a key contribution to make in exploring what the patterns in complexity and coping strategies might be, how far they can be generalized between different contexts, and at what level of abstraction from the empirical detail. New complexity might generate new patterns that tightly framed research might miss, because it is couched in terms of concepts that are not necessarily sensitive to the characteristics of the new phenomenon. The study of school reorganization was a starting point, but it was an investigation of just one case of change in one public service at one time. We still know little about how systemic reform is orchestrated within and between different public services and sectors, and the salience of contingent contextual factors.

At the time of writing, a new research investigation designed to contribute to this agenda is getting under way, entitled 'Developing Organization Leaders as Change Agents in the Public Services'. The study focuses on how training and other learning support offered by national leadership development bodies and other agencies to acculturate organization leaders as change agents relates both to UK government programmatic change to implement public service modernization and personalization, and to fostering independent, locally emergent improvement efforts. National leadership development bodies represent a strategic innovation in themselves, with a service sector or system-wide brief to improve the quality of service organization leadership in general, and the role of leaders as change agents in particular – whether on behalf of government or their own institution.

Second, we need to draw on a wider range of social science-informed ideas than those (such as transformational leadership mentioned earlier) prevailing in the knowledge-for-action and instrumentalist literature. Possibly the most prominent approach in this literature that does squarely address the complexity of public service change and its relative unmanageability is not even based on social science ideas. According to the review in Chapter 2, it offers only limited potential for deepening understanding or informing practice.

Other ideas which are more social science related sometimes unrealistically assume that a high degree of managerial control is possible in principle, whether over hearts and minds to shape implementers' disposition to adopt specific practices, or over the practices themselves. Alternative ideas that assume less managerial controllability are to be found in several traditions of social science-based literature developing knowledge-for-understanding about organizational life and change. They are also to be found in the sociological literature developing knowledge-for-critical evaluation about the impact of public service change on professional work. The pluralistic orientation informing the enquiry into complex change discussed here, and the ironic perspective to be elaborated in Chapter 4, represent a conscious attempt to bring in selected ideas from this wider social science base.

The conception of complex and programmatic change put forward in this chapter represents one way of foregrounding the relative unmanageability of change and the coping strategies that render change as manageable as possible. One important task is to conceptualize emergent coping strategies for dealing with multiple change in the context of sustaining normal provision. Firestone and Shipps make a significant contribution in Chapter 11. They explore the idea of maximizing coherence as far as is feasible in setting the direction for changing practice at the service organization level, despite multiple external and internal pressures. Another conceptual task is to elaborate the notion of a hierarchical system-wide network of orchestrators, whose hallmark is extensive indirect and often unknowing interaction, especially across administrative system levels.

In short, there is no shortage of empirical and theoretical work to do. Between them, the chapters that follow begin to take forward selected elements of this agenda. The rest of Part I explores conceptualizing the complexity of public service change, Part II examines the tortuous process of policy making for public service reform that generates so much complexity, and Part III focuses on the complexity of change within and between service and administrative organizations.

REFERENCES

Bolman, L. and Deal, T. (1991) *Reframing Organizations: Artistry, Choice and Leadership*. San Francisco: Jossey-Bass.

Davies, B. (1997) Re-engineering and its application to education. *School Leadership and Management*, **17**(2), 173–85.

Ferlie, E., Hartley, J. and Martin, S. (2003) Changing public service organizations: current perspectives and future prospects. *British Journal of Management*, **14**, S1–S14.

Foster, C. and Plowden, F. (1996) *The State under Stress*. Buckingham: Open University Press.

Kanter, R., Stein, B. and Jick, T. (1992) *The Challenge of Organizational Change*. New York: Free Press.

Leithwood, K., Jantzi, D. and Steinbach, R. (1999) *Changing Leadership for Changing Times*. Buckingham: Open University Press.

Levin, B. and Wiens, J. (2003) There is another way. *Phi Delta Kappan*, **84**(9), 658–64.

Louis, K. and Miles, M. (1990) *Improving the Urban High School: What Works and Why*. New York: Teachers College Press.

McNulty, T. and Ferlie, E. (2002) *Reengineering Health Care: The Complexities of Organizational Transformation*. Oxford: Oxford University Press.

Moore, A., George, R. and Halpin, D. (2002) The developing role of the headteacher in English schools: management, leadership and pragmatism. *Educational Management and Administration*, **30**(2), 175–88.

Newman, J. (2001) *Modernising Governance: New Labour, Policy and Society*. London: Sage.

Office of Public Service Reform (2002) *Reforming our Public Services: Principles into Practice*. London: OPSR.

Osborne, D. and Gaebler, T. (1992) *Reinventing Government: How the Entrepreneurial Spirit is Transforming the Public Sector*. Reading, MA: Addison-Wesley.

Pollitt, C. and Bouckaert, G. (2000) *Public Management Reform: A Comparative Analysis*. Oxford: Oxford University Press.

Rhodes, R. (1997) *Understanding Governance: Policy Networks, Reflexivity and Accountability*. Milton Keynes: Open University Press.

Wallace, M. (2004) Orchestrating complex educational change. *Journal of Educational Change*, **5**(1), 57–78.

Wallace, M. and Pocklington, K. (2002) *Managing Complex Educational Change: Large-Scale Reorganization of Schools*. London: RoutledgeFalmer.

Wallace, M. and Wray, A. (2006) *Critical Reading and Writing for Postgraduates*. London: Sage.

Weick, K. and Quinn, R. (1999) Organizational change and development. *Annual Review of Psychology*, **50**, 361–86.

Weick, K. and Sutcliffe, K.M. (2003) Hospitals as cultures of entrapment: a re-analysis of the Bristol Royal Infirmary. *California Management Review*, **45**(2), 73–84.

CHAPTER 2

APPLYING COMPLEXITY THEORY TO PUBLIC SERVICE CHANGE: CREATING CHAOS OUT OF ORDER?

Mike Wallace and Michael Fertig

Weight is added in this chapter to the case for social science-informed approaches to understanding the complexity of public service change and informing practice to cope with it. The chapter scrutinizes the strongly deductive approach towards basing practical prescriptions for public service change on chaos and complexity theory. Mike Wallace noted in Chapter 1 his rejection of such a deductive use of complexity theory. Here he and Michael Fertig provide the evidence that informed Wallace's view about the greater potential of a more inductive, social science-informed approach.

Their intellectual project was to develop knowledge-for-understanding, being open-minded at the outset about the nature and quality of the literature and what it might offer in terms of grasping patterns in the complexity of public service change. They evaluated any support for various claims about the applicability of concepts from chaos and complexity theory. The outcome of this evaluation suggested that the more ambitious claims made by some advocates are insufficiently warranted to be compelling.

The heavily theoretical nature of the literature means that the acceptability of the prescriptions for improving practice in the public services stands or falls on how convincingly complexity theory can be translated from its origins in studying the natural world to prescribing effective practice in the human social world. The validity of making this translation depends, in turn, on whether relevant parallels between the two worlds are more significant than the differences. The review concludes that as a loose metaphor this approach to theorizing has the potential (on a par with many other metaphors including orchestration) to inform practitioners' thinking about their practice, but not to prescribe what they should do.

Performative Theory, Convenient Metaphor or Management Fad?

> Complexity theory is not simply a metaphor or an analogy that is convenient for senior managers to use to exhort employees to work or to extort innovations from them. If that is all it is then it is little more than another 'management fad' . . . and it should command little attention. No, complexity theory is a reality; it is happening; it is working in practice, whether we like it or not. Though its message is unsettling, for it argues that long-range planning is futile, that control is a chimera and that the power of bosses is limited, it is *descriptively* accurate. One cannot play Canute and ignore it; it exists. It is a *theory* that explains how and why to practise particular leadership practices (Morrison 2002: 189).

This most forceful of assertions comes from an enthusiastic advocate of complexity theory as the key to effective school leadership. Complexity theory is held to *be* in some way the phenomenon it describes. Not only is the theory a 'reality', but it is 'happening' on the ground and cannot be ignored. The theory is held also to be 'working in practice' by providing a sound explanatory basis for evaluating and prescribing school leadership. As Hoyle (2003: 214) has commented: 'it almost appears as if complexity theory is functioning as what one might term a *performative* theory, the statement of the theory effectively constituting the phenomena that it purports to explain'. In his enthusiasm, Morrison may have inadvertently overstepped the bounds of logic in eliding complexity theory with the empirical phenomenon of social complexity. But is he still onto something?

Not all advocates of complexity theory as a route to public service improvement would take such a forceful view in asserting its literal – rather than more impressionistically metaphorical – applicability. Haynes (2003: 30) is perhaps more representative. He makes the relatively moderate assertion that the concepts of complexity theory 'can change the way managers and professionals think about the world of public organizations and the process of public service management'. Here complexity theory remains distinguishable from the thinking and practice that it may valuably inform. Is Haynes more convincingly onto something? Could applying complexity theory to the public services be a promising way forward for understanding and improving the management of public service change?

Many academics and consultants think so. Whether taken as literal truth, convenient analogy or metaphor, complexity theory is increasingly being applied to public service change as part of a wider movement to improve organizational effectiveness. Subscribers to this movement such as Morrison would reject the notion that it is merely another short-lived fad (e.g. Mitleton-Kelly 2003). Some claim that we are witnessing nothing less than a paradigm shift across the natural and social sciences. The outmoded, mechanistic and predictive 'Newtonian–Cartesian' paradigm is being superseded by the complexity paradigm which 'can shed fresh light on a range of organizational problems and issues, and suggest innovative and ground-breaking ways of reshaping the organizational world so that it is more in tune with the times' (McMillan 2004: 3).

Complexity theory is an umbrella term that incorporates chaos theory, its pre-decessor. The term covers a variety of ideas derived from mathematics and nat-ural scientific disciplines such as meteorology and social biology. It would be an overstatement to imply that all advocates of complexity theory for organizational management in general and the public services in particular agree on their choice of concepts from this accreting array, their preferred definition of certain concepts, or how to apply them to specific phenomena (Burnes 2005). What they do share is the core assumption that complexity theory ideas can be legitimately and fruit-fully translated not only to the realm of 'social' animals (such as colonies of ants) but also to the more sophisticated social world of people. Complexity theory is their lens for explaining what happens and prescribing what should happen.

Whether the phenomena of public service provision and change have become increasingly complex is scarcely in question. The underlying premise of these scholars may therefore seem unexceptionable. Contemporary organizational and more systemic changes are complex and relatively unmanageable, so unpacking this complexity is necessary, both to help practitioners manage change as effec-tively as possible, and to inform policy-makers. Yet it is much more contestable which approaches to conceptualising and investigating complexity are likely to prove most fit for their advocates' purpose in prescribing practice.

Alternative approaches arise because no 'one best way' can exist to theorize human social phenomena. The enduring philosophical problem over whether there is a social reality out there independent of one's conceptualization of it reflects the fact that experience of the human social world and the capacity to communicate that experience do not rest on the senses alone. The human social world is only 'real' insofar as a conceptual reality is constructed that gives meaning to inter-action between people and the social structures they create to facilitate or control that interaction. This conceptual reality can be shared only through the medium of language. Therefore there can never be a one-to-one correspondence between whatever social reality may exist and the linguistic ability to conceptualize it. Complexity theory is an empirical reality in that it comprises a bundle of related concepts that some advocates are applying to public service change through lan-guage embodied in the literature. But complexity theory is not the same thing as the public service change that those involved experience as being complex to manage. Other ways of interpreting such change abound.

This is so, in part, because focusing simultaneously on all aspects of complex social phenomena through all conceptualizations available is self-evidently beyond human capacity. Reductionism is inevitable, however social reality is conceived. Any conception – complexity theory included – will therefore back-ground certain aspects that other conceptions place in the foreground, and vice versa. It is so, also, because values intrinsically inform which aspects of phenomena are considered significant and which are to be ignored. Values underpin any ensu-ing practical prescriptions. The prevalence of value pluralism and the incompat-ibility of some of these values mean that those espoused by prescribers may or may not be acceptable to those whose practice they seek to influence. Applying complexity theory to public service change is one way of theorizing this human social phenomenon which, demonstrably, can be done. But how insightfully for deepening understanding, and how usefully for informing practice?

Our purpose in this review chapter is to address the question: what are the problems and potential of employing complexity theory to inform and improve the management of change in the public services? The popularity of complexity theory as a foundation for practical prescription gives rise to the need to take stock and critically to assess its applicability to contemporary public service change. Rather than attempting to synthesize the burgeoning literature applying complexity theory to organizational management or exploring the divergence among advocates (for reviews see Maguire and McKelvey 1999; Burnes 2005), we will concentrate primarily on selected texts that focus on the public services. We will also refer to indicative examples of the more generic literature that has influenced the authors of these texts.

The rest of the chapter is divided into four sections. First, we briefly consider the scope of academic interest in and the dominant types of literature produced by advocates of complexity theory, why, and with what consequences. Second, we summarize claims about the applicability of complexity theory to the public services in particular, reflecting the wider concern to apply this way of thinking to organizations in general. Third, we evaluate the extent to which a convincing case has been made for this 'paradigm shift' in understanding the complexity of public service change and prescribing how to manage it effectively. Finally, we conclude that inherent problems with this intellectual endeavour restrict its potential to become more enduring than a management fad. These limitations reinforce the need to seek social science-informed approaches to addressing the complexity of public service change.

Where are Advocates of Complexity Theory Coming from?

Applying complexity theory to organizations is a growth industry. From the late 1980s, a steadily expanding minority of practice-oriented scholars of organizations, consultants and trainers (e.g. Nonaka 1988; Stacey 1991, 1992; Wheatley 1992) have drawn for inspiration on ideas from the emerging literature on chaos and, more recently, complexity theory in the natural sciences (for a history see McMillan 2004). Special attention has been paid to popular works (e.g. Gleick 1988; Waldrop 1994) introducing these new developments to a general audience. Most advocates have adopted a broad focus on organizational management, though they often refer mainly to the private sector (e.g. Pascale, Milleman and Gioja 2000; Stacey 2003). There has also been some concern with translating complexity theory to the voluntary sector (Donaldson, Lank and Maher 2005), generically to the public services (Haynes 2003), and to individual services including education (Fullan 1993, 2001; Morrison 2002; McMillan 2004) and health (Anderson and McDaniel 2000; Higginbotham, Albrecht and Connor 2001). The expansion of academic interest is reflected in the establishment of interdisciplinary research centres whose coverage includes the public services (e.g. the Centre for Complexity Research at the University of Liverpool), of learned societies (e.g. the Complexity Society) and of journals (e.g. *Non-Linear Dynamics, Psychology and Life Sciences*).

The proliferation of practical interest is reflected in the emergence of networks, some formalized, as with the US-based Plexus Institute (2005). Members of this not-for-profit organization are invited to subscribe to the mission of 'fostering the health of individuals, families, communities, organizations and our natural environment by helping people use concepts emerging from the new science of complexity' through participation in conferences and other exchange opportunities. Some trainers and consultants working in the public services also draw on complexity theory to frame ideas for improving the effectiveness of organizational change and collective learning. One UK instance is a course on managing the delivery of social care where complexity theory informs consideration of the interaction between carers and those for whose care they are responsible (Harrogate Training and Development 2005).

The dominant type of frontline academic literature is theoretical – amply supported by textbooks (e.g. Haynes 2003) and training guides (e.g. Zimmerman, Lindberg and Plsek 1998). This is hardly surprising, given the novelty of complexity theory, the common concern with improving practice, the necessity of arguing the case for translating complexity ideas from the natural to the human social world and the size of the textbook market for advanced management courses. However, the theory developed takes a strongly applied form. It leans towards the hortatory, and is designed primarily to inform practitioners' thinking about how to enhance their practice. Far from adopting a sceptical stance, the prevailing point of departure is one of commitment: an 'act of faith' (Wheatley 1992) that complexity theory *can* be applied insightfully to the human social world (whether literally, analogously or metaphorically). Authors proceed to specify how it provides the basis for prescribing practice in managing organizational change. This literature can be located within the practically oriented tradition of management theory (Hoyle 1986), as distinct from the social scientific tradition of organization theory, which is driven more by an interest in deepening understanding.

The main 'intellectual project' (Wallace and Wray 2006), or purpose for study, that these authors pursue is to develop 'knowledge-for-action': creating theoretical and research knowledge with practical application from a positive standpoint towards current practice and policy, whether in the public services or in any organizational system. The aim is to inform improvement efforts from within the prevailing ideology framing practice. So in the case of the UK public services, such authors are more concerned with implementing changes, including central government-driven modernization, than with questioning the tenets of modernization, its managerialist heritage and its unintended consequences. The subsidiary intellectual project, producing less literature, is 'instrumentalism': imparting practice knowledge and skills through training and consultancy aimed directly at improving practice, also from within the prevailing ideology. The primacy of these intellectual projects in the field has resulted in a paucity of more sceptical literature assessing the extent to which complexity theory is applicable to the human social world, of more critical accounts highlighting aspects of social phenomena which complexity theory downplays, and of social science-informed enquiry to understand the nature of complexity in social life and how people cope with it. Proselytizing dominates over critique.

How is Complexity Theory Applied to Public Service Change?

First, we mentioned above how the concepts employed to build this change focus are lifted from the complexity theory of mathematics and natural science. The procedure is legitimated by the claim that complex natural and social systems are both expressions of the one phenomenon: the dynamically complex system. Therefore complex natural world phenomena (originally identified inductively) are seen to have their correlates in the human social world, whether by direct parallel (Morrison) or looser metaphor (Haynes). The core translation task for those who wish to apply complexity theory to the public services is deductive: either to determine which public service phenomena count as correlates of natural phenomena, or to build on the work of pioneers (such as Stacey) in the generic field of organizational management by searching for public service instances of correlates already identified there. Mathematical and natural scientific complexity theory comes first. Finding a fit with the human social world comes second. Finding a precision fit with narrower public service phenomena comes last. In Table 2.1 we have summarized some key concepts and indicative examples in the public services. Juxtaposing the concepts gives a strong sense of the *Gestalt* they offer of public service organizations and service systems: too complex to understand fully or control tightly, and constantly changing through myriad interactions while held together by common values and relatively stable routines.

Not only do advocates tend to view public service change management as a subset of organizational change management, but they also converge on the same bundle of concepts and a similar set of practical prescriptions as their generic organization counterparts. There is little problematizing of these concepts or their application among either group. Any discrepancy noted often refers to points of definition or translation. Indicatively, for the study of organizations Mitleton-Kelly (2005) prefers the term 'complex co-evolving system' (CCES) over the original natural scientific term 'complex adaptive system'. A CCES does not merely adapt to the environment but also affects it, so both system and environment co-evolve.

Second, we also noted earlier that treating the public services conceptually as a system is central to this approach. Complexity theory is at heart a holistic theory of relationships between interacting elements within and between entities that are system-like: each entity amounts to more than the sum of its parts. The notion of a system is applied equally to a single organization (such as a hospital) and to a set of related organizations (such as a regional grouping of hospitals and

Table 2.1 Applying complexity theory to public service change (drawing on Haynes 2003; McMillan 2004)

Concept	Illustrative public service application
Bifurcation	The process of transformation, or radical change, through which a service organization makes the transition from a period of instability to a new form of order through unfolding interaction among staff.
Complex adaptive system	Staff constantly adapt to changing circumstances and, through their interaction, learn collectively to alter or develop new practices.
Edge of chaos	A state where organizations continually reinvent themselves through the ferment of ideas among staff whose work contains a mix of ongoing activity and aspects that are changing, so maximizing their collective potential for fruitful creativity.
Emergence	The evolution of changes in staff practices as they collectively experiment in their work and adapt to shifting environmental demands.
Feedback	The way in which interaction between people, information and structures contributes to the indeterminate range of infiuences affecting the evolution of change.
Fractals	Units of similarity within and between organizational levels, as in the operation of project teams, administrative committees, working parties and management teams whose members all share the same guiding principles and codes of behaviour.
Self-organization	Staff spontaneously work together collaboratively to respond continuously to environmental demands and bring about change which improves their practice according to their professional service values.
Sensitive dependence on initial conditions	A small leadership initiative may unpredictably produce large immediate and long-term effects as a result of subsequent interaction between staff.
Strange attractor	The subliminal sense of order that draws staff together through attraction to certain values and behaviours, enabling the short-term direction of change to be forecast despite organizational diversity and unpredictability.

primary care trusts). But these are 'complex adaptive' (or 'complex co-evolutionary') systems, where change is the norm. The *dynamic* view of systems is held to distinguish them from the older notion of 'open systems', where it is assumed that a stable state of equilibrium between the constituent parts is attainable. In contrast, the relationships between complex system elements, which define them as complex, are characterized by inherently unpredictable change, due to varying interaction between varying groups of elements. So advocates of complexity theory for the public services foreground change. They seek to explain why it is endemic, and how it can be harnessed for improvement, both in individual organizations and across a regional or national service system.

Third, a strong claim is made about the limits imposed by complexity in the public services, as with organizations more broadly, for trying to comprehend and control change (through the knowledge-for-action intellectual project). Complexity renders systems indeterminate to a significant degree. Indeterminacy rules out researchers identifying and weighting all possible variables, and then demonstrating major linked causes or single cause explanations, even in principle. (Thus the precise, if non-linear, calculations that generated complexity ideas in mathematics are not deemed feasible in the human social world.) Causation is non-linear and variably networked: multiple, direct and distant causes result in multiple direct and distant effects which, recursively, may feed back to cause further effects. Small causes can have big direct or distant effects. Therefore a public service system is endemically unstable, in part. It is continually prone to change in ways that are unpredictable in their specifics. But service system processes that are never identical are still recognizably similar, lying inside more predictable parameters. These processes are claimed to be subject to 'strange attractors': organizing forces comprising allegiance to certain values and behaviours. They delimit diversity at the level of detail and generate partial stability.

Fourth, as non-linearly evolving systems marked by a mixture of instability and stability, the public services are poised at 'the edge of chaos'. This 'far from equilibrium' state of 'bounded instability' can be enduring. The service organization or system may neither collapse into chaos (too much change), nor ossify (too little change) in the face of shifting environmental pressures. Indeed, Stacey (2003) normatively asserts that only by operating at the edge of chaos can any complex system have the ability to transform itself in order to survive.

In this state, new forms of order unpredictably emerge as changing and similar (but not identical) patterns in the behaviour of organization members. The process by which this ongoing but irregular changing occurs is 'self-organization', as individuals and groups in the complex adaptive system learn collectively through their interaction in response to evolving circumstances. Each member of a public service (or any other) organization is conceived as an individual *agent* with the freedom to act in unpredictable but interconnected ways. Each agent adjusts her or his behaviour in interacting with other agents. The overall pattern of organizational and system behaviour emerges from the sum of agents' interactions. The edge of chaos state is where the capacity for self-organization and creativity are greatest. Prescriptively, this state is held to offer the optimal potential for improvement through creating conditions favouring self-organization among spontaneously forming groups, directed towards enhancing the effectiveness of their contribution to achieving official service goals.

Fifth, somewhat paradoxically in the face of the indeterminate complexity of system elements and their interaction, promoting and sustaining operation at the edge of chaos is quite feasible for managers to achieve. Creating new order out of chaos occurs through self-organization: generating emergent, productive new forms of order through the operation of a few simple order-generating rules. These rules allow restricted disorder and instability within relative order and stability. In other words, unpredictability is governed by strange attractors, which keep it within predictable and manageable bounds. However, advocates (such as Stacey) acknowledge that, in contrast to natural systems, order-generating rules do not directly or automatically generate self-organization in human social systems, since people may pursue idiosyncratic objectives and come to diverse interpretations of events.

The endpoint of the application of such ideas to public service change is to articulate managerial prescriptions. Illustratively, managers should:

- harness the natural creativity of organization members and other stakeholders through facilitative leadership which allows variation in practice entailing some uncertainty (Plsek and Wilson, 2001);
- encourage people to make small changes in their sphere of influence because they may turn out to have large and beneficial effects (McMillan 2004);
- design management structures to maximize horizontal networks and minimize vertical hierarchies (Morrison 2002);
- develop and support project teams and networks (Haynes 2003);
- educate organization members for capability, enabling them to adapt to change, generate new knowledge and continually improve their performance (Fraser and Greenhalgh 2001).

What Evidence is there that Complexity Theory Applies to Public Service Change?

Advocacy among academics, consultants and trainers working in the public service field evidences the spread of faith in the validity of these claims. But how robust is the empirical grounding to bolster this new faith? Empirical research literature is conspicuous by its relative absence (Rosenhead 1998). Many accounts of real organizational change are case studies, whether in business (Mitleton-Kelly 2003) or a public service such as higher education (McMillan 2004). An alternative strategy is to take others' findings, which were not framed by complexity theory, to support claims about its application to the public services. Thus, Morrison (2002: 84–5) uses the outcomes of research by Hoy, Tarter and Kottkamp (1991) on school climate to argue that the 'open' climates identified are the most productive for encouraging self-organization and emergence. Later, Morrison (2002: 191) does acknowledge the weak connection between findings and theory that is consequent on adopting this strategy: 'It can be argued that several of the ideas in this book can stand by themselves without *requiring* complexity theory'.

Only now are we beginning to see major funded research projects, and even here the methodology tends towards action research and co-production of knowledge, rather than professional research conducted from a less committed and more sceptical standpoint. A recent instance is 'Integration of Complex Social Systems', a substantial research project based at the London School of Economics. It entailed collaborative action research whose aim was 'to co-create with our business partners an enabling environment to facilitate integration and the emergence of a new organizational form' (ICOSS 2005). There appears to be little research designed to assess the logically prior issue of *whether* complexity theory is fully applicable to the human social world and, if so, with what consequences for the sort of findings and prescriptions that flow from its application.

Rosenhead (1998: 10) points to the limitations of heavy reliance on anecdotal evidence to back claims about the application of complexity theory concepts to organizational management (encompassing, therefore, the public services):

> The problem with anecdotal evidence is that it is most persuasive to those who experienced the events in question, and to those who are already persuaded. For others it can be hard to judge the representativeness of the sample of exhibits. This is especially so if, even unintentionally, different standards of proof or disproof are used for different sides of an argument. Such distortions do occur in Stacey (1992). Thus the advantage of opportunistic policies is supported by presenting examples of success, while the perils of formal planning methods are driven home by examples of failure. Yet obviously opportunism has its failures, and analytic techniques even have their modest achievements – which are not cited.

Overall, a missing link remains between advocates' initial deductive theoretical step of translating concepts from mathematics and the natural sciences to the human social world (and so to the public services), and their subsequent normative step of formulating practical prescriptions. The necessary link is empirical verification: that the conceptual translation is valid, and that prescriptions really do lead to the improvements claimed for them. Evidence is needed about the nature of complexity and of practice to cope with it in public service contexts to which the new ideas are applied. One obvious omission connected with the UK public services is the policy context that advocates tend largely to ignore. A highly centralized approach to reform has long tightened national government control over essentials across the public services, such as the school curriculum or healthcare protocols. At the same time this approach has decentralized control over inessentials, such a devolved operating budget (Taylor-Gooby and Lawson 1993). Room for 'self-organization' has been narrowly circumscribed. Social science-informed research suggests that emergence has been as much connected with mediating reforms as with local innovation (see Hoyle and Wallace 2005).

Lack of evidence confirming the applicability of complexity theory to the public services is compounded by controversy over the original development of complexity theory in mathematics and the natural sciences. There has been criticism of the limited empirical basis for the inductive derivation of certain complexity theory concepts (see Burnes 2005). Much of such evidence as underlies several complexity ideas, including 'sensitive dependence on initial conditions' and 'self-organization', is not empirical. It is based on computer simulations where certain parameters and rules are first set, and then the computer program is run to see what develops over time. But simulations are not, by definition, the real thing. Virtual reality is neither natural world nor human social world reality. Computer simulation evidence can do no more than offer a simplified model (Lissack and Richardson 2001), and modelling is not the direct empirical study of the real world. So a mathematically derived model cannot demonstrate whether the real world actually operates that way, as opposed to having some coincidental intuitive parallel with the model.

How Adequate is the Theoretical Base to Support Prescription?

If the empirical base remains underdeveloped, how robust is complexity theory as a normative frame for prescribing how to manage public service change? It seems unlikely that the prescriptions listed earlier would strike many public service managers as either extreme or particularly novel. They have similar face validity as other lists of prescriptions to be found in the popular management literature, appealing to recognizable characteristics of common experience at a high level of abstraction from the details of particular contexts and practices. Who is going to argue with the advice to give professional staff in public service organizations some scope to experiment collaboratively with ways of improving practice in their sphere of activity? This prescription happens to resonate with the long-established practice of facilitating 'quality circles' (Robson 1984), so is hardly new. But the authority for prescriptions drawn from complexity theory comes primarily from their theoretical foundations, rather than from the inductive synthesis of empirical evidence. So how solid are these theoretical foundations? A verdict of 'shaky' is suggested by several logical and conceptual problems.

First, there are deep-seated logical difficulties with arguing that a particular prescription is likely to produce a desired outcome on the basis of predictive theoretical ideas about the unpredictability of phenomena. If the future is in principle unknowable, how can one know whether a desired outcome is likely to follow from a prescribed practice? Rosenhead (1998: 21) signals such logical problems in his comment that advocates 'provide rational arguments against rationality, as well as forecasting with great confidence the impossibility of forecasting, and planning for the absence of planning'. The insights that concepts from complexity theory provide about the nature of unpredictability are not well suited for the purpose of deriving prescriptions. The latter rely for their authority on predicting – at least implicitly – that their implementation will produce particular desired outcomes. If managers *should* promote self-organization, it is because doing so is predicted to stand a good chance of enabling staff (and so also managers) to reap the proclaimed benefits of self-organization.

Further, casting the flow of interaction in terms of such a multiplicity of diverse causes and proximal and distant effects militates against identifying some causes as operating more powerfully and directly than others. If everything causes everything, then nothing causes anything. Yet advocates wish to argue at the same time that the management practices they prescribe *are* likely to make a difference, resulting in enhanced organizational or service performance. If, say, developing horizontal management structures is advocated to facilitate productive self-organization, then implicitly a significant cause–effect linkage between management structure and desirable creativity is being posited. Even where it is acknowledged that the likelihood of other contingent factors renders this linkage a probability rather than a certainty, a particular cause and its effect are being singled out as both important and open to managerial intervention (with relatively predictable results).

Second, the legitimacy of translating ideas from the natural world to the human social world is open to question. Observable regularities or laws may be adduced which appear to govern the workings of the natural world. But the human social world is fundamentally different, obeying a 'double hermeneutic' (Giddens 1976) where, say, staff in public service organizations construct their own interpretations of their experience. Influences on their interpretation include academic theories which filter down, as when staff receive training in the application of complexity theory. They may be positively influenced by or react against claims about regularities of their behaviour and related prescriptions. To the extent that they all possess a significant degree of agency (the capacity to choose between alternative actions), they retain the capacity to respond in line with their own interpretation, whether consistent with the tenets of complexity theory or not. Structuration theory (Giddens 1984) draws our attention to the way actors' behaviour is not totally determined, though their agency is limited by pre-existing social structures (such as conventions and organizations connected with schooling and health care) that are themselves the largely unwitting product of agency expressed in the past.

There is thus an inherent degree of indeterminacy of meaning in the human social world, lying within structural limits which bound what is considered doable and thinkable. It has no parallel in the natural world. The observed behaviour of social animals like ants, inanimate entities like laser beams or mathematical phenomena like fractal geometrical shapes means nothing to them. But meaning-making is integral to human social life, and so to the work of public service professionals.

Deductively translating a holistic theory of relationships from the natural to the human social world runs the risk of losing sight of the contested arena of meaning-making that puts the humanity into the human social world. While advocates like Stacey emphasize agency, the overall thrust of complexity theory is to foreground the systemic whole. There is abundant unhelpful 'reification', where a public service organization may be referred to as if capable of corporate action independent of the people who constitute its parts. Attention is then deflected from the contribution of incompatible interpretations, of contradictory values, and of conflicting interests and differential levels of access to power among members of the organization to the managerial complexity of organizational and system-wide public service change.

Berger and Luckmann (1967: 106) define reification as the 'apprehension of the products of human activity *as if* they were something other than human products – such as facts of nature'. Nouns describing collectivities – school, university, hospital, healthcare system – are inescapable. But reification in conceiving public service organizations as complex adaptive systems gives rise to mystifying conceptual shorthand, such as '... if an organization wants to exist at the edge of chaos ...' (McMillan 2004: 95). An organization does not literally want to exist. Individual organization members do, they may value incompatible things, they may compete against each other to get what they want and they may change their minds. Reification tends to gloss over the possibility that the parts of an organization or system are as capable of conflicting with each other as fitting neatly and harmoniously into the evolving whole.

Third, there is an inherent tension for advocates between the extent of the parallel between the natural and human social worlds that they wish to assert and the potential for realistic prescription. The quotation from Morrison that heads this chapter implies the most direct of parallels. Complexity is the same in the natural and human social worlds. The view of Stacey (2003) that human social groups *are* complex adaptive systems runs Morrison close. Complexity in the natural world is analogous to complexity in the human social world. There is extensive (but not necessarily complete) overlap between corresponding elements of complexity in the two spheres. Where there is overlap, specific elements of complexity in the natural world equate to specific elements in the less well understood human social world. If the parallel is indeed this strong, then what is observed to happen in the natural world forms a predictive basis for prescribing what should happen in the human social world. But acceptance of its prescriptive force hinges on the scarcely sustainable view that similarities between the two worlds far outweigh their differences. We saw above that the double hermeneutic of the human social world distinguishes it radically from the natural world.

Where a looser parallel is implied, as does Haynes in relation to the public services, the approximation of metaphor (rather than the more precise equivalence of analogy) allows for a more elastic and impressionistic overlap between the natural and human social worlds. A dictionary definition of metaphor is 'a figure of speech by which a thing is spoken of as being that which it only resembles' (Chambers 2001). Therefore, applying complexity theory as an extended metaphor allows for the natural and social worlds to remain worlds apart. The one may resemble the other in some ways but they are not, by definition, the same phenomenon. Resemblance allows for relatively superficial parallels to be drawn without implying the tighter equivalence of analogy. This approach is entirely consistent with the common practice in management theory of using metaphors to inform practice by drawing attention to intuitively recognizable, but hitherto unnoticed, patterns in organizational experience.

However, as Morgan (1986) has demonstrated, there is no obvious limit to the variety of metaphors that can stimulate managerial thought. Very different phenomena have some resemblance to each other – witness the metaphor of organizations as brains. So positing only a more distant parallel weakens the prescriptive potential of complexity theory. It becomes demoted to just one of many possible metaphors, highlighting many possible resemblances between diverse phenomena. Moreover, pointing to resemblances gives no backing for the normative claim that what happens within one phenomenon should happen in another. Suppose it is accepted that self-organization observed in the natural world may legitimately be highlighted as a metaphor to stimulate thinking about how to create space for local experimentation in managing complex public service change. It does not follow that managers should necessarily promote activities that resemble self-organization, or that doing so will produce desirable outcomes, since it is also accepted that the two worlds are different.

Fourth, the initial act of faith in the applicability of complexity theory to the human social world, including the public services, creates pressure to make the full set of concepts fit – whether the parallel is argued to be direct, analogous or metaphorical. Demonstrating sufficient parallel for face validity sometimes requires language that distorts the one phenomenon to make it fit the other. Referring to any interpretive framework as a 'uniframe', Minsky (1985: 299) notes that:

> Good metaphors are useful because they transport uniframes, intact, from one world into another. Such cross-realm correspondences can enable us to transport entire families of problems into other realms, in which we can apply them to some already well-developed skills. However, such correspondences are hard to find since most reformulations merely transform the uniframes of one realm into disorderly accumulation in the other realm.

In other words, the more two realms differ, the greater the potential of inadvertently inducing 'disorderly accumulation' when transporting a uniframe from one realm to the other. An early account by Stacey (1996: 330) illustrates the difficulty. He draws a parallel between the interpretation of self-organization whereby gas molecules form a laser beam and self-organization in the human social world. Heating the gas makes the molecules in it become more unstable, increasing their random movement until they come to a critical point. Then they:

> ... appear to communicate with each other and suddenly they organize themselves to all point in the same direction. The result is a laser beam casting its light for miles. The sudden choice of molecules all to point in the same direction is not predictable from the laws of physics. There is no central intention or law prescribing this behaviour; it emerges out of instability through a self-organizing creative process.

Further on, Stacey (1996: 333) proceeds to define self-organization in the human social world as 'the spontaneous formation of interest groups and coalitions around specific issues, communication about those issues, cooperation and the formation of consensus on and commitment to a response to those issues'. Senior organization managers in situations marked by some uncertainty are advised to provide conditions that foster creative problem solving through spontaneous self-organization.

The original concept of self-organization within the uniframe of natural science is neatly transported to that of the human social world, through at the price of some 'disorderly accumulation'. Stacey relies on a linguistic sleight of hand, minimizing the gap between gaseous and human contexts by anthropomorphizing the gas molecules in the laser beam account. Implying that molecules 'communicate' with each other, 'organize themselves' or make a 'choice' to point in the same direction makes the parallel appear closer that managers can create conditions where colleagues in situations of uncertainty are likely to intercommunicate, to organize themselves spontaneously, and to make a choice to work towards a shared goal of which managers would approve. Gas molecules, of course, do not literally communicate, organize themselves or make choices. But it helps to render the concept of self-organization translatable between the natural and human social worlds if the degree of correspondence between them is exaggerated. Ironically, the language used here to describe self-organization in the natural world is actually metaphorical: using 'a figure of speech by which a thing is spoken of as being that which it only resembles'. The behaviour of gas molecules may resemble that of people in organizations, but in only a superficial way.

Even where complexity theory is applied consciously as a metaphor, there is a temptation for advocates to gloss over differences in seeking to maximize the apparent resemblance. Instead of anthropomorphizing the natural world, this resemblance is made to seem closer by reifying the human social world. Illustratively, when Haynes (2003: 34) applies the notion of bifurcation (Table 2.1) to public service change, he initially acknowledges that he is translating the term loosely: 'Strictly speaking, bifurcation refers to a complete separation, a new order and breaking of one system into two'. The translation begins with the reifying claim that 'Many public organizations may recognize this process in their attempts at reorganization'. (In what sense do organizations, literally, recognize anything?) The resemblance is then elaborated by referring to increasingly complex demands on public service organizations and responsive attempts to reorganize them. Haynes (2003: 34) concludes that:

> Many organizations have found a bifurcation of processes and purposes in recent years. The challenge is to find new and less rigidly defined structures and processes that assist what is required, rather than hindering it. Often, such organizations feel that they really are *on the edge of chaos*. What this means is that boundaries are less clear and managers have to find a new dynamic comprising formal and informal agreements about what is good and acceptable practice with a flexibility of approach.

The meaning that Haynes accords to bifurcation in the realm of the public services is diluted in comparison with the original. Far from reorganization amounting to the radical 'breaking of one system into two', it turns out to entail the evolutionary development of more flexible structures and processes and ongoing negotiation over what is to count as acceptable practice. Thus Haynes has contributed to disorderly accumulation because he has to shoehorn the natural scientific concept of bifurcation to make it fit the world of the public services as well as he does. In the process he underplays the very significant differences between the two realms.

Fifth, it is questionable whether the application of complexity theory provides authoritative support for advocates' implicit claim that the values embodied in their prescriptions are morally just, and so should be accepted. Values are integral to the dominant intellectual projects of knowledge-for-action and instrumentalism. The authoritative force of advocates' prescriptions rests on the interpretation they give to complexity theory concepts when applying them to the human social world. But, as Morrison (2002: 190) acknowledges, 'complexity theory is amoral'. So any values that are attached to it must derive from the inferences drawn by advocates. Their central focus on the evolving relationships between interacting elements of systems leads to their strong emphasis, noted already, on promoting ongoing change through self-organization.

Creating conditions that facilitate good communication is a common prescription. Some advocates (including Morrison) go so far as to suggest that public service or other organizations should operate according to democratic principles. Their members will then have the freedom to communicate as required for self-organization. Yet the value placed on organizational democracy does not flow automatically from the original (amoral) notion of self-organization in the natural world. Those who translate complexity theory to the human social world inject their values when making their interpretation of what is to count as self-organization in, say, public service organizations. Democratic values come first. Their justification through conceptualizing the nature of self-organization in the human social world comes second. So complexity theory, in itself, cannot justify holding democratic values in the workplace. Justification might come later if empirically it was demonstrated that establishing organizational democracy did lead to more effective change and more effective operation (as judged according to values underpinning what counts as effectiveness). This step has yet to be taken.

How Consistent is the Application of Complexity Theory with Others' Work?

Complexity theory advocates attempt to show, quite appropriately, how their approach differs from and offers more than whatever has gone before. However, many succumb to the temptation to create 'straw persons' when reviewing older traditions. What are actually diverse and disputed areas of enquiry get lumped together in creating a rather simplistic and overly homogeneous account of the 'mechanistic' theories within 'conventional wisdom' (Morrison) or the 'Newtonian–Cartesian paradigm' (McMillan) that complexity theory is to transcend. Thus there is plentiful criticism of hierarchical command-and-control structures, goal-setting or long-range forecasting. At the same time, uncritical approval is given to theories that are interpreted as challenging this mechanistic view in line with advocates' interpretation of complexity theory ideas. A much-used example is where the notion of the 'learning organization' (Senge 1990) is associated with the potential for productive self-organization. Problems with such a conception (see Hoyle and Wallace 2005), and counter-evidence from research (here on collective organizational learning) are largely ignored. It remains unclear what is actually new, especially when considering the prescriptions that flow from the application of complexity theory.

These prescriptions, as we argued earlier, resonate with many in conventional literatures following the knowledge-for-action and instrumentalist intellectual projects in public service fields. For example, the tradition of school improvement research, theorizing and training has long promoted consultative – even democratic – operation, encouraged teachers to innovate, fostered their continual professional development and promoted organizational learning (e.g. Joyce, Calhoun and Hopkins 1999; Hopkins 2001; Stoll, Fink and Earl 2003). The congruence between complexity theory and other traditions reinforces the sense that advocates of complexity theory for the public services are indeed onto something. But conversely, this congruence also suggests that they are missing the same aspects of the phenomenon of complex public service change as their counterparts working in other knowledge-for-action and instrumentalist traditions.

Most significant perhaps, these different approaches embody much well-intentioned but unrealistic wishful thinking, based on the twin assumptions that organization members possess both sufficient agency to interact spontaneously, and a shared desire to collaborate in bringing about change for improvement as defined by managers and politicians. Findings of the sociologically oriented public service research and theorizing that lean more towards the knowledge-for-understanding intellectual project call those assumptions into question. (UK examples include Moore, George and Halpin 2002; Wallace and Pocklington 2002; McNulty and Ferlie 2002; Dopson and Fitzgerald 2005; Hoyle and Wallace 2005.) As we argued above, in reifying public service change, complexity theory advocates downplay the integral part played by incompatible interpretations, conflicting interests, contradictory values and differential access to power – whether among government politicians who seek to regulate and mould the direction of public service change, or among the staff in public service organizations who seek to endorse, mediate or subvert it.

Finally, we note, in passing, that the human side of organizational change depicted in the sociologically oriented work intuitively resonates much more strongly with our personal experience (as school teachers and university academics) than the reified picture conjured up by the prescriptions of complexity theory advocates.

Incompatible interpretations of the same social situation coupled with conflictual uses of authority and influence to achieve contradictory interests were the stuff of the research that one of us conducted into his own managerial practice some years ago (Wallace 1986). The findings could be reinterpreted thus, using complexity theory ideas. Managers' well-intentioned innovatory and consultative managerial activity created a bifurcation point. Among the managed it stimulated a shared sense of threat to their professional autonomy. Their collegial self-organization was designed to subvert the endeavours of the managers, resulting in a new form of order. All innovatory and consultative managerial activity was forced to cease, and the status quo was restored.

The Problems and Potential of Complexity Theory for Informing Public Service Change

Let us now take stock. On the downside, the prospects do not seem strong for complexity theory to become widely accepted, either as a performative theory or as a proven source of valid prescriptions that render it more enduring than a management fad. There is little novelty about the ensuing prescriptions. There is little empirical evidence that they actually work, and some social science-informed research to suggest that they fail adequately to address endemic ambiguities in meaning-making, associated uses of power and contextual factors delimiting agency. There is little possibility of circumventing the logical and conceptual flaws connected with such a strongly deductive theoretical basis for applying complexity theory ideas to public service change. Predicting the unpredictable, scrambling causes and effects, conceiving resemblances as equivalents, reifying change, force-fitting an entire uniframe into a radically different realm, and grounding prescriptions in an amoral theory all contribute to creating the 'chaos' of disorderly accumulation.

On the upside, advocates *are* on to something: they do seek to address aspects of phenomena related to human social life in general and to the complexity and relative unmanageability of public service change in particular. The conceptualization of complexity is new, and it does focus squarely on what is widely recognized to be one hallmark of contemporary change in the public services. Its very novelty gives it scope as a vehicle for challenging managers' assumptions and offering constructive ideas for their consideration in trying to render complex change as manageable as possible. Some practitioners reportedly do find the prescriptions, the co-production of knowledge activities and associated training experiences useful.

So our answer to the review question we posed is that, on the one hand, there are major problems with the application of complexity theory to prescribe public service change practice. But, on the other hand, complexity theory does have some modest potential as a convenient metaphor, one among many that may inform thinking about how to manage complex change effectively. The deductive approach adopted by advocates of complexity theory for the public services may amount to starting at the wrong end: with the natural world. Greater potential to inform practice seems likely to be offered by approaches that start at the other end: with public service change contexts. Here concepts from the social sciences provide orienting concepts as a sensitizing device for more inductive generation of ideas about the nature of complexity in the change process and how people cope with it.

REFERENCES

Anderson, R. and McDaniel, R. (2000) Managing health care organizations: where professionalism meets complexity. *Health Care Management Review*, **25**(1), 83–92.

Berger, P. and Luckmann, T. (1967) *The Social Construction of Reality*. Harmondsworth: Penguin.

Burnes, B. (2005) Complexity theories and organizational change. *International Journal of Management Reviews*, **7**(2), 73–90.

Chambers (2001) *The Chambers Dictionary*. Edinburgh: Chambers Harrap.

Donaldson, A., Lank, E. and Maher, J. (2005) Connecting through communities: how a voluntary organization is influencing health care policy and practice. *Journal of Change Management*, **5**(1), 71–86.

Dopson, S. and Fitzgerald, L. (eds) (2005) *Knowledge to Action? Evidence-Based Health Care in Context*. Oxford: Oxford University Press.

Fraser, S. and Greenhalgh, T. (2001) Complexity science: coping with complexity; educating for capability. *British Medical Journal*, **323**, 799–803.

Fullan, M. (1993) *Change Forces: Probing the Depths of Education Reform*. London: Falmer Press.

Fullan, M. (2001) *The New Meaning of Educational Change*, 3rd edn. New York: Teachers College Press.

Giddens, A. (1976) *New Rules of Sociological Method*. London: Hutchinson.

Giddens, A. (1984) *The Constitution of Society*. Cambridge: Polity Press.

Gleick, J. (1988) *Chaos: Making a New Science*. London: Heinemann.

Haynes, P. (2003) *Managing Complexity in the Public Services*. Maidenhead: Open University Press.

Harrogate Training and Development (2005) Management and leadership in social care. http://www.htd.org.uk/cf/main10.htm (accessed November 2005).

Higginbotham, N., Albrecht, G. and Connor, L. (2001) *Health Social Science: a Transdisciplinary and Complexity Perspective*. Oxford: Oxford University Press.

Hopkins, D. (2001) *School Improvement for Real*. London: RoutledgeFalmer.

Hoy, W.K., R.B. (1991) *Open Schools, Healthy Schools*. London: Sage.

Hoyle, E. (1986) Overview. In E. Hoyle and A. McMahon (eds) *The Management of Schools*. London: Kogan Page, pp. 11–26.

Hoyle, E. (2003) Review of Morrison (2002). *Educational Management and Administration*, **31**(2), 213–16.

Hoyle, E. and Wallace, M. (2005) *Educational Leadership: Ambiguity, Professionals and Managerialism*. London: Sage.

ICOSS (2005) ICOSS Project. http://www.psych.lse.ac.uk/complexity/icoss.htm (accessed November 2005).

Joyce, B., Calhoun, E.F. and Hopkins, D. (1999) *The New Structure of School Improvement*. Buckingham: Open University Press.

Lissack, M.R. and Richardson, K.A. (2001) When modelling social systems, models ≠ the modelled. *Emergence*, **3**(4), 95–111.

Maguire, S. and McKelvey, B. (eds) (1999) Special issue on complexity and management: where are we? *Emergence*, **1**(2).

McMillan, E. (2004) *Complexity, Organizations and Change*. London: Routledge.

McNulty, T. and Ferlie, E. (2002) *Reengineering Health Care: the Complexities of Organizational Transformation*. Oxford: Oxford University Press.

Minsky, M. (1985) *The Society of Mind*. New York: Simon & Schuster.

Mitleton-Kelly, E. (2003) Ten principles of complexity and enabling infrastructures. In E. Mitleton-Kelly (ed.) *Complex Systems and Evolutionary Perspectives on Organizations*. Oxford: Elsevier.

Mitleton-Kelly, E. (2005) World futures: a complexity approach to co-creating an innovative environment. *World Futures*. Special issue on complexity and innovation. http://www.psych.lse.ac.uk/complexity/ICoSS/Papers/World_Futures_article1.pdf (accessed November 2005).

Moore, A., George, R. and Halpin, D. (2002) The developing role of the headteacher in English schools: management, leadership and pragmatism. *Educational Management and Administration*. **30**(2), 175–88.

Morgan, G. (1986) *Images of Organization*. Newbury Park: Sage.

Morrison, K. (2002) *School Leadership and Complexity Theory*. London: RoutledgeFalmer.

Nonaka, I. (1988) Creating order out of organizational chaos: self-renewal in Japanese firms. *California Management Review*, Spring, 57–73.

Pascale, R.T., Milleman, M. and Gioja, L. (2000) *Surfing the Edge of Chaos*. London: TEXERE Publishing.

Plexus Institute (2005) Plexus Institute homepage. http://www.plexusinstitute.org/ (accessed November 2005).

Plsek, P. and Wilson, T. (2001) Complexity science: complexity, leadership, and management in health care organizations. *British Medical Journal*, **323**, 746–9.

Robson, M. (ed.) (1984) *Quality Circles in Action*. Aldershot: Gower.

Rosenhead, J. (1998) Complexity theory and management practice. Operational Research Working Paper No. 98.25. London: London School of Economics and Political Science.

Senge, P. (1990) *The Fifth Discipline: the Art and Practice of the Learning Organization*. New York: Doubleday.

Stacey, R. (1991) *The Chaos Frontier: Creative Strategic Control for Business*. Oxford: Butterworth-Heinemann.

Stacey, R. (1992) *Managing the Unknowable*. San Francisco: Jossey-Bass.

Stacey, R. (1996) *Strategic Management and Organizational Dynamics: the Challenge of Complexity*, 2nd edn. London: Pitman Publishing.

Stacey, R. (2003) *Strategic Management and Organizational Dynamics: the Challenge of Complexity*, 4th edn. Harlow: FT/Prentice Hall.

Stoll, L., Fink, D. and Earl, L. (2003) *It's About Learning (and It's About Time)*. London: RoutledgeFalmer.

Taylor-Gooby, P. and Lawson, R. (1993) Where we go from here: the new order in welfare. In P. Taylor-Gooby and R. Lawson (eds) *Markets and Managers: New Issues in the Delivery of Welfare*. Buckingham: Open University Press.

Waldrop, M. (1994) *Complexity*. New York: Penguin.

Wallace, M. (1986) Towards an action research approach to educational management. Unpublished PhD thesis. Centre for Applied Research in Education, University of East Anglia.

Wallace, M. and Pocklington, K. (2002) *Managing Complex Educational Change: Large-Scale Reorganization of Schools*. London: RoutledgeFalmer.

Wallace, M. and Wray, A. (2006) *Critical Reading and Writing for Postgraduates*. London: Sage.

Wheatley, M. (1992) *Leadership and the New Science: Learning about Organization from an Orderly Universe*. San Francisco: Berrett-Koehler.

Zimmerman, B., Lindberg, C. and Plsek, P. (1998) *Edgeware: Insights from Complexity Science for Health Care Leaders*. Irving, TX: VHA Inc.

CHAPTER 3

THE EMERGENCE OF NEW ORGANIZATIONAL FORMS: NETWORKS OF INTEGRATED SERVICES IN HEALTH CARE

Lise Lamothe and Jean-Louis Denis

This chapter shows how insightful social science-informed approaches to theorizing can be in deepening our understanding of complex public service change through social science theory-based research. Lise Lamothe and Jean-Louis Denis pursue knowledge-for-understanding, employing new institutional theory as a conceptual framework for interpreting how a government initiative to create networks of integrated healthcare services across the Canadian province of Quebec was mediated. They note that the initiative amounted to a complex change expressing in some way all the characteristics of complexity identified by Wallace (Chapter 1). New institutional theory offers a more elaborate conceptualization of the context-dependence characteristic, theorizing the influence of institutional history and external contextual factors on the perceptions and values of those involved in changing practice.

The shift to new arrangements for providing local health care, in which a range of service organizations share in offering a seamless array of services, ran counter to patterns of beliefs and values among clinical professionals and managers about the appropriateness of existing arrangements. The transition to integrated health care implied the development of new organizational forms, routinized ways of providing services through a network of interrelated organizations. Lamothe and Denis highlight the importance of exploring not just contextual factors but also the micro-dynamics of change: the interplay of power within and between key groups of stakeholders, legitimated by their existing or possibly altered beliefs as they gradually negotiate a new order of internal organizational and inter-organizational relationships.

Their research shows how contradictory historical and interpretive forces led to the emergent hybridization of organizational forms, comprising networks of only partially integrated healthcare provision. They may be temporary phenomena, or they could become legitimated and so institutionalized as the new norm.

Introduction

In recent years, healthcare systems have been subjected to major reforms. These have been driven by demographic, technological and economic pressures and have led to various forms of cost cutting and restructuring. At the same time, there has been a universal perception of the need to implement more integrated systems of care, although the struggle to find the best way to conceive and implement them is still ongoing. Over a decade ago, Shortell *et al.* (1993) proposed a definition for these integrated delivery systems. Judging by the frequency of references to it, this definition has generated considerable consensus and has become an ideal towards which healthcare systems should aim. An integrated system of health care is defined as:

> a network of organizations that provides or arranges to provide a coordinated continuum of services to a defined population and is willing to be held clinically and fiscally accountable for the outcomes and the health status of the population served.

Experience shows that the implementation of these networks of integrated services is very complex. It forces a redefinition of the core of healthcare services and in doing so, challenges embedded dynamics. While attempting to resolve system deficiencies, networks of integrated services challenge the micro-dynamics of healthcare production. In that sense, they are revolutionary and call for the emergence of new organizational forms.

The development and implementation of networks of integrated services represents a major change in healthcare systems because it implies changes in the status and autonomy of existing organizations, and changes in the way professionals conceive their responsibilities towards patients. Looking more closely at the components of complex organizational change, as described by Wallace and Pocklington (2002), networks of integrated services express the characteristics of complexity.

1   Complex change is large-scale. Multiple stakeholders are involved; they come from public, private and community organizations and they influence change from multiple (local to national) levels of decision making. Also, the presence of an extensive range of healthcare specialists, who promote different change initiatives and the means to achieve them, increases the importance of micro-dynamics.
2   Complex change is componential. Integrated services imply the creation of multiple new organizational and inter-organizational arrangements built on existing modes of functioning.
3   Complex change is systemic. Cross-level discourses are entailed in making these new arrangements. Differentiated power relationships are at play between professionals, between professionals and decision-makers, and among decision-makers at all levels.

4   Complex change is differentially impacting. Some groups need to make deeper changes in their practices; a shift towards more developed primary care services is expected.
5   Complex change is contextually dependent. Planned changes need to incorporate rapidly emerging technological developments and public health practices (prevention and health promotion). In the healthcare industry, understanding context is of major importance.

In previous works, we observed that the implementation of multidimensional change required the emergence of collective leadership based on the cooperation of leaders with multiple sources of expertise and legitimacy (Denis, Lamothe and Langley 2001b). This type of leadership is congruent with the phenomenon of 'orchestration' identified by Wallace and Pocklington (2002) in their study of major educational change, also discussed in Chapter 1.

Here we first briefly review how organizational forms and their transformation have been accounted for by new institutional theorists. Their focus is on the constitutive beliefs that are required to delineate organizational forms (Scott 1995) and how they are imported from broader institutional frameworks to provide legitimacy and routines of behaviour. Using this conceptual framework, we then draw on our research on the creation of networks of integrated services to expose and reflect on the dynamics taking place during the transition to these new organizational forms. We argue that these new forms are subjected to both contextual and micro-level factors. Better understanding of the micro-dynamics taking place at the professional level and their interactions with organizational and supra-organizational dynamics is essential to comprehend whether and, if so, how integrated systems will become institutionalized forms of healthcare delivery.

Reflecting on the challenges that these new forms impose on existing organizational features, we suggest that the organic evolution towards implementing networks of integrated services puts the system into a hybrid form. This hybridization may be interpreted as the tangible expression of the contradictory forces applied. Some of these forces may be seen as inertia flowing from the historical heritage. If this is the case, the system may risk remaining stuck in the middle. However, the experimental changes conducted have been a stepping stone in the process of emergence of these new organizational forms. Their implementation – albeit localized and variable – has increased their legitimacy.

The Transformation of Organizational Forms

Literature on organizational forms focuses mainly on description, leading to their categorization in various ideal types or configurations (Mintzberg 1979). Defined as 'the degree to which an organization's elements are connected by a single theme' (Miller 1999: 31), the concept of configuration aims at capturing the complexity of organizations and exposing their inner logic. The idea is that organizational elements often coalesce into a limited number of relatively stable common types or configurations that could describe a large proportion of high-performing organizations (Miller 1987). In this sense the concept of configuration is related to those of 'basic patterns' (Van de Ven and Drazin 1985), 'gestalts' (Miller 1981), types (Mintzberg 1989) and archetypes (Miller and Friesen 1977, 1978; Greenwood and Hinings 1993).

However, according to Miller (1996, 1999), what is often missing in the literature is the search for configuration itself: the search for complex systems of interdependency brought about by central orchestrating themes. By favouring categorizing over analysing over a long period, academic research on configurations has developed only limited understanding of how configurations or archetypes emerge and are being transformed over time. Their emergence and transformation appear to be the outcome of ongoing processes of interactions between partners involved. Therefore behind ideal types, dynamic construction processes take place. Their complexity carries much uncertainty, which poses a challenge to the management of change in order to promote and sustain coherence and cohesiveness.

Studying the transformation of organizational forms, institutional theorists put an emphasis on the social forces that extend beyond organizational boundaries (DiMaggio and Powell 1991; Scott 1995), suggesting that an action taken by an organization is not considered as a choice among a series of possibilities determined by internal arrangements but rather as a choice among a series of legitimate options determined by a group of actors forming the organizational field (Scott 1991). Contextual dynamics may induce a need for organizational adaptation (Leblebici et al. 1991; Oliver 1991); actions are then influenced by exchange dynamics where actors are engaged with partners in the field (Greenwood and Hinings 1996).

Institutional change may occur, but the transition revolves around what Scott (1995) has called the pillars of institutions: their regulative (or legal), normative (or social) and cognitive (or cultural) aspects. One of the pillars may exercise more influence at one point in time but the three coexist and are interrelated. The regulative aspects are essentially rules that guide or even coerce institutional actions. Normative aspects are generally expressed through policies and procedures, practice standards and training curricula. Institutional actions and beliefs are then guided in part by professionalization (or social obligation) and motivated by a need to conform to norms imposed by universities or professional associations. Cognitive aspects are expressed through symbols (vocabulary, signs) and the cultural frameworks that help decode reality and bring meaning. They help legitimize actions. Therefore, the context influences institutions through rules, norms and beliefs that together describe reality for the organization, explaining what is and what can be done. These institutional frameworks provide legitimacy and routines of behaviour (Meyer and Rowan 1977). In sum, new institutional theory enables us to understand how social choices are moulded and channelled by the institutional environment.

This seems to imply that the adaptation of institutions to contextual dynamics is incremental, but events may introduce debates and modify issues in such a way that discontinuities may appear in the course of events (Lorange, Scott Morton and Ghoshal 1986; Hoffman 1999). Facing uncertainty, organizations need to innovate, experiment, even engage in restructuring processes in order to be able to deal with the new rules (Meyer 1982; Meyer, Brooks and Goes 1990). In that respect, Hoffman argues that organizational fields are structured around issues rather than markets or technologies. This notion introduces the idea that organizational fields are centres of debates where, because of the presence of divergent interests, negotiations take place on how to interpret issues. The formation of an organizational field is then not a static process. Events stimulate the introduction of new forms of debate which induce a modification in the composition of the field and in the patterns of interactions between partners concerned. Partners in the field (government, organizations, associations or corporations) then form a complex system where the interpretation of issues and the objectives pursued vary. New organizational forms may emerge.

Studies of the emergence of new organizational forms have emphasized that the latter evolve over time and that consequently their history is of major importance (DiMaggio and Powell 1991). Organizational forms are then the emergent product of dynamics occurring in a specific context or organizational field (DiMaggio and Powell 1983) and their legitimacy will draw on existing beliefs in the community of organizations in the field. The processual character of their evolution is marked by periods where ideas and intentions are being circulated with respect to the creation of new organizational forms, where there are social movements that secure resources for their development, and where there are regulations that identify new forms as legitimized organizational roles (Tucker, Singh and Meinhard 1990). It also appears that the transition relies on the presence of interested actors, 'institutional entrepreneurs' who can use collective action to foster the cognitive and socio-political legitimacy of the new forms.

The new institutional perspective offers an insightful approach for analysing the transformation of organizational forms. Not only does it allow analysis to take into account various forces influencing the relationships between organizations of the same community, it also allows analysis to capture the dynamic aspects of change. This approach is then useful to analyse the dynamics occurring across the community of organizations that comprises a healthcare system. However, with an emphasis on contextual factors, new institutional theorists may have neglected the influence of micro-dynamics occurring within and between organizations. In healthcare organizations, as in other professional organizations, professionals carry their own beliefs and have autonomy and control over production processes. Therefore, the creation of integrated networks of services, as emerging new organizational forms, is subjected to influences from both contextual and micro-level factors.

Probing into the inner dynamics of hospitals as examples of such organizations, Bucher and Stelling (1969) illustrated that they were intensely political and fluid entities, resulting in what Cohen, March and Olsen (1972) called 'organized

anarchies' characterized by considerable ambiguity and uncertainty. The interactions between professionals, and between professionals and managers, result
in highly complex organizational forms, especially when different types of professionals interact, as in a hospital. Developments in science and technology have
greatly increased the complexity within hospitals, adding new types of professionals, changing the nature of their work and increasing their interdependencies.
The complexity of these professional organizations relies greatly on the complexity
of inter-professional relationships at play.

In order better to understand inter-professional relationships, Freidson (1970)
documented the existence of a 'professional dominance' relationship between professional groups (that is, dominance by doctors). Bucher and Stelling (1969) argued
that professionals create their own social order within the organization as a whole.
Their 'negotiated orders' (Strauss *et al.* 1963; Strauss *et al.* 1964) develop and
stabilize through informal ongoing interactions and tacit rules and mutual trust
developed over time help to hold operating units together (Lamothe 1999). A
state of conflictive equilibrium (Crozier 1964) emerges as individuals and groups
develop strategies to position themselves favourably within the organization and
try to maximize their control over sources of uncertainty (Crozier and Friedberg
1978). Professional influence is therefore differentiated and, in hospitals, physicians have traditionally been the dominant group. Professional domains are then
constantly being redefined (as also explored in Chapter 8) and some professional
groups are hierarchically subordinated to others (Abbott 1988).

The web of reciprocity relations among professionals extends to the upper level
of professional organizations, dilutes the role of management and creates a need
for collaboration and emergent negotiation not only in the operating core but also
right to the top of the organization (Denis *et al.* 1999). The administrative group
then exercises largely indirect – integrative and support – roles (Mintzberg 1979)
and through these processes, the clinical operating core has often had considerable
immunity from managerial influence. The interplay of these contradictory forces
at the top contributes to the stabilization of the system.

Overall, this analysis of aspects of emergent collaboration in professional
organizations paints a more complex portrait of the context in which changing
ideologies of healthcare delivery must take root. It reveals certain fundamental
dynamics that will affect attempts to traverse boundaries at all levels (Denis *et al.*
1999). If networks of integrated services are to become institutionalized organizational forms, they will need to emerge, over a period of time, from these inter-
professional and inter-organizational dynamic processes.

Networks of Integrated Services in Health Care

In Quebec, as in most countries, the healthcare system has been historically structured around a series of organizations with a specific mission (hospitals, primary
care and long-term care organizations). Over time, these organizations have

developed specific cultures, adopting specific interpretive schemes and structural arrangements. Such fragmentation of the system, with organizations functioning quasi-independently, has resulted in deficiencies in terms of access, continuity and adaptation of services.

In the early 1990s, reforms were implemented with the aim of improving the performance of the system. They were built on existing logic by focusing on structures (vertical and horizontal mergers) and emphasizing specific missions. This strategy did not allow for the achievement of objectives. However, during this period, another logic for reforms has gradually made headway: the system needs to be conceived differently, according to production processes in an inter-organizational context. This logic was supported by new technology developments pushing for more ambulatory care and at the same time creating a need for better recognition of organizations' interdependencies. Also, public health concerns encouraged the development of more community-based services. Transition to this new logic for reforms slowly penetrated the system, which was struggling to conceive and implement better integrated networks of services.

From the late 1990s, in order to stimulate learning and renewal in the system, the federal government has invested in research to allow short-term pilot experiments to be implemented. Many projects were aimed at introducing and evaluating new modes of integrated delivery systems, while promoting various means to achieve them. As we were associated as evaluation researchers in four of these pilot projects (Simard *et al.* 2001; Lamarche *et al.* 2001; Contandriopoulos *et al.* 2001; Touati, Denis and Langley 2001), we were frontline observers of the dynamics leading to the creation of networks of integrated services.

The four projects were implemented in Quebec and are labelled SIPA, Laurentians, Capitation-Montérégie and PACTE. All the experiments aimed at improving access and continuity of services by adapting existing modes of functioning. These projects were formulated in the belief that better primary care and home care services would have positive effects on population health and help control increasing healthcare costs and utilization of resources.

The four projects are mainly grass-roots initiatives. SIPA emerged from an alliance between academics and clinicians. Physicians concerned with the deficiencies of the care provided to the frail elderly and academics in the area of healthcare policy pooled their expertise to develop an original model of integrated delivery. Sites for implementation were selected and professionals and managers were co-opted after the model had been worked out by clinical and academic leaders.

The Capitation-Montérégie and PACTE projects were initiated by managers concerned with the lack of continuity in the care provided to the frail elderly in their geographical area. Both suggest various adaptive means to increase the efficiency of healthcare delivery, based on extended use of primary care and networking between the organizations involved. Unlike the SIPA project, academics became involved mostly at the implementation and evaluation stages.

Finally, the Laurentians project was also aimed at achieving efficient integrated systems. But it differs from the others because no funds to support operational changes were provided: the project involved evaluating an ongoing attempt by a regional health agency to implement integrated systems in each of its five sub-regions. In this case, the promotion of specific models was left to local practitioners. Academic involvement was restricted to in-process discussions with practitioners and to evaluation. In spite of the differences between the projects, similar observations may be made about their implementation processes.

After two and a half years, none of the projects had managed to achieve a stable network mode of functioning. All the networks had evolved into a hybrid form, keeping features of the previous modes of functioning alongside attempting to introduce horizontally integrated services. Some within the Laurentians project remained embryonic. Emergent forms varied from one context to another, and they even varied between the Laurentian sub-regions. Their main differences related to the number of producers involved, resulting in a more or less fully deployed form of network. Those involving fewer producers tended to revolve around hospitals. We observed that the more deployed networks were generally associated with care and cure services for patients with chronic clinical conditions, while networks having hospitals as their focal point were associated with ambulatory medicine. The various horizontal processes implemented were influenced by existing professional and organizational practices, and also by the existence or not of professional consensus over beliefs about how care and cure services should be offered to specific clienteles. Progression towards a network mode of functioning followed a rhythm specific to each context and influenced by interactions between the actors involved.

Our observations suggest that the pilot projects to implement networks of integrated services have stimulated debates on the issue among all actors involved (Hoffman 1999). In that sense, they may be seen as a 'social movement for their development'. Debates within the organizational field are at the core of the processes involved in the emergence of new organizational forms. It is through participation in debates and controversies that various actors negotiate plausible pathways within their own context to materialize new organizational forms.

Debates generated are part of a complex interactive process where interpretive ideas, experiments and regulation mutually influence each other in a dynamic way. Emergent organizational forms are therefore the outcome of the interplay between the three. This is consistent with new institutional theory where change is seen as the outcome of the dynamic interrelationships between the pillars of institutions and organizational forms as the emergent product of dynamics occurring in a specific context. Our view may, however, be opposed to that of other authors (Conrad and Shortell 1996; Barber *et al.* 1998) who position most integrated delivery systems at the second of a four-stage lifecycle process.

Also consistent with new institutional theory, our observations suggest that the debates on the issue of networks of integrated services modify the composition of the field and the patterns of interactions. But, because of the complexity of the field and the nature of professional organizations, debates take place at more then one level and are the vehicle for the promotion of partners' individual interests. All three levels of debates influence each other.

Debates at the field level

At this level various discourses interact and influence actions that lead to the emergence of the new organizational form:

- Those involved should come from various sectors of activity (public policy discourse).
- Services should be community based (public health discourse).
- Services should be adapted to technological pressures (technological discourse).
- The complexity of services forces the adoption of a global perspective in understanding clients' needs and the reorganization of work processes to promote collegiality, interdisciplinarity and complementarity (services discourse).
- Services should be more efficient (managerial discourse).

These various discourses may be interpreted as the expression of the ideological position of their promoters. But they are also one of the means used to influence ideas on models of integrated delivery systems and their implementation process. For example, the public health discourse feeds arguments for the realignment of the focal centre of the system from hospitals to primary care organizations. At the same time, the technological discourse tends to keep the hospital at the centre of the system. Leaders in the managerial, clinical and academic domains are very active. They often use public arenas to promote their beliefs and their vision of the best model, and to obtain the necessary resources for its implementation. Their use of collective action helps to foster the cognitive and socio-political legitimacy of these new forms (Aldrich and Fiol 1994). Some of the promoters of the experiments studied were very active in this respect, investing a lot of energy in trying to influence decision-makers in the supra-organizational centres (regional boards and the ministry). Since they tend to protect individual interests, ideological debates at the field level influence debates and actions at the other levels, and do not always allow for other, more specific sub-issues at stake to be uncovered.

Debates at the organizational level

The implementation of networks of integrated services forces culturally different organizations to renegotiate their structural or systems arrangements in an inter-organizational context. Our observations of the four projects suggest that autonomy (even survival) of organizations is a major issue. It generates complex interactions between organizations. Among the projects, the relative importance given to this issue was influenced by some of the traits of the organizations (management style, historic inter-organizational relationships) and by the local geographical and socio-demographic characteristics. The inter-organizational dynamics were influenced by structural, economic and normative incentives used by the supra-organizational decision centres (regional boards and the ministry).

Negotiations also took place between organizations and these decision centres. It appears that the adaptation of structural or systems arrangements needs to emerge from a collective learning process subjected to the combined influence of all these organizational actors. But negotiations are not restricted to organizational actors. Professionals also participate, promoting their own vision and defending their own turf.

Debates at the professional level

Debates at this level reflect the complexity of clinical work, and are linked to the organizational characteristics. Healthcare organizations, and more generally professional organizations, are characterized by emergent operating units, differentiated professional influence and diluted managerial control (Lamothe 1999). Understanding the nature of these emergent structures of collaboration at the operating level is crucial. It is here that fundamental boundaries are defined, and it is here that most concrete boundary-crossing initiatives must penetrate and take root if they are to be successful (Denis *et al.* 1999).

Although professional organizations have been described as a federation of autonomous experts in control of operations (Mintzberg 1979), a closer look reveals that in reality, various specialists and professional groups need to collaborate to get the work done. Depending on the uncertainty of the task and the technology used, a variety of semi-autonomous operating units organically emerge around different categories of patients. These distinctive forms of coordination among professionals do not have any formal existence in the organizational chart, but they form the *de facto* elementary structures of the organization (Lamothe 1999). Also, these operating units adopt various modes of functioning (a heterogeneous operating core) depending on the nature of the clinical work that needs to be done.

Implementation of networks of integrated services forces the destabilization of existing negotiated orders within organizations to extend them between culturally different ones (hospitals and primary care organizations). For the most part, the specific culture (the cultural position) of organizations in the system reflects the differing professional consensus within each group and their ideological foundations. These professional groupings help define the mission of the organizations and characterize their differing modes of functioning. A historical 'climate' of opposition may even entail competition when budget reductions are pending. Our observations confirm that the transition to networks of integrated services relies heavily on the willingness of professionals to engage in new negotiation processes and to modify their practices to create new operating units expanded in space (in a multi-organizational context) and time (as in the follow-up of chronic diseases).

The development of new trust relationships appears to be a central issue at the heart of debates. Differing ideologies generate considerable tension concerning modes of collaboration even when there is agreement that linkages are needed.

For example, primary care organizations (adopting a public health discourse) whose traditional ideology and emphasis has been on preventive and home care may be reluctant to be obliged to develop new patterns of behaviour for dealing with acute post-operative patients (a technological discourse) (Denis *et al.* 1999). Still, as observed, new trust relationships are essential for the development of new professional consensus (new negotiated orders) in an inter-organizational context. The legitimacy and efficiency of liaison mechanisms (such as protocols) essentially depend on the level of trust achieved in the creation of a new professional consensus. A collective learning process needs to take place and in that respect, effective clinical leadership appears to be a crucial element of success. Professionals had to go through this process before being willing to share information and coordinate their work in a non-competitive way.

Our observations also confirm that these new operating units may take various forms depending on the nature of their clinical work. Various factors (including chronic clinical conditions, the central role of technology) seem to command specific forms of networks. So far, little is known on this matter. Finally, an efficient network requires a coherent adaptation of organization structural or systems arrangements, which stimulates debates across levels.

Debates across levels

Diluted managerial control over processes forces the creation of a collective leadership in which professionals (especially dominant groups) are involved. Their co-optation in the design of models to be implemented appears crucial for the generation of new ideas and for ensuring their implementation (Denis, Lamothe and Langley 2001a). In that respect, it has been demonstrated that in such pluralistic organizations, the creation of a collective leadership in which members play complementary roles is of key importance for the effective management of change (Denis, Lamothe and Langley 2001b). In such a context, professional issues are intertwined with organizational ones. Networks of integrated services imply the creation of a collective leadership in an inter-organizational context. The forum of negotiations is then widened to include multiple organizations and it involves supra-organizational decision centres (regional boards, the ministry). These more distant structures may have wider leverage over direct and indirect mechanisms for managerial action that are capable of producing potentially positive change (including regulation, control over resource allocation, structures and incentives). The action of such coordinating agencies may also be less constrained by the entrenched patterns of professional power described earlier (Denis and Valette 1998).

The experiments have revealed some positive and negative effects of supra-experimental conditions on changes: some constraints were commonly experienced. The integration of doctors was considered a major constraint and their mode of payment, one of its causes; multidisciplinary work was slowed down by legal professional jurisdictions and union contracts; information systems could be adapted only with difficulty, and legal considerations restricted the flow of clinical information between professionals of different organizations. In addition, system integration may ultimately open the door to inter-sectoral boundary crossing as regional or local health agencies (engaging in public policy discourse) collaborate with other kinds of public and private organizations, such as educational institutions and municipal services, having a potential impact on health (Denis *et al.* 1999). It appears that debates across levels are essential to keep coherence in the overall system. Networks of integrated services, as with any complex organizational change, cannot be implemented without the mobilization of facilitating conditions, which are found at various levels of a given organizational field. In this case, a set of policy, managerial and clinical conditions must be put in place to make the implementation of networks possible.

The interactive influence of debates and actions at all three levels of the system tends to modify the composition of the field and the patterns of interactions (Meyer 1982; Meyer, Brooks and Goes 1990). Debates on the issue of networks of integrated services tend to penetrate at all levels while raising other sub-issues (organizational survival, protection of a professional domain). Pushed by institutional entrepreneurs (leaders in the clinical, managerial and academic domains), ideas, experiments and regulation mutually influence each other in a complex dynamic way and stimulate learning through the transition process. Networks of integrated services emerge, taking various forms, and influenced by contextual and micro-level factors. Better understanding of the emergent processes of organizing leads us to believe that various forms of networks of integrated services may actually be needed to adapt services to cope with complex and multifaceted factors.

Learning generated from experiments and the progressive implementation of networks of services has recently allowed for modifications of the laws governing health and social services. These regulative measures are in line with recommendations formulated by the Clair Commission (Clair 2000), mandated to propose solutions for the health system's deficiencies. The main recommendations, inspired by experiments that had been conducted, focused on the development and reinforcement of primary care organizations and the implementation of networks of integrated services. It also brought attention to the supra-organizational conditions that the experiments had exposed as needing to be changed. The new regulative measures address most of these conditions (including union accreditations, professional jurisdictions, the allocation of resources and flow of clinical information). They also impose new structural arrangements.

From an organizational point of view, the government bases its reform on three major changes: the implementation of local health networks; the creation of formal linkages between local health networks and specialized care; and the redefinition of the roles of regional authorities as agencies with transitional status devoted to the implementation of these networks. The local networks are based on the structural integration of some healthcare organizations named 'Centers for Health and Social Services' (community health organizations and long-term care institutions with or without the inclusion of acute care hospitals), together with alliances or virtual integration with physicians in private practices, teaching hospitals, community pharmacists and non-governmental community organizations. The new Centers for Health and Social Services are held responsible for the health status of the local population, so population health considerations need then to be introduced into the management of these organizations and networks.

Since they have introduced obligation and a sense of urgency (through the monitoring of results), these recent legal measures have greatly stimulated debates at all levels between professionals and organizations. The quest for locally adapted forms of networks of integrated services, which remain coherent with the overall system's objectives and constraints, is ongoing.

Discussion

Over the years, healthcare systems and their organizations have adopted the main features of bureaucracy (hierarchical control with top-down authority and relatively fixed boundaries). In organizations where the operational control is mainly in the hands of professionals, bureaucratization has contributed to maintaining and maybe increasing the relative independence of the production system (the black box of these organizations) and to restricting organizational capacity to learn and adapt (Child and McGrath 2001). Also, the predominance of a structural logic for organizing has led to fragmentation and rigidity. If networks of integrated services are to become institutionalized organizational forms, a horizontal shift has to occur. So far, the apparent consensus on the need to put integrated services in place hides the fact that divergent conceptions of what they should be coexist (multiple discourses). This may be responsible for the slow passage towards tangible new modes of organizing. Further progress in the transition requires better reconciliation of discourses. As illustrated, this lack of reconciliation may be partly responsible for the complexity of the transition processes.

In integrated service delivery, the locus of production is no longer within the boundaries of a single organization but at the nexus of relationships between various parties that contribute to the production function (Schilling and Steensma 2001). The provoked explosion of professional and organizational boundaries forces parties to focus on their interdependencies and be more tightly coupled. But paradoxically, the system as a whole becomes more loosely coupled, structured on various interlinked production processes or networks (Orton and Weick 1990).

Schilling and Steensma argue that generally, in industries where production processes are heterogeneous in terms of inputs and demands, a higher level of modularity would be associated. Rapid technological changes would also exercise pressure in that direction. Since these factors apply to healthcare organizations, greater value on flexibility would be required. Greater flexibility implies redefining the core of healthcare services along a variety of small self-organizing units adapted to the nature of clinical work. Flexibility is then recombined into a variety of configurations. An organizational form is created where both differentiation and integration are increased (Powell, Brock and Hinings 1999) and where rapid adaptation to changes is made possible because space is left for emergent patterns of interaction. This requires an emphasis on learning within and between constitutive units. Efficiency then relies on the flow of information between the parties involved. Greater flexibility also implies joint *ad hoc* decision making between all levels in the system. To deal with contradiction and paradox, governance needs to focus on integrative mechanisms across multiple networks that share resources.

Even if such complex organizational forms make sense conceptually, and if they appear to bring solutions in a dynamic environment where potentially conflictive strategies are being pursued (Malnight 2001), they remain hard to translate into tangible organizational features. Still, they rely on the conviction that in a changing environment, planning does not come from reduction of uncertainty and complexity but from its increase, allowing for creativity.

At this point in time, the organic evolution towards implementing networks of integrated services puts the system into a hybrid form which may be interpreted as the tangible expression of the contradictory forces applied. Some of these forces may be seen as inertia carried from historical heritage. If this is the case, the system may risk remaining stuck in the middle. In the projects studied, networks of integrated services tended to overlay horizontal structures on existing vertical ones. Structural resistance even altered features of the projects. In PACTE, although the project aimed at integrating mentally ill elderly patients within the integrated services for elderly patients, this could not be achieved. The primary care organizations belonged to two different programmes. In Capitation-Montérégie, the desire to respect the autonomy of the institutions has impeded the development of a common governance structure for an integrated local health system. In SIPA, the fact that physicians in private clinics are paid on a fee-for-service basis limited their involvement with the new integrated system. In all four projects, information systems had to be put in place and existing systems were of little help with horizontal processes and developing adequate performance indicators. Existing vertical structures and systems are hard to adapt. Also, in PACTE and Laurentians, innovative services were intended to be negotiated with community organizations and private long-term institutions (through public policy discourse). But existing professional norms tended to be reproduced and in that respect, the objectives were not achieved.

But the experiments have been a stepping stone in the process of emergence of these new organizational forms. Their – albeit localized and variable – implementation has increased their legitimacy (Denis, Lamothe and Langley 2001a) and has stimulated new debates. The government's recent legal measures are attempts to reconcile the various ideological positions, eliminate some of the contextual constraints, and propose new structural or systems arrangements for the system that may be more supportive of local change objectives.

Our studies tend to suggest that Shortell *et al.*'s definition (1993) of integrated delivery systems may not be an ideal towards which healthcare systems should aim, but an ideal type to which none would really correspond. Nevertheless, further analysis of their emergence may allow us better to identify their characteristics and conditions for implementation, and maybe help propose a typology of their configurations.

Conclusion

In this chapter, we used new institutional theorists' ideas to show how the debates over the issue of integrated networks of services are transforming the organizational field and the patterns of interactions between the organizations involved. We also illustrated that in the complex environments of healthcare systems, both contextual and micro-level factors need to be taken into account if we are to grasp how the debates penetrate all levels of actions and become the vehicle for promoting partners' individual interests (sub-issues). So far, it seems that micro-level factors may have been neglected by new institutionalists. If networks of integrated services are to become institutionalized new organizational forms, they will be the emergent product of the interactive dynamics occurring at all levels of this specific context.

Further analysis of these dynamics is needed. They imply redefining the core of healthcare services along a variety of small self-organizing units adapted to the nature of clinical work. Therefore the analysis of networks of integrated services needs to focus on the changing professional and organizational boundaries, and the discrete processes of the production system. 'Focusing on the structuring of processes provides a potentially important lens for investigating patterns of emerging internal structural complexity' (Malnight 2001: 1189). Descriptions of new modular (or processual) organizational forms tend to be abstract; more emphasis on the socio-cultural dynamics of these adaptive evolving organizational forms is necessary in order to comprehend their complexity (Galunic and Eisenhardt 2001). Our analysis of emerging integrated networks of services in health care is an attempt in that direction.

Orchestration of such complex change is challenging. The dual (top-down and bottom-up) dynamics of change and their mutual influence must be acknowledged and addressed. This is where orchestration becomes crucial. Debates may allow us to negotiate pathways to make change possible. Debates between leaders based in different organizations in the emerging networks may therefore be required to instigate new practices. But to translate them into tangible or concrete modes of functioning, debates need to be associated with the use of various levers capable of channelling actions in the desired direction. Our analysis, based on new institutional theory, highlights the limitations of attempts to build shared values and beliefs beyond individual organizations in the networks because of intra-institutional and intra-professional allegiances. There is a need for monitoring how they work out in practice, and to take corrective action to steer the change towards the desired goal of more integrated modes of functioning.

Employing new institutional theory enabled us to analyse the emergence of networks of integrated services as new organizational forms in the complex context of the healthcare industry. But additional research is needed to understand in greater depth the nature of networks as new organizational forms, and their process of emergence. Hybridization of modes of functioning as an intrinsic part of the emerging process may be identified as a focus of additional research. This focus would put more emphasis on the micro-dynamics of change and help build theory to address the limitations of new institutional theory in that respect. Comparative analyses with other healthcare systems or other complex industries, including education systems, are also required.

REFERENCES

Abbott, A. (1988) *The System of Professions*. Chicago: University of Chicago Press.

Aldrich, H.E. and Fiol, M.C. (1994) Fools rush in? The institutional context of industry creation. *Academy of Management Review*, **19**(4), 645–70.

Barber, J., Koch, K., Parente D., Mack, J. and Davis, K. (1998) Evolution of an integrated health system: a life cycle framework. *Journal of Health Care Management*, **43**(4), 359–77.

Bucher, R. and Stelling, J. (1969) Characteristics of professional organizations. *Journal of Health and Social Behavior*, **10**(1), 3–15.

Child, J. and McGrath, R.G. (2001) Organizations unfettered: organizational form in an information-intensive economy. *Academy of Management Journal*, **44**(6), 1135–48.

Clair, M. (2000) *Emerging Solutions: Report and Recommendations*. Quebec City: Commission for Health and Social Services.

Cohen, M., March, J. and Olsen, J. (1972) A garbage can model of organizational choice. *Administrative Science Quarterly*, **17**, 1–25.

Conrad, D.A. and Shortell, S. (1996). Integrated health systems: promise and performance. *Frontiers of Health Services Management*, **13**(1), 3–40.

Contandriopoulos, A-P., Denis, J-L., Sicotte, C., Touati, N., Rodriguez, C. and Nguyen, H. (2001). Projet de capitation dans la municipalité de comté du Haut Saint-Laurent. Evaluation report presented to the Health Transition Fund, March.

Crozier, M. (1964) *The Bureaucratic Phenomenon*. Chicago: University of Chicago Press.

Crozier, M. and Friedberg, E. (1978). *L'Acteur et le Système*. Paris: Seuil.

Denis, J-L., Lamothe, L., Langley, A. and Valette, A. (1999) The struggle to redefine boundaries in health care systems. In D. Brock, R. Hinings and M. Powell (eds) *The Transformation of Professional Organizations*. London: Routledge.

Denis, J-L. and Valette, A. (1998) Décentraliser pour transformer la régulation: la création des agences régionales d'hospitalisation. Paper presented at the Seminar of the Institut National de la Santé et de la Recherche Médicale, Paris.

Denis, J-L., Lamothe, L. and Langley, A. (2001a) Government-funded experiments as resources for renewal in health care? Paper presented at the Academy of Management Conference, Washington.

Denis, J-L., Lamothe, L. and Langley, A. (2001b) The dynamics of collective leadership and strategic change in pluralistic organizations. *Academy of Management Journal*, **44**(4), 809–37.

DiMaggio, P. and Powell, W. (1983) The iron cage revisited: institutional isomorphism and collective rationality in organizational fields. *American Sociological Review*, **48**(2), 147–60.

DiMaggio, P. and Powell, W. (1991) Introduction. In W. Powell and P. Di Maggio (eds) *The New Institutionalism in Organizational Analysis*. Chicago: University of Chicago Press.

Freidson, E. (1970) *The Profession of Medicine*. New York: Dodd Mead.

Galunic, D.C. and Eisenhardt, K.M. (2001) Architectural innovation and modular corporate forms. *Academy of Management Journal*, **44**(6), 1229–49.

Greenwood, R. and Hinings, C.R. (1993) Understanding strategic change: the contribution of archetypes. *Academy of Management Journal*, **36**(5), 1052–81.

Greenwood, R. and Hinings, R. (1996) Understanding radical organizational change: bringing together the old and the new institutionalism. *Academy of Management Review*, **21**(4), 1011–54.

Hoffman, A.J. (1999) Institutional evolution and change: environmentalism and the US chemical industry. *Academy of Management Journal*, **42**(4), 351–71.

Lamarche, P.A., Lamothe, L., Bégin, C., Léger, M. & Vallières-Joly, M. (2001) Effets des modes d'intégration des services en émergence dans la région socio-sanitaire des Laurentides. Report presented to the Health Transition Fund, February.

Lamothe, L. (1999) La reconfiguration des hôpitaux: un défi d'ordre professionnel. *Ruptures*, **6**(2), 132–48.

Leblebici, H., Salancik, G.R., Copray, A. and King, T. (1991) Institutional change and the transformation of interorganizational fields: an organizational history of the US radio broadcasting industry. *Administrative Science Quarterly*, **36**(3), 333–63.

Lorange, P., Scott Morton, M. and Ghoshal, S. (1986) *Strategic Control Systems*. St Paul: West Publishing Company.

Malnight, T.W. (2001) Emerging structural patterns within multinational corporations: toward process-based structures. *Academy of Management Journal*, **44**(6), 1187–210.

Meyer, A. (1982) Adapting to environmental jolts. *Administrative Science Quarterly*, **27**(4), 515–37.

Meyer, A., Brooks, G. and Goes, J. (1990) Environmental jolts and industry revolutions: organizational responses to discontinuous change. *Strategic Management Journal*, **11**, 93–110.

Meyer, J.E. and Rowan, B. (1977) Institutionalized organizations: formal structures as myth and ceremony. *American Journal of Sociology*, **83**(2), 340–63.

Miller, D. (1981) Towards a new contingency approach: the search for organizational gestalts. *Journal of Management Studies*, **18**, 1–26.

Miller, D. (1987). The genesis of configuration. *Academy of Management Review*, **12**(4), 686–701.

Miller, D. (1996) Configurations revisited. *Strategic Management Journal*, **17**(7), 505–12.

Miller, D. (1999) Note on the study of configurations. *Management International Review*, **39**(2), 27–37.

Miller, D. and Friesen, P. (1977) Strategy making in context: ten empirical archetypes. *Journal of Management Studies*, **14**(3), 253–80.

Miller, D. and Friesen, P. (1978) Archetypes of strategy formulation. *Management Science*, **24**(9), 921–33.

Mintzberg, H. (1979) *The Structuring of Organizations: A Synthesis of the Research*. Englewood Cliffs, NJ: Prentice-Hall.

Mintzberg, H. (1989) *Mintzberg on Management – Inside our Strange World of Organizations*. New York: Free Press.

Oliver, C. (1991) Strategic responses to institutional processes. *Academy of Management Review*, **16**(1), 145–79.

Orton, J.D. and Weick, K. (1990) Loosely coupled systems: a reconceptualization. *Academy of Management Review*, **15**(2), 203–23.

Powell, M.J., Brock, D.M. and Hinings, C.R. (1999) The changing professional organization. In D.M. Brock, M.J. Powell and C.R. Hinings (eds) *Restructuring the Professional Organization*. London: Routledge, pp. 1–19.

Schilling, M.A. and Steensma, H.K. (2001) The use of modular organizational forms: an industry-level analysis. *Academy of Management Journal*, **44**(6), 1149–68.

Scott, W.R. (1991) Unpacking institutional arguments. In W. Powell and P. DiMaggio (eds) *The New Institutionalism in Organizational Analysis*. Chicago: University of Chicago Press, pp. 164–82.

Scott, W.R. (1995) *Institutions and Organizations*. London: Sage.

Shortell, S., Gillies, R., Anderson, D., Mitchell, J. and Morgan, K. (1993) Creating organized delivery systems: the barriers and facilitators. *Hospital and Health Services Administration*, **38**(4), 447–67.

Simard, J-Y., Blanchette, L., Trottier, J-G., Lamarche, P-A., Lamothe, L. and Saint-Pierre, M. (2001) Projet d'action concertée sur les territoires (PACTE): une gestion locale des services du réseau de la santé et des services sociaux en réponse aux besoin des personnes âgées. Report presented to the Health Transition Fund, May.

Strauss, A., Schatzman, L., Bucher, R., Ehrlich, D. and Sabshin, M. (1964) *Psychiatric Ideologies and Institutions*. New York: Free Press.

Strauss, A., Schatzman, L., Ehrlich, D., Bucher, R. and Sabshin, M. (1963) The hospital and its negotiated order. In E. Freidson (ed.) *The Hospital in Modern Society*. London: Collier-MacMillan, pp. 147–69.

Touati, N., Denis, J-L. and Langley, A. (2001) L'analyse de la dynamique d'implantation du SIPA. Working paper prepared for the evaluation of the SIPA program, the Health Transition Fund.

Tucker, D.J., Singh, J.V. and Meinhard, A.G. (1990) Organizational form, population dynamics and institutional change. *Academy of Management Journal*, **33**(1), 151–78.

Van de Ven, A.H. and Drazin, R. (1985) The concept of fit in contingency theory. *Research in Organizational Behavior*, **7**, 333–65.

Wallace, M. and Pocklington, K. (2002) *Managing Complex Educational Change: Large-Scale Reorganization of Schools*. London: RoutledgeFalmer.

CHAPTER 4

AN IRONIC PERSPECTIVE ON PUBLIC SERVICE CHANGE

Mike Wallace and Eric Hoyle

This chapter sets out the main concepts of a novel ironic perspective on organizations and applies these generic ideas to the complexity of change in the public services. The ironic perspective informed part of Wallace's conceptualization in Chapter 1, which addresses the relative unmanageability of complex and programmatic change. The core concept of 'irony' is linked with ideas drawn from the extensive tradition of organization theory which focuses on the degree of ambiguity, or uncertainty in meaning, that is endemic in organizational life. (This tradition has many affinities with new institutional theory employed by Lamothe and Denis in Chapter 3, especially the emphasis on alternative and often incompatible bases for the legitimation of actions and organizational arrangements.) Wallace and Hoyle contend that the ironic perspective offers a sensitizing device for understanding the inevitable increase in the extent of ambiguity brought by public service change, and the consequences of this heightened ambiguity for coping strategies.

Their intellectual project is a hybrid. They harness insights from knowledge-for-understanding to inform knowledge-for-action that, they argue, could in turn support more realistic policy making and leadership and management practice to improve public services under conditions of endemic ambiguity. They argue that rationalistic efforts to strengthen control over the complex change process in the interests of reducing ambiguity are vulnerable to generating the inadvertent irony of adding to ambiguity and further reducing the already limited manageability of change. Wallace and Hoyle advocate a more temperate approach to policy making and coping with change. It would imply learning to live with a degree of unmanageability and attempting marginally to increase the degree of control within the limits of what is realistically feasible, and promoting local innovation to improve local practices in diverse settings.

Best Practice: Elusive or Illusory?

It is not hard to find evidence at any level of public service systems that practice is not yet perfect, despite decades of effort and investment to bring about
more or less radical change for public service improvement across many western
countries. At the international level, US expenditure on health care runs at over
13 per cent of gross domestic product, an economic burden that is one-fifth greater
than any other country (Docteur and Oxley 2003). But although the US, like other
nations, has engaged in long-term healthcare reform, the population remains less
healthy as measured by premature deaths and life expectancy than countries whose
rate of expenditure is less than half the US rate. Why has all that extra economic
power to support reform not delivered comparably better health outcomes?
At the national system level, the central government strategy for modernizing
the National Health Service (NHS) in England has resulted in the proliferation of
expensive 'arm's length bodies' (ALBs), government agencies set up incrementally to provide a better aspect of the service or to promote improvement. Now
further investment in a review (Department of Health 2004a) has brought the
central government decision to cut them back from 38 to 20 by 2008, heralding
another change within the modernization strategy whose implementation will
affect ALB staff and other stakeholders over several years. At the organization
level, 'superheads' – experienced headteachers appointed as part of a central
government policy to turn round failing English secondary schools – have met
with widely varying success. Of the first nine superheads appointed to schools
located in socially deprived areas, three resigned in a single week (*Times
Educational Supplement* 2000).

These three instances reflect, indirectly or directly, good intentions to improve
public services coming unstuck in some way – consistent with what Fink (2003:
105) calls the 'law of unintended consequences . . . for every policy initiative there
will be unpredicted and unpredictable results'. The comparatively low performance
of US health care is an unintended consequence of its unique history of private
and voluntary sector involvement in provision and decentralized governance. What
is good for business or for the managed health organization is not necessarily good
for preventive and restorative health care across the nation (especially the quarter of the population with no health insurance). The burgeoning of costly ALB
agencies in the NHS in England is an unintended consequence of incremental
decisions by different government ministers to create more ALBs as a standard
solution to the problem of improving particular aspects of health care. The
demise of a significant proportion of superheads is the unintended consequence
of a particular government minister's idea for solving the problem of how to improve
the most demonstrably underperforming secondary schools across England.
What doubtless seemed like a good idea at the time was based on the generalized
assumption (probably shared by appointees) that formal leaders who have per-
formed superlatively in a particular context have the capacity and endurance, in

another context, to shift entrenched cultural attitudes and structural conditions of social deprivation. Sometimes yes, sometimes no.

Why is problematic practice such a common unintended consequence of well-intentioned improvement activity? Is the root cause simply failure to use the right techniques, the 'best practice' often advocated by policy-makers and not a few consultants and researchers? Or is it actually unrealistic to consider that a single best practice exists which is universally applicable across public service settings? Indicatively, UK government protocols detailing research-based best practice for medical conditions have been disseminated to doctors across the NHS. But doctors have not systematically applied these protocols because they do not allow for the complexity of doctors' decision-making processes, which include their own experience of different treatments, what treatment peers are giving and what local facilities are available (Dopson *et al.* 2005). Best practice is contextualised. Making it work entails learning how to adapt it to suit contingent circumstances. In the process, the original formulation of best practice gets morphed into a variety of locally determined good practices. As Glatter and Kydd (2002: 6) point out: 'The idea of "learning from best practice" implies bottling a prescription formula. Learning in a social context is a more dynamic process and "building a learning system for improvement" may provide a better focus for sustainable development.' The attempt to spread the use of best practice protocols may have been unrealistic because it did not support doctors with learning how to adapt these protocols in creating context-sensitive good practices. (The importance of fostering the adaptation of knowledge of good practice ideas to make it work in new contexts is underlined in Chapter 9.)

Here, echoing Voltaire, the best is the enemy of the good. A more profitable direction for improvement activity might be to 'build a learning system for improvement' by promoting the development of system-wide capacity for coping with change as effectively as possible in contextually diverse and relatively uncertain circumstances. This approach would accept that unintended consequences cannot be eliminated. Our purpose in the present chapter is to develop the detailed argument that underlies Mike Wallace's contention (in Chapter 1) that contemporary public service change is, intrinsically, relatively unmanageable. Attempts reflected in many reform efforts to tighten control over the change process and its outcomes (as with protocols for medical conditions) risk the unintended consequence of reducing its manageability further, so undermining the achievement of change agents' improvement goals. One alternative is to stop trying so hard. A more temperate approach would be to accept the limited manageability of change and seek to maximize the modest degree of control that may be possible within these limits. Fostering incremental local development of good practices that work in contingent circumstances may turn out to be both more manageable and more productive than single-solution endeavours to identify best practices and apply them to all change situations.

Conceptual tools are needed to build our argument. We will draw on a tradition of organization theory focusing on the extent of ambiguities that are endemic to organizational life. Change inherently increases these ambiguities within broad structural parameters – economic and ideological – that delimit what is considered to be doable and even thinkable (Chapter 1). The remainder of this chapter falls accordingly into four sections.

First, we introduce the ironic perspective on organizational life with particular reference to change embodied in policy implementation across multiple organizations. Ambiguity, or uncertainty at the level of meaning, creates conditions for the ironies of unintended consequences and of intended or unintended ambiguities in language about practice (for a detailed treatment see Hoyle and Wallace 2005). Change, whether emergent or connected with the implementation of planned policy initiatives, exacerbates the endemic level of ambiguity and so enhances its potential for generating irony. Second, we list different sources of such ambiguity and consider how they are magnified by change. Third, we explore the irony that planned changes designed greatly to reduce endemic ambiguities in public service provision may stimulate practitioners' responses that serve to increase these ambiguities, and so generate unintended consequences that undermine the change instigators' well-intentioned actions. We hypothesize that some mediatory responses may be both principled and underpinned by an ironic orientation towards professional practice and change. Finally, we outline how a temperate approach to organizational change and policy implementation involves developing good practices in coping with irony framed by this ironic orientation towards managing change, rather than attempting to control out of existence the ambiguities that create conditions for irony to arise.

An Ironic Perspective on Organizational Change

Irony has diverse connotations. They span amusement over unexpected coincidences, cynicism where the literal meaning of the words used contradicts what was actually intended, and rueful acknowledgement of things turning out unexpectedly despite one's best endeavours. All draw attention to the limited capacity of people to make sense of their own and others' lives, to get what they want and to control what happens to them. We have chosen this term as the basis for a new perspective because no other concept so closely captures the phenomenon of limited human capacity at the heart of organizational life and of the change process. And since there is no canonical definition of irony, we feel free to concentrate on those connotations that best suit our analytical purposes.

Our claims for this perspective are modest. Like the practical planning framework for coping with complex and programmatic change proposed in Chapter 1, our perspective has neither the explanatory range of a theory, nor the conceptual consistency of a model. But the ironic perspective does offer a new sensitizing device. It directs attention to the empirical gap between intention and outcome or between concept and experienced reality, and the conceptual gap between declared and implied meaning, that together contribute to the limited manageability of organizational life and change. It offers a starting point for considering how to cope as effectively as possible with endemic ambiguities of meaning and unintended consequences in public service provision, and with their exacerbation by change – whether planned improvement efforts or emergent responses to environmental pressures.

We conceive irony as referring to some disjunction between what is intended and what happens, or what is stated and what is meant. Two forms of organizational irony may be distinguished. *Situational irony* refers to those ironies that are part of social reality. The key manifestation of situational irony is the unintended consequence: most commonly when good intentions have unfortunate consequences, but sometimes conversely where apparently unfortunate occurrences bring unanticipated benefits.

Semantic irony refers to ironic uses of language, either intended by a speaker or writer, or unintended but still detectable by an observer. Intentional irony includes wordplay or banter where the meaning conveyed contradicts the words used, as when an organizational mission statement is quoted cynically to underline how an organizational practice is perceived to transgress the official missionary sentiment. We recognize that it is often difficult to establish intentionality, especially where people feel under pressure to adopt new management terminology. Contemporary public service examples include 'keeping the vision', 'incentivizing', 'deliverables', 'performance measurement'. While some people may employ such terms with unreflective sincerity, others may use them with intentional but covert insincerity because they perceive that their career prospects depend on appearing to be sincere. Visionary rhetoric, increasingly prevalent in public service discourse, is particularly vulnerable to semantic irony. By design, there is a gap between the inspirational and often unreachable aspiration which is expressed (how many 'world-class' organizations and practices can there be?) and the more prosaic reality of organizational experience.

Multiple sources of *ambiguity* create preconditions for irony. Ambiguity implies uncertainty in meaning. Actions, organizational structures and language are all capable of being accorded different meanings, generating some degree of uncertainty or unpredictability. A dictionary definition of 'ambiguous' – 'doubtful; undetermined; of intermediate or doubtful nature; indistinct; wavering; having more than one possible meaning; equivocal' (Chambers 1998) – resonates with this aspect of common experience. Doubt about what is going on, wavering between different interpretations, or equivocation over what should be done can often be reduced, but never eliminated altogether.

Some element of change is endemic to all organizations, even those in relatively stable settings. Endemic change contributes to organizational ambiguity. It creates uncertainty relating to whatever individuals and groups must learn to do and think in putting the change into practice. Since they cannot fully comprehend what it is like to operate in new ways until they have tried them out, ambiguity surrounds the meaning of these new practices until the change is institutionalized. The mere passage of time brings periodic turnover and the redistribution of responsibilities among organization members. Newcomers have to familiarize themselves with their new work setting, while their colleagues must adjust to new faces. Most learning required to fulfil tasks that are new for any particular individual entails tacit *incidental learning* (Marsick and Watkins 1990) through the job experience, perhaps supported by reflection on action and by preparatory or ongoing training. Adding planned innovations to the endemic element of change, typically based on one group's conception of improvement, increases ambiguity for a time due to the extra learning required to put the innovation into practice. Even change on a modest scale can challenge the current practices and assumptions of people in and around the organizations involved.

They cannot fully understand and so gain clarity about the new practice before they have experienced it for themselves, so initially its meaning will be ambiguous. Nor can they be sure how to implement the change before doing so. Preparatory support inevitably stops short of providing them with what they can learn consciously or incidentally only through attempting to modify their practice in their work setting. Knowing how to change practice emerges from changing practice, even if informed by others' ideas about 'best practice'. People come fully to make sense of a significant change only when it becomes assimilated into their practice repertoire, when its hitherto high degree of ambiguity recedes.

Any endeavour to change the practice of people in a multiplicity of public service organizations, and especially those across an entire regional or national system, adds ambiguity of a different order. It occurs where a locally emergent change gathers momentum, becomes regarded by powerful advocates as the new norm, and is then rapidly adopted across much or all of a service system (as with the hospitalist movement discussed in Chapter 8). Greater ambiguity is generated where government-led public service reform policies and accountability checks drive system-wide changes in practice to implement these policies. The evolutionary profile of innovations that programmatic reforms generate has to be implemented in intermediate administrative agencies and service organizations. Each innovation may be at a different stage of implementation, and is likely to compete for priority with other innovations, responses to unplanned chronic environmental pressures or temporary crises and the rest of ongoing service provision. Greater still is the ambiguity flowing from change designed to promote multi-agency working across existing service boundaries (as with the introduction of integrated systems of health care discussed in Chapter 3). This form of change can bring together multiple services. Witness early childhood programmes that attempt to bring together educational, health care and social service components into a seamless service for young children and their families. Greatest of all must be the ambiguity flowing from programmatic reform of an entire national public service system, as with the UK central government's modernization strategy (Office of Public Service Reform 2002).

Normal practice in public service organizations is affected by multiple and interrelated factors connected with the mix of organization members, the system of which their organization is a part, and the social milieu in which they are located. To the extent that individuals and groups possess agency, they have some choice over their course of action and response according to their interpretation of the situation at hand (Giddens 1984). The potential of all involved in organizational life to act in alternative ways according to beliefs that cannot be directly controlled generates a perennial measure of ambiguity. Organizational change adds complexity. The outcome of many actions cannot be assured until they have happened. System-wide reform policies increase this complexity still further (as reflected in the 'characteristics of complexity' outlined in Chapter 1). The capacity of practitioners in the organizations making up a service system to express some degree of agency inevitably creates potential for ambiguity through the possibility of different responses, including covert or overt resistance, or even subversion by harnessing a change to achieve alternative goals. Research evidence includes, in education, Wallace (1998a), Moore, George and Halpin (2002), Farrell and Morris (2003, 2004), Deem (2004); in health, Dopson (1997), McNulty and Ferlie (2002), Mueller *et al.* (2003), Dopson *et al.* (2005). This potential militates against policy-makers assuring faithful implementation on the ground. Conditions favouring the generation of irony are integral to the change process.

Sources of Ambiguity that are Exacerbated by Change

The chronic shortfall between the lofty official goals that tend to be proclaimed for public service organizations and the possibility of their achievement has long been observed. It has even been built into the currently fashionable practice, noted earlier, of articulating an organizational or service vision and mission. The intention of inspiring organization members to achieve greater things implies that they should attempt to modify what they do now in the direction of achieving the vision. The visionary statement must therefore embody goals that are beyond immediate reach. The result is endemic *organizational pathos* (Hoyle 1986), a variable gap between the goals of official aspiration and the more mundane reality of organizational practice.

Planned change designed to bring a shift in practice across multiple organizations produces inherent *policy pathos*, some disjunction between the aspirational goals expressed by policy-makers that promise a brighter future and the extent to which they are achieved throughout the service system. Here is a health service illustration. Central government reform of the National Health Service in England has, since the New Labour government came to power, included the visionary commitment to 'giving the people of this country the best system of health care in the world' (Department of Health 1997). In his foreword to an NHS plan for improvement, seven years on, the Prime Minister noted that 'with the journey to a world-class health service in all, not just some parts, of the NHS still to be completed, now is not the time to falter.' (Department of Health 2004b: 3) The ambition of the original rhetoric has deflated somewhat – from best in the world to world-class, but the scope for enduring policy pathos is obvious.

Policy-makers at one administrative level can have, at most, limited familiarity with organizations elsewhere into which their policy initiatives are introduced.

When new policies are launched their impact cannot be wholly predetermined. The greater the range and scope of new policies, the greater the novelty and effort for implementers in target organizations, and the greater the potential for divergence between the espoused goals of policy-makers and their realization in the sites of implementation. Less-than-faithful implementation, especially of policies initiated at one administrative level for implementation at another, has long been recognized, encapsulated in concepts such as the 'implementation gap' or 'mutual adaptation' of a planned change between the initial vision promulgated by policy-makers and the practice of its implementers (Odden 1991; McLaughlin 1991). The potential for infidelity derives from and contributes to the limited manageability of change. Official goals are not the only goals. Various operational goals may be held by individuals and groups, including covert ones that may be inconsistent with the official line. An example might be a doctor's unarticulated goal of limiting the time spent reassuring patients at the bedside in order to maintain a desired work–life balance.

Organizational and policy pathos endure in part because deliberately ambitious goals for improvement are unattainable in full. But they also endure because pursuing such goals never occurs in a vacuum. As discussed in Chapter 1, any change takes place in the context of all activity in each organization, including other changes and the day-to-day provision of the existing service. Overall, the combination of official and unofficial goals being pursued in any organization and across a service system is likely to be both *diverse and diffuse*. The National Health Service in England has long been subject to reform. In the document alluded to above, the Prime Minister reiterated the aim 'to reshape the NHS . . . so it is not just a national health service but also a personal health service for every patient . . .' (Department of Health 2004b: 4), implying increased patient choice among alternative care providers. But reshaping the NHS has been ongoing for well over two decades. So in each health service organization, today's push for the personalization of care comes on top of an existing clutch of official goals still being pursued to implement yesterday's round of central government reforms, which included reducing waiting times for treatment. Those goals had already been added to the many perennial goals that are entailed simply in maintaining routine service provision.

It is this diversity of accreting goals, as much as the diffuseness of any one goal, which creates ambiguity. Restricting the scope and tightening the specification of a particular goal does not remove the ambiguity surrounding the pursuit of this goal in relation to all the other goals that different stakeholders hold for the organization or service system. Some goals may be incompatible with others. Personalization of health care requires a modicum of surplus capacity to provide the basis for patients to exercise choice between alternative providers within a short waiting time. The pursuit of greater efficiency, a long-term goal for the NHS, exerts a contrary pressure to minimize surplus capacity. But the more a service is operated at full stretch for maximum efficiency, the more likely waiting times are to increase if a particular provider becomes popular with patients trying to exercise their newfound choice.

As the range of goals associated with programmatic change increases, the more difficult it becomes to pursue them all with equal vigour. Abundant evidence suggests that the goals of current policies, to which any extra resources are likely to be directed, get prioritized. 'Perverse effects' of the UK government's recently adopted target regime for public service improvement did not take long to surface: attention became channelled towards meeting the targets, and away from the rest of service provision.

It is inevitable that some goals become subordinated because not everything can be prioritized all of the time. Ambiguity also arises where goals cannot be meaningfully operationalized in terms of measurable performance. The broader the goal, the less of the aspiration behind it can be covered by the substitution of a small number of 'proxy measures' (such as the waiting time for a particular operation) from which performance statistics can be compiled. A world-class health service demonstrably adds up to more than performance along a few discrete measures of specific components of service provision.

Another key source of ambiguity lies in the inherent *limits to rationality* of organizational life and policy implementation. March and Simon pointed long ago to the *bounded* nature of rationality in organizations, because members are not realistically capable of weighing up all the possible consequences of all the possible decision choices before selecting the optimal way to go. Rather, they *satisfice* (1958: 140–1):

> Most human decision-making, whether individual or organizational, is concerned with the discovery and selection of satisfactory alternatives; only in exceptional cases is it concerned with the discovery and selection of optimal alternatives. To optimize requires processes several orders of magnitude more complex than those required to satisfice. An example is the difference between searching a haystack to find the sharpest needle in it and searching the haystack to find a needle sharp enough to sew with.

Satisficing captures the commonplace experience of public service providers, especially when coping with change: making iterative, fast-paced decisions in evolving and significantly ambiguous conditions. Electronic data management and communication systems can increase the information base for decision making but cannot get round the following limits to rationality.

First, *cognitive* limits are imposed by the impossibility of knowing in advance what all the possible immediate and longer term outcomes of a particular change decision will be. Individuals – including policy-makers – will have variable, but always limited, awareness of what is happening inside and outside their own and other organizations. They will have even less idea about what will happen in future that turns out to impinge on the decision outcomes. No one can have a fully comprehensive overview of complex or programmatic change because no one can experience the experiences of maybe thousands of people involved or affected. Extensive consultation, monitoring, inspection and outcome measurement can provide only snapshot information about how a change interacts with other aspects of diverse organizational contexts. The greater the endeavour to gather intelligence, the greater is the probability of distracting implementers who are the sources of this information from coping with the change itself.

Second, *logical* limits are imposed where individuals' pursuit of a particular goal can prevent this goal being achieved when others in the same setting also pursue it. Personalization of a service implies increasing individual consumer choice among different service providers. We have noted already that collective consumer choice will be delimited by the pattern of alternative provision on offer because of the impracticability of providing unlimited choice. So if more individuals turn out to make the same choice than the level of provision can cater for, they may collectively inhibit each other from attaining their individual choice. Personalization of health care risks frustrating choice because the content and aggregate of individual choices cannot be directly manipulated to ensure a smooth match with available provision.

Third, *phenomenological* or interpretive limits arise where people come to differing interpretations of the same events or change proposals. Although a hospital has a material reality in terms of buildings, organizational membership and organizational structure, as a social institution it may be construed very differently by, say, senior managers and nursing staff. The potential range of constructions is constrained by the parameters for official healthcare goals, the unequal distribution of power among those associated with them, and constraints that constructions can impose on perception and action (Giddens 1979). But incompatible perspectives will be regarded as 'rational' by their protagonists. Room for incompatibility expands with the range of people involved and the complexity of change they may face, as Chapter 3 insightfully portrayed through the application of new institutional theory.

The frames of reference governing social constructs may relate to contradictory beliefs, norms (rules about how people should behave) and values held by individuals or groups. The ambiguity of incompatible perceptions about the same situation will be familiar to any public service manager who has arbitrated when colleagues come into conflict. The account offered by each protagonist seldom matches up to that of his or her adversaries. Yet all were party to the same situation. Contradictory values are rife. Pursuing efficiency through changes to minimize the resources required to achieve given outcomes often constrains simultaneous changes in pursuit of greater effectiveness. Conflict is especially prone to arise where pursuing effectiveness requires additional resources.

Fourth, *control* limits flow from the likelihood that no one in normal organizational life can achieve absolute control over anyone else. Control ambiguity arises through the potential of those whose practice must change to act and react in ways that may not be wholly predictable from the perspective of change agents. Power is distributed – however unequally – within and between organizations. Whatever central or local position of authority formal leaders may hold, and whatever the official sanctions available to them, they depend ultimately on the cooperation of those whom they lead. All members of organizations have some recourse to informal influence, not least the capacity to resist or subvert work towards the achievement of service improvement or reform goals.

Another source of ambiguity is the persistence of unresolvable *dilemmas*, whether for individuals, groups, organizations or service systems. Action oriented towards one pole of the dilemma brings negative consequences that build pressure for action towards the opposite pole. No stable cost-free balance is achievable between both poles. Thus, what works for system reform may not work so well for all the individuals whose additional effort is necessary to make it happen. Desired change may not be achievable while also preserving a desired healthy work–life balance and job satisfaction (Evans 2000). A dilemma arises over what balance to try and strike between pace of change and sustainability.

Public service improvers or reformers face a centralization–decentralization dilemma. A strongly centralized 'profile of innovations' approach maximizes the capacity for central direction and speed according to particular political values, employing prespecified innovations. But it incurs costs: inhibiting desirable innovativeness in service organizations, restricting the scope for adapting reforms to contingent circumstances, favouring attention to the appearance rather than the reality of change, and requiring expensive surveillance to ensure compliance. A strongly decentralized 'change agenda' approach maximizes the capacity for local ownership and voluntary effort, and for incremental improvement activity that is sensitive to local circumstances. But it also incurs costs: creating conditions allowing minimal response or local innovativeness in directions that are unacceptable to policy-makers, inhibiting concerted and systemic effort in a coherent direction, and offering restricted potential for measuring and publicly demonstrating improvement. A mixed approach incurs some of the benefits and costs of both centralization and decentralization strategies, plus the cost of inconsistency between centralized and decentralized elements.

In sum, these various sources of ambiguity create conditions in which change efforts are likely to generate unintended consequences, whether judged to be good or bad. Those that are negative from the perspective of the people responsible for managing change may inhibit them from achieving their goals. Such consequences also tend to stimulate ameliorative policy making, bringing the situational irony of more change with its accompanying ambiguity. Such corrective action, in turn, creates favourable conditions for further unintended consequences, and so the likelihood of yet further amelioration.

Public Service Reform, Ironic Response

The greater the ambition of public service change, the more it stands to exacerbate the endemic level of ambiguity for those involved in its implementation. Nowhere, therefore, is the potential for situational irony greater than the programmatic public service reforms introduced over recent decades by many national and regional governments in response to global economic and technological pressures. An underlying thrust has been radically to reduce ambiguity in public service organizations by tightening the link between political goals and service practice. The endeavour to do so has entailed curbing the autonomy of professions at the heart of service provision, which had contributed both to the diversity of organizational goals and to politically unacceptable variations in practice. Service organization leaders have often been harnessed as conduits for reform, held accountable for managing change on behalf of politicians (and ultimately the public users of services whose votes gave the politicians their mandate). The profile of innovations for each public service embodied in what is widely conceived as 'managerialism' or 'new public management' has evolved as ideologies of public service reform have developed. The UK can be conceived as having witnessed local innovation followed by three phases of central government-driven reform:

- *Corporatism*, reflected till the 1980s in a service provider ideology and 'bureau-professionalism' mode of governance, largely controlled by professionals (Clarke and Newman 1997) and marked by piecemeal innovation and experimentation at service organization and local administrative levels.
- *Neo-liberal managerialism*, surfacing in the 1980s from the New Right critique of corporatism (Newman 2001), reflected in marketization reforms embodying industrial management techniques such as staff appraisal, site budgets and competitive tendering, alongside strong accountability mechanisms including external inspection and publicized performance league tables.
- *'Post-new public management'* (Ferlie, Hartley and Martin 2003), from the mid-1990s, synthesising technocratic managerialism and populist consumerism through 'managed markets' and networks (Newman 2001), featuring target setting, workforce remodelling, performance measurement coupled with performance-related pay, and direct participation by service users culminating in the 'personalization' of public services (Leadbeater 2003).

The rhetoric of reform tends towards the radical, as with the emphasis on 'transforming our public services' (Office of Public Service Reform 2002: 2) in the UK. Service organization leaders are exhorted to transform their organizations (e.g. National College for School Leadership 2003; NHS Leadership Centre 2003). But where transformational goals are set centrally, a semantic irony arises that belies the transformational rhetoric. What is actually being sought of service organization leaders is faithful *transmission* of political goals and the promotion of activity to implement them, not transformation of their organizations according to their own diverse beliefs and values and those of other local stakeholders. Further, the ambition of such transformational goals belies the limited capacity of public services to spearhead radical social change. Structural social and economic forces, which are much more powerful, ensure that public services remain largely responsive and function to support social reproduction rather than revolution. Educational organizations have no more potential to eliminate the social and economic determinants of inequitable educational outcomes than healthcare organizations have to eliminate the social and economic determinants of lifestyles that generate health problems such as obesity.

The very reforms designed to achieve transformational goals and rein in the local innovation of the corporatist era by reducing professional autonomy have actually contributed to situational irony. They have reduced the scope for professionals in service organizations to develop good practices either by adapting externally specified changes to their circumstances, or by instigating modest local innovations. The additional ambiguity brought by reforms creates fertile conditions for the situational irony of unintended consequences.

Especially ironic is the additional ambiguity caused by the – often contextually insensitive – reforms designed to reduce it. An example in UK education is school development planning, a managerial innovation designed to support school staff with implementing other managerial innovations connected with marketization, alongside those concerned with teaching and learning. The lock-step annual planning cycle and prespecified limit to the number of priorities that could be addressed each year did not square well with the incremental imposition of further central government innovations. Nor did it encompass ameliorative adjustments to deal with existing innovations that proved to be unworkable in themselves or to clash with other innovations. The annual cycle was too rigid for the relatively turbulent planning environments into which it was introduced, yet it had to be followed. The form of the innovation did not cater for the need for incremental updating of plans. It exacerbated endemic ambiguity for school leaders brought by the dilemma over long-range direction setting versus short-term flexibility to adapt to unpredictably evolving circumstances.

One common response revealed by research was to compile the development plan as required, especially once the external inspection regime came to include examining each school's development plan document. But then informal incremental planning, conducted alongside development planning, actually guided practice because it gave the necessary flexibility that the annual development planning cycle could not (Wallace and McMahon 1994; Wallace 1998b). Adaptation was necessary to cope with a reform which may have been well suited to the relatively stable pre-reform school contexts from which it was developed. But it proved ill-suited to the more turbulent contexts of programmatic change in which it was to be implemented.

A UK health service example is the introduction of individual district general managers into the NHS during the mid-1980s. They were to replace 'consensus management' where district management teams containing representatives of different healthcare professional groups had been expected to operate through reaching consensual decisions. The more streamlined line-management structure led to greater bureaucracy, confusion over the roles of managers and their relationships within the NHS structure, less involvement by nurses in decision making, scepticism among doctors (few of whom were willing to take up management posts) – all serving to inhibit local service provision (Dopson 1997).

We noted earlier that research into the impact of reforms on the experience and practice of professional staff suggests that they respond in different ways. We will categorize these responses as compliance, non-compliance or mediation. Compliance connotes that reform goals are accepted, whether with enthusiasm implying belief in these goals, or resignation implying no more than belief that behavioural acquiescence is prudent in the face of accountability mechanisms and associated sanctions. The response of compliance reduces ambiguity for policy-makers as long as reforms are workable. Non-compliance connotes everything from retreatism, covertly continuing with present practice in the expectation of not being caught out, to overt resistance. This response generates ambiguity for policy-makers over how to determine the extent of non-compliance or how to increase compliance.

Mediation is of a different order. We suggest that it can constitute an ironic form of response where service organization staff attempt, as far as possible, to adapt the imperatives of particular reforms to develop what they regard as good practices according to their existing professional values in their contingent circumstances. Professional workplace research implies that such mediators are principled, characterized neither by slavish compliance nor by resistance but by the sincere endeavour to work round externally imposed requirements (e.g. Woods et al. 1997; Osborn et al. 2000). They appear to express what we will term 'principled infidelity': infidelity because they do not fully adhere to policy-makers' expectations, and principled because they seek to sustain their professional values rather than overlay them with the values underpinning reforms.

The deployment of agency to mediate reforms adds further to the increase in ambiguity already brought by the change process embodied in implementation. Things are not what they seem: what may be presented for accountability purposes as dutiful compliance masks what, according to practitioners' professional values, are actually divergent good practices, the best that they can achieve in their situations and often despite, rather than because of, reforms. Ironically, to the extent that reforms like development planning are contextually insensitive, covert adaptation by mediators may render them more workable than would have been the case if they had been fully compliant. Principled infidelity may thus undermine achievement to the letter of policy-makers' goals where they are deemed unworkable in a particular context. At the same time principled infidelity contributes to the spirit of these goals by making a related, more realistic practice work (as happened with school development planning). Mediators may successfully moderate some of the negative unintended consequences of reforms by giving priority to the interests of staff and local service users over those of policy-makers.

Principled mediators may be regarded as committed ironists. We suggest that their approach to coping with relatively unmanageable change, which is largely not of their making, is both appropriate and to be encouraged. Little research has been done on the perceptions and attitudes of such practitioners. But our hunch is that ironists express an *ironic orientation* towards professional practice and change. We assume that they are sceptics who are committed to improving public service practice. But they are not cynics. Their scepticism derives from their habitual experience of endemic ambiguity and the ironies that often ensue, and their often well-founded reservations about the impact of reforms on their practice and on the interests of the local users of the service they provide. They are likely to adopt the position which, Moore et al. (2002) in their research on schools, labelled 'principled pragmatism'. This term was applied to headteachers who seek to balance reforms with their personal educational beliefs and values. They are also likely to adopt a perspective on change which, while open to new ideas, is also coloured by a sense of contingency. External reforms or other changes are assessed against the perceived needs of local service users and service organization staff, examined for their workability in these circumstances, and compromises sought where necessary to cope with unrealistic expectations.

Coping Effectively with Ambiguity and Irony in the Change Process

If ambiguity is endemic to organizational life, if the change process can only add to it, if changes to reduce ambiguity beyond a certain point only create yet more ambiguity, and if sufficient agency for the irony of mediation can never be eliminated, what potential is left for improving the public services? An ironic perspective suggests that there are grounds for optimism. Learning to live with irony offers considerable potential for managing change as effectively as possible within the limits of manageability. But counter-intuitively for many policy-makers and service organization leaders, that potential is founded on moderation rather than missionary zeal, on the modest pursuit of incremental improvement rather than rapid transformation, and on coping with the risks imposed by the relative unmanageability of change rather than attempting to eliminate them through ever-tighter control.

Particularly in countries with a recent history of large-scale public service reform, politicians may feel that moderation, incrementalism and coping would be politically unattractive because the electorate has long been groomed to expect stirring visionary rhetoric and quick results. As Levin points out in Chapter 7, democratic political dynamics create pressure for ambition and speed with an eye always on building capital for the next general election. But that same electorate may also have been groomed for cynicism about political promises if past rhetoric has not been borne out by the reality of their contingent experience as public service users. It is notable that politicians in the UK and other western countries consistently feature in public opinion polls as one of the least trusted of occupations.

What might a more temperate approach to policy making and the nature of policies look like for public service improvement and for dealing with unplanned pressures? Indicatively, including representatives of those groups on whom implementation depends in setting the political agenda could act as a reality check for politicians' broad-sweep ideas and foster implementers' initial willingness to cooperate (consistent with Karen Seashore Louis's argument in Chapter 5). There is a risk for politicians of opening up the potential for 'provider capture' to suit provider interests over those of service users. But it is balanced against the risks of non-compliance, ameliorative policy making to address problems generated by unrealistic innovations, unfulfilled public expectations and loss of voter support.

Second, adopting an incremental strategy for evolutionary improvement (which allows for addressing new problems as they emerge) could maximize the capacity for smooth adjustment, or even for revising the strategy itself in the light of unfolding consequences and emerging factors. There is a political risk of appearing myopic and timid by withholding from the attempt to envision and control a very much brighter future. It is balanced against the risks of promising more than can be delivered, of sunk investment in unworkable innovations whose retraction will be deemed a policy U turn, and of disaffecting and burning out service providers on whose committed improvement effort everything depends.

Third, building some flexibility into innovations flowing from the policies that do get onto the agenda could be designed to encourage the measure of principled infidelity needed for implementers to develop good practices in their contingent circumstances. There is a risk of unacceptable mediation or non-compliance. It is balanced against the risk of overly rigid requirements, which can inhibit the adaptation needed to make innovations work in detailed settings for which they could not feasibly be designed.

Fourth, promoting the development of generic capacity to cope with sources of ambiguity delimiting the manageability of change could help service providers in two ways: to pre-empt ironies that striving for impossible certainty can trigger; and to deploy routine strategies for assimilating and addressing those that slip through. There is a risk of drift through chronic imprecision and opacity. It is balanced against the risks of derailing implementers whenever the latest solution for a 'wicked problem' turns out to generate unintended consequences, and of lowering their morale whenever things go wrong despite their best efforts.

Fifth, developing unobtrusive monitoring and modest accountability mechanisms that maximize the use of new technology could safeguard against, and alert policy-makers to, any extremes of service providers' behaviour that represent consensually unacceptable malpractice or incompetence (such as compromising patient safety). Concentrating on extremes could minimize the distraction that accountability mechanisms can impose on the conscientious and competent majority. There is a political risk of having insufficient information to demonstrate system-wide quality of service performance to users. It is balanced against the risk that strong surveillance will prove very costly, soaking up resources that could otherwise have been used to support service provision. It is also balanced against the risk of heavy demands for information deflecting implementers' attention away from improving service provision towards providing a 'glossy' account of their practice to please their evaluators.

And what of a temperate approach for those responsible for leading change in intermediate administrative and service organizations? Parameters for their work are set in part by policy-makers. But as we have argued, whether policy-makers are intemperate or temperate in their approach, sufficient agency is likely to remain for those elsewhere in the public service system to practise principled infidelity: whether to protect frontline service provider colleagues from changes imposed by policy-makers, to adapt such changes, to support wholeheartedly their implementation, or to promote local innovation.

The ambiguity generated by complex or programmatic change offers scope for what one of us (Wallace, Chapter 1) has termed 'orchestration' as a key coping strategy. It includes considering whether and how to respond to externally instigated change (consistent with the approach to dealing with multiple accountabilities advocated by Firestone in Chapter 11). But it mainly encompasses active promotion and organization to get change under way, and continual monitoring and adaptive action whenever required to cope with the unfolding consequences of ambiguity. Orchestration could enable formal leaders to take the strain off their colleagues and to absorb some of the stress induced by reform through the three sub-themes of flexible planning (for rapid response to unintended consequences while sustaining a broad direction), culture building and communication (for fostering a sense that coping with change is a collaborative effort within and between organizations), and differentiated support (for helping frontline professionals and other staff to cope effectively with their contextualized tasks). There is a managerial risk of being held to account for colleagues' less-than-faithful implementation of externally instigated changes. It is balanced against the risk of overloading and overstressing staff, who then provide a less-than-optimal service to users.

Second, temperate leadership of change implies expecting and fostering good professional practice, whether in relation to externally instigated change or local innovation. It could include encouraging staff and ensuring that they operate professionally through exercising the judgement that is necessary for the assiduous performance of their tasks, and act professionally through developing and sustaining appropriate relationships with colleagues and service users. It could run to fostering ongoing individual and collective professional learning within the 'community of practice' (Wenger 1998). Doing so implies protecting the necessary degree of autonomy required for making change work in each individual's context, which is unique in its detail. There is a managerial risk of losing control over the boundaries of colleagues' practice in implementing change. It is balanced against optimizing their capacity to express principled infidelity in making change work for the sake of high-quality service provision.

Third, change leaders could actively encourage the emergence of ideas, techniques and procedures from professional practice within the boundaries of acceptability, through identifying, supporting and achieving congruence between emerging good practices and externally shaped requirements. Leaders could expand the scope for (unequal) distribution of change leadership, creating favourable conditions for emergent practice among different specialised groups. There is a risk of unworkable innovation or unacceptable divergence from regulatory norms. It is balanced against the risk of failing to find new context-sensitive ways of doing the things that matter most to staff and service users.

Finally, promoting a climate of 'high trust-with-verification' could help set the expectation that staff will take responsibility for operating professionally, and so not abuse the degree of autonomy accorded them to foster local innovation and emergence. An initial presumption of trust, rather than the mistrust that strong surveillance and accountability mechanisms imply, stands to maximize capacity for coping with the increased ambiguity accompanying change. There is a risk that staff might betray this trust (hence the continuing need for verification through accountability mechanisms). It is balanced against the risk that a low-trust climate marked by obtrusive surveillance is likely to militate against staff willingness to take responsibility for their professional conduct.

We readily acknowledge that temperance promises relatively little, so is unlikely to seem politically attractive. Intemperate approaches promise so much more, and therein lies their attraction to politicians. But they inherently increase the bad risk of debilitating irony because of their very ambition. This ambition stands to be deeply undermined, whether through the stipulation of new practices which unintentionally inhibit local experimentation necessary to find what works in different contexts, through raised expectations that cannot be met, or through perverse side effects such as change appearance taking precedence over change reality.

A temperate approach minimizes (though it cannot remove) the bad risk of generating serious ironic consequences of this kind. Since it does not promise overmuch, it is practically realistic. It embraces the good risk of generating mildly ironic consequences: moderate diversity of incrementally changing practice and outcomes. In sum, a temperate approach offers politicians and leaders of change for service organizations no guarantee of success, but the least-worst prospect of failure.

REFERENCES

Chambers, W. and R. Ltd (1998) *The Chambers Dictionary*. Edinburgh: Chambers Harrap Publishers Ltd.

Clarke, J. and Newman, J. (1997) *The Managerial State*. London: Sage.

Deem, R. (2004) New managerialism in UK universities: manager-academics' accounts of change. In H. Eggins (ed.), *Globalization and Reform in Higher Education*. Buckingham: Open University Press, pp. 55–67.

Department of Health (1997) *The New NHS: Modern/Dependable*. Cm 3807. London: Department of Health.

Department of Health (2004a) *An Implementation Framework for Reconfiguring the DH Arm's Length Bodies: Redistributing Resources to the NHS Front-line*. London: Department of Health.

Department of Health (2004b) *The NHS Improvement Plan: Putting People at the Heart of Public Services*. Cm 6268. London: Department of Health.

Docteur, E. and Oxley, H. (2003) *Health Care Systems: Lessons from the Reform Experience*. Paris: OECD.

Dopson, S. (1997) *Managing Ambiguity and Change: the Case of the NHS*. London: Macmillan.

Dopson, S., Fitzgerald, L., Ferlie, E. and Gabbay, J. (2005) *Knowledge to Action? Evidence-Based Health Care in Context*. Oxford: Oxford University Press.

Evans, L. (2000) The effects of educational change on morale, job satisfaction and motivation. *Journal of Educational Change*, **1**, 173–92.

Farrell, C. and Morris, J. (2003) The neo-bureaucratic state: professionals, managers and professional managers in schools, general practices and social work. *Organization*, **10**(1), 129–56.

Farrell, C. and Morris, J. (2004) Resigned compliance: teacher attitudes towards performance-related pay in schools. *Educational Management Administration and Leadership*, **32**(1), 81–104.

Ferlie, E., Hartley, J. and Martin, S. (2003) Changing public service organizations: current perspectives and future prospects. *British Journal of Management*, **14**, S1–S14, Special Issue, December.

Fink, D. (2003) The law of unintended consequences: the 'real' cost of top-down reform. *Journal of Educational Change*, **4**, 105–28.

Giddens, A. (1979) *Central Problems in Social Theory*. Berkeley: University of California Press.

Giddens, A. (1984) *The Constitution of Society*. Cambridge: Polity Press.

Glatter, R. and Kydd, L. (2002) 'Best practice' in educational leadership and management: can we identify it and learn from it? Paper presented at the National College for School Leadership first invitational international conference 'An International Future: Learning from Best Practice Worldwide'. October, Nottingham.

Hoyle, E. (1986) *The Politics of School Management*. London: Hodder & Stoughton.

Hoyle, E. and Wallace, M. (2005) *Educational Leadership: Ambiguity, Professionals and Managerialism*. London: Sage.

Leadbeater, C. (2003) *Personalization through Participation*. London: Demos.

March, J. and Simon, H. (1958) *Organizations*. New York: Wiley.

Marsick, V.J. and Watkins, K. (1990) *Informal and Incidental Learning in the Workplace*. London: Routledge.

McLaughlin, M. (1991) The RAND change agent study: ten years after. In A. Odden (ed.), *Education Policy Implementation*. Albany, NY: SUNY Press.

McNulty, T. and Ferlie, E. (2002) *Re-engineering Health Care: the Complexities of Organizational Transformation*. Oxford: Oxford University Press.

Moore, A., George, R. and Halpin, D. (2002) The developing role of the headteacher in English schools: management, leadership and pragmatism. *Educational Management and Administration*, **30**(2), 175–88.

Mueller, F., Sillance, J., Harvey, C. and Howarth, C. (2003) A rounded picture is what we need: rhetorical strategies, arguments and the negotiation of change in a UK hospital trust. *Organization Studies*, **25**(1), 75–93.

Newman, J. (2001) *Modernizing Governance: New Labour, Policy and Society*. Buckingham: Open University Press.

National College for School Leadership (2003) *School Leadership 2003*. Nottingham: NCSL.

NHS Leadership Centre (2003) *An Introduction to the NHS Leadership Centre*. London: Department of Health.

Odden, A. (ed.) (1991) *Educational Policy Implementation*. New York: SUNY Press.

Office of Public Service Reform (2002) *Reforming our Public Services: Principles into Practice*. London: Office of Public Service Reform.

Osborn, M., McNess, E., Broadfoot, P. with Pollard, A. and Triggs, P. (2000) *What Teachers Do. Changing Policy and Practice in Primary Education*. London: Continuum.

Times Educational Supplement (2000) Whatever happened to the heroes? 5 May.

Wallace, M. (1998a) A counter-policy to subvert educational reform? Collaboration among schools and colleges in a competitive climate. *British Educational Research Journal*, **24**(2), 195–215.

Wallace, M. (1998b) Innovations in planning for school improvement: problems and potential. In A. Hargreaves, A. Lieberman, M. Fullan and D. Hopkins (eds), *International Handbook of Educational Change*. Dordrecht, Netherlands: Kluwer Academic Press, pp. 1181–202.

Wallace, M. and McMahon, A. (1994) *Planning for Change in Turbulent Times: the Case of Multiracial Primary Schools*. London: Cassell.

Wenger, E. (1998) *Communities of Practice: Learning, Meaning and Identity*. Cambridge: Cambridge University Press.

Woods, P., Jeffrey, B., Troman, G. and Boyle, M. (1997) *Re-structuring schools, Re-structuring Teachers: Responding to Change in the Primary School*. Buckingham: Open University Press.

PART II

EXPLORING THE COMPLEXITY OF POLICY MAKING FOR PUBLIC SERVICE REFORM

CHAPTER 5

MANAGING COMPLEX CHANGE: BRINGING MESO-POLITICS BACK IN

Karen Seashore Louis

Extending our understanding of the complexity of public service change entails embracing more than just the change process and associated coping strategies on which the earlier chapters have concentrated. In countries where particular public services or the public services as a whole are subject to major political reform efforts, the policy-making process and its outcomes contribute very significantly to the complexity of change. They set many parameters – whether through legislation, mandates, resource allocation or accountability mechanisms – circumscribing how coping strategies must operate.

As discussed in Chapter 1, Karen Seashore Louis's previous research on the change process was instrumental in conceptualizing the problem coping and 'steady orchestration and coordination' that are endemic to implementation. Here she adopts a complementary focus on the policy-making process within public service reform, which contributes so much to the need for orchestration and coping strategies. Her literature review is directed primarily towards developing knowledge-for-understanding, exploring the process of public policy agenda setting and choosing among alternative policy options. She makes the case for attending more to the non-rational elements of reform policy making including the interplay of power, much of which occurs outside the public domain (see Chapter 7). The macro-politics of policy making parallel the micro-politics entailed in the interaction between alternative rationalities highlighted by research on implementation (and theorized in Chapter 4).

The outcomes of the literature review are used to inform the development of 'knowledge-for-action'. The normative argument is developed that expanding the contribution of diverse stakeholder voices to policy agenda setting would help to make policy making more realistic, by maximizing the degree of coherence between policies, and favouring reform decisions whose implementation is a practical proposition. (A complementary case is made in Chapter 11 for an ongoing endeavour at service organization level to maximize coherence in responding to multiple pressures for change.)

Introduction

This chapter has one objective: to make a case for discussions about public service reform to focus more on models that attend to the non-rational elements of policy making. This argument is not new, and I cite many studies published years ago. In education, this research has focused on what happens to programmes during implementation, a perspective that has brought attention to the street-level bureaucrat and teacher's influence on policy. While not ignoring implementation, my approach is different, emphasizing the need to understand the *policy-making process* and its implications for managing for complex change.

I develop my argument in five sections. First, I deal with the alternative perspectives that can be applied to policy making for complex change; second, I examine the earliest stages of policy agenda setting; third, I discuss what is known about how policy options are shared and become legitimated; fourth, I look at the problem of creating policy coherence in complex governance settings; and finally, I present some implications for considering the role of power in orchestrating complex change.

Perspectives on the Relationship between Policy and System Change

There are three common images of the relationship between policy and complex social change in the literature. A *technical policy perspective* is found in most policy analysis texts and among those advocating rational choice models (Ostrom 1999). Policy-makers need information, including frameworks for understanding the sector that they are trying to affect, in order to make sensible legislative and regulatory decisions and to monitor policy impacts. Policy analysis should, therefore, focus on rational choices to be made once a policy issue is on the agenda (Stokey and Zeckhauser 1978; Weimer and Vining 1999). In general, when complex policy models are adopted, there is an emphasis on understanding the accepted 'rules' of decision making that govern the policy process.

Other scholars emphasize a *political perspective*, focusing on a naturalistic explanation of how policies are made, and how they spread. Both the indeterminate nature of the policy-making process and the inevitable slippage that occurs as additional policy refinements accrue during implementation are fodder for explaining how policies succeed or fail (Forrester and Adams 1997; Kingdon 1995). In contrast to explaining the gaps between policy intent and impact as the consequence of loose implementation processes, the focus is on agenda setting. The levers for incrementally shifting policies are often less important than understanding how a particular policy issue got the committee's attention (Sabatier and Jenkins-Smith 1993).

A *practitioner perspective* emerges from studies of public sector administrators and civil servants, and examines how the strain towards autonomy in interpreting policies affects the broader process of complex change. Professionals who will be affected by proposed changes often see new policies and regulations as distractions from their 'real work', and therefore interpret them to fit their needs (Weatherly and Lipsky 1977). Rather than being passive recipients of policy, they are creative actors in the policy-making process. Recent research suggests that professionals in schools, for example, have opportunities to pick and choose from the inducements and constraints that are offered by policy-makers to maximize their own interpretations of those policies (Honig and Hatch 2004) as they orchestrate the *local* policy process (Wallace 2003, 2004).

Each of these perspectives has validity. But they are seldom integrated in applied policy analyses, creating frustration for everyone who wants to understand how we ended up in our most current public service mess. This observation leads to questions that must be addressed as we think about managing public service change:

1 How do issues get defined and taken seriously as policy options?
2 How do clusters of policies – systemic efforts at reform – get embedded and transmitted to create impact?
3 How does local autonomy shift the process of system change?

These questions are consistent with the broad assumptions set out by Wallace (Chapter 1) which focus on power: both formal authority and informal influence. I agree with his emphasis on the role that authority at all levels creates for leveraging complex social change, but in this chapter I place more emphasis on the role of informal, often non-positional, influences. As Gandhi pointed out, most elites, including designated 'orchestrators,' are only temporarily in power. While their effect may be large in the short run, we also need to look at the broader context and processes that may lead to the longer range success or failure of public service reforms, particularly those in education.

The literature related to the questions posed above reflects three premises about the nature of the change process. First, I assume that policies are made at national and local levels in processes that are quasi-independent. In education, for example, initiatives, rules and mandates are created by intermediate governance units (municipalities or local education authorities) as well as in government ministries and departments of education. Second, even when local authorities are required to implement national policy, there is still an adoption process that includes interpreting policies to make them applicable in a particular context. Local autonomy always exceeds the latitude that has been formally delegated. Finally, adoption and implementation processes are influenced by factors that are largely out of the control of national policy actors. These assumptions are based on distinct theoretical perspectives. The first, from political science, draws on research around agenda setting and the role of policy networks and interest groups. The second two, from sociology, emerge from research on knowledge use, and from 'new institutionalism', which emphasizes implicit informal rules conditioning organizational choices (as explored in Chapter 3).

Defining the Issues: Agenda Setting in Complex Public Service Change

The agenda-setting process, which begins long before large-scale policy reforms become laws, is multifaceted and largely hidden from public view. In this murky arena, non-rational and serendipitous social influences further obscure how issues are framed. Why some options wind up on the table while others receive little attention is not well understood, which makes altering or influencing this early process extremely complicated.

Wicked problems and complex change

Problems are wicked when they are resistant to resolution through any single set of policy initiatives (Basu, Dirsmith and Gupta 1999; Rittel and Webber 1973). In the world of wicked problems, promising policies often conflict with other equally attractive policies that address the same problem. A current example is the effort to provide more stable educational experiences to immigrant children by ensuring that they attend the same school even if their families move frequently, a goal based on research suggesting that changing schools depresses achievement. In practice, this solution conflicts with other policies that are designed to avoid segregating minority and 'at risk' children. They are based on research findings that socio-economic isolation depresses achievement. Conflict among policies designed to provide adequate services for children of recent immigrants that solve the educational transience problem bumps up against housing and racial segregation issues. This interconnectedness inevitably leads to efforts (or the lack thereof) related to economic support of immigrants, the concentration of immigrants in urban centres and so on. In this case I emphasize the knowledge–policy connection because it foreshadows the dilemma of formulating public service reforms that appear to be based on rock-solid findings but are actually built on shifting tectonic plates.

Setting the policy agenda to address complex change

At this juncture there is no research that supports comprehensive solutions addressing all of the educational, housing and work issues facing immigrants. Policies that address complex social problems in manageable chunks continue to be made because they are the best that we can do. How then do different options or clusters of options make it to the table?

Research on the policy-making process has been one of the most robust areas of overlap between policy analysts and theoretical political scientists (Sabatier 1991). Most of this research has been driven by the observation that studying government decision making in isolation ignores the core processes of influence that characterize democracies. In fact, much of the action in policy making occurs before any votes are taken, during the period when new ideas are introduced and become policy issues for the legislative body and the public. The most frequently cited models of policy development emphasize the chaotic and pluralistic aspects of the process.

Until the 1970s, little attention was paid to how particular policy alternatives were determined, and research on agenda setting tended to look for (and find) elite influence (Putnam 1976). An alternative, while acknowledging elite bias and resistance to change in the formal system of influence, makes a key additional assumption: that 'pre-political, or at least pre-decisional, processes are often of the most critical importance in determining which issues and alternatives are to be considered . . . and which choices will be made' (Cobb and Elder 1971). This may include 'non-decisions', one process by which ideas are eliminated from formal consideration. While elites may determine which issues come up, it is at this juncture that non-elite groups joust to get their knowledge and ideas into the discussion. The pre-decision process is often biased and politicized, but in other cases there are multiple points of entry, and 'outsiders' who have ideas can market them freely (Edmondson 2005).

The role of knowledge in agenda setting

Those who best understand the complexity of the social problems to be addressed by policy are often scholars and practitioners. In education, most researchers are ill equipped to participate in the policy-making process because they do not understand it. While educational researchers occasionally become active policy analysts, they are more likely to play an entrepreneurial role, 'selling' their own findings or acting as a behind-the-scenes adviser. Researchers complain that their firm results are often ignored, while policy-makers argue that the research is not useful. At the same time, professional associations representing educators are regarded as weak sources of knowledge for policy (Louis *et al.* 2005). Whoever is complaining, the outcomes are the same: limited attention paid to the value of rigorous research or practice-based knowledge (Rosenbaum 1996; Ryan 1999).

The point is not that policy deliberately ignores research and rigorous examination of effective practice (although it sometimes does), but that the policy-making process always takes into account that 'what we know', at least in service sectors, is swamped by what we do not know. Focusing on these uncertainties often stimulates debates that further undermine the credibility of knowledge.

Alternative modes of agenda setting

A recent example in the US illustrates the problem of incorporating research and practice perspectives into agenda setting. The federal Reading Excellence Act was based on the goal of ensuring that every child would read by the third grade *and* on the assumption that we know how to teach reading. However, competing views among various actors – individuals, professional associations and well-placed policy advisers – undermined these reasonable assumptions (Edmondson 2005). Schisms concerned the best way to teach reading, whether reading should be taught in pre-school or earlier, and other issues. Rather than rallying the expected coalition of stakeholders, the legislation precipitated lingering divisions between agencies and researchers committed to understanding and promoting reading. If promoting reading in the early grades can be politically volatile and create vituperative debate we cannot expect that managing change in more complex parts of the system will be less so.

Policy initiatives can also become resistant to empirical or rational analysis. For example, recent technical and further education policies in Australia were influenced primarily by corporate opinions and a neo-liberal rhetoric linking further education to economic expansion and work, in spite of limited empirical evidence supporting the payoff of such a shift (Ryan 1999; Symes *et al.* 2000). This policy process apparently lacked the pluralistic and chaotic discourse characterizing the development of the Reading Excellence Act in the US. But it incurred the cost of discouraging the inclusion of alternative ideas that might have led to a more comprehensive education policy. There is little evidence that the policy change made much of a difference in the routines and practices of universities, except on the margins (Symes *et al.* 2000).

What can we conclude? First, the use of knowledge in the agenda-setting process is contested and poorly understood. Second, using rigorous practitioner or research-based knowledge to sway opinions once the agenda is set has little impact (sad news to all of the social scientists who prepare for legislative or parliamentary testimony). Third, certainly in education, research on agenda setting is very limited. We know more about how legislative agendas are set in the small, left-leaning state of Minnesota (Mazzoni 1993) than we do about larger and perhaps more typical states, much less about other countries.

Kingdon's (2003) model identifies three arenas in which competing ideas operate: a 'problem stream' that determines which social needs are viewed as important, a 'solution stream', composed of competing policies, and a 'political stream' that consists of potential key actors. The collision among these streams was apparent in the *post hoc* analyses of the Reading Excellence Act. All three operate quasi-independently, which means that the combination of issues, solutions and active participants is often difficult to predict. It is the quasi-organized, fluid nature of the agenda setting and subsequent policy decision process (which often cannot even be described to an outsider) that accounts for the uncertain fate of good ideas in affecting decisions. My emphasis on the agenda-setting process suggests that if we hope for research-based decisions, scholars must become involved even before public awareness is activated (Easton 1969).

A focus on agenda setting stands in contrast to efforts to develop and apply modified rational-choice theories to the development of public policy (Kato 1996; Ostrom 1999). Rational choice theorists have much to add to discussions about choosing among policy alternatives, yet they rarely address agenda-setting, even though agendas can develop in ways that limit options and make rational choice more problematic later on.

How Ideas about Complex Change Diffuse

Political scientists rarely investigate explicitly how new ideas are incorporated into the policy process. In this section I turn to what sociologists tell us about the problems of managing complex change from their research on knowledge diffusion and use. This encompasses both how research makes its way into policy, as well as how policies cross boundaries and spread between government units.

Many scholars focus on the characteristics of knowledge as a predictor of use. According to various writers, educational research is likely to influence policy development when it: (i) is compatible with existing belief structures; (ii) diffuses rapidly throughout the organizational field so that it becomes legitimized; (iii) has *prima facie* utility in local sites; and (iv) is 'processed' or discussed within the potential user group in ways that make it fit with local preferences (Wejnart 2002). Research increasingly pays attention both to the nature of the knowledge and the characteristics of the setting.

Weak ties and diffusion

The 'strength of weak ties' is a concept that explains the unexpected finding that new ideas transfer most rapidly between groups that share only a few members (Granovetter 1973). The underlying explanation is that *very strong ties* foster 'groupthink'. Little disagreement about preferred policy solutions occurs among groups that share common ideologies, and therefore genuinely challenging information is unlikely to be exchanged. The *absence of ties* between groups means that innovative policy ideas will not be shared at all because of limited opportunity to meet. *Weak ties*, in contrast, permit both the development of diverse ideas in independent groups, and also the occasional *ad hoc* communication that is associated with the more rapid spread of new ideas. Weaker ties between units within the same social system can be important in generating a broader range of solutions to identified problems, or help in identifying new problems (Hansen 1999).

Recent research on policy formation and agenda setting incorporates network studies that examine weak and strong ties. In particular, research on policy networks has turned from an emphasis on bargaining to one that also includes information transfer (John 2001) and the diffusion of innovations in the public sector (Wejnart 2002; Louis *et al.* 2003;). This shift expands the framework to account for the emergence of competitive 'issue networks', and also moves beyond examining privileged or 'elite' communication relationships to more inclusive and loosely regulated forms of information exchange. A network approach argues that most connections are fluid and bound together by the trading of valuable ideas and not just the exchange of favours.

The implications for conceptualizing complex social changes are stunning. If policy-makers at all levels in the educational system are held in a large but diffuse network in which different ideas circulate, but in which some ideas may come up against unpredictable exclusionary boundaries, the problem of managing change becomes more complex than is even suggested by the notion of 'wicked problems'. In large systems, managing complex change requires managing the flow of knowledge – something that has become increasingly difficult in the information age. Rather than managing change, we are driven to a worldview in which embracing the apparent chaos and disorder of an evolutionary process provides the only logic for making the world better (Wheatley 1999; Wheatley and Crinean 2004). It is the nature of the idea and whether it 'sticks' that creates structures – not the command and control apparatus.

Strong ties: the influence of elite networks on complex change

The weak ties concept is compelling, but may be less applicable when complex knowledge needs to be transferred. The weak ties approach suggests that countries or states will look for solutions to educational problems quasi-independently. One government's choices will not dictate an approach to others. 'Successes' are, however, communicated through a variety of venues. They range from invitational expert conferences to Organization for Economic Cooperation and Development (OECD) meetings, and governments compete to be the first to adopt solutions that look good (Berry and Berry 1999). The problem with this pattern is that the information communicated can be weak and poorly researched, and that spread may be based more on the immediate needs of officials to 'look good' than on careful analysis. Further, the more complex the information, the more likely it is to be distorted during transfer.

To compensate, officials develop stronger ties with information providers, turning to trusted groups for information on complex issues. In general, when faced with complex problems, most policy-makers look for acknowledged expertise that has proven helpful in the past (Salisbury *et al.* 1989). Experts may become members of the policy elite as part of their role in regularly providing information, a trend that accelerates when legislators are faced with ever more complex research results and policy options.

Sustained interactions are a key to the effective transfer of complex knowledge. This is the strong ties–weak ties dilemma: trust creates networks that facilitate the flow of complex knowledge, but may also serve to crowd out divergent voices and ideas. Sustained interaction facilitates consistency in 'mental models' or the worldviews of parties (Huberman 1999), and emerging research suggests that people simply do not remember factual information that challenges their mental model (Mishra and Brewer 2003; Brandon and Hollingshead 2004). Perhaps fortunately, networks connecting researchers and policy-makers rarely generate stable or formalized strong ties. Reliance on experts does not make decision-makers powerless recipients, because they pick and choose who to listen to (Lupia and McCubbins 1994; Mintrom and Vergari 2003).

Whose voice?

Weak ties–strong ties help to explain characteristics of Kingdon's political actors stream. I alluded previously to the cacophony of voices that emerged during the agenda-setting process for the Reading Excellence Act in the US, and the opposite problem that occurred when divergent voices were crowded out in the Australian technical and further education policies. Studies of specific agenda-setting situations do not, however, explain the conditions under which some voices become prominent or stifled (Campbell 2002). A case can be made, for example, that the policy focus on 'direct instruction' occurring in some countries is a consequence of purging research voices that recommend a more complex set of options for improving classroom teaching (Beard 2000). In the US, however, the scholarly advocates of 'direct instruction' (a behaviourist pedagogy that provides students with specific task-focused instructions, teacher-led practice, independent practice and immediate corrective feedback) did not silence scholars during the national debates whose research suggested different models (Edmondson 2005). But direct instruction advocates had more influence during the development of some states' policies (Allington 1999). We could not easily predict these differences with one common theoretical framework, although Kingdon's policy streams model can be applied *post hoc*.

Expanding networks and the spread of complex change

How can we account for the rapid spread of some policy options (for example school-based accountability or direct instruction) while other policies that have strong empirical support remain localized? While this is an under-investigated topic, there are some hints in the literature (Wejnart 2002; Mintrom and Vergari 2003). The spread of policy innovations between states in the US is rather idiosyncratic, and is, to some extent, based on unpredictable contacts between members of the policy elite. At the same time there are also more structured networks of policy actors that influence the diffusion and adoption of policies (Soule and Zylan 1997).

In education, one example of an organization that maintains a low profile with high influence is the Education Commission of the States, a 50-year-old association that brings together representatives from all states on a regular basis to discuss educational issues. While it conducts policy analyses, it relies primarily on synthesizing ideas from research, policy and practice in ways that are useful to governors and legislators. It carries out the role of 'trusted servant', while refraining from making judgements about policy initiatives being contemplated in any state. It is not a household word, even to the readers of national newspapers. In the US ideas also spread between culturally and economically similar states, which generally cluster by region. Thus, weaker networks nationally and stronger local or regional networks permit rapid and varied searches for innovations, as well as facilitating effective dissemination of more complex information as it becomes available.

While there is less research on how policy ideas become diffused across larger areas, policy knowledge clearly flows across national borders (Wilson and Al-Muinhanna 1985). In most cases, the international flow of knowledge is through the uncoordinated involvement of multinational corporations and organizations, as well as being transmitted through loose international policy networks – classic 'weak ties'. This helps to explain, for example, why educational policy discussions in England are picked up more quickly in Australia (physically distant but culturally connected) than in France (close, but culturally remote). It is likely that this is true in other parts of the world. It is no surprise that the complex changes associated with 'new public management' diffused rapidly to many of the countries that are active in the OECD, where the term was introduced for group discussion (Kaboolian 1998).

Overlapping networks may contribute to the rapid diffusion of some research ideas. Equally useful ideas related to complex social change languish because they cannot find their way into a network. Increasingly, however, we see efforts to systematize international policy coordination, and these are often led by knowledge-based experts rather than politicians (Haas 1992). Thus, a key to understanding the uncertain development of reforms lies in examining the role of 'policy entrepreneurs', or individuals who assume a central role as brokers in the policy-making process (Mintrom 1997).

Mintrom demonstrates that the presence of individual policy entrepreneurs significantly increased the probability that one educational issue – school choice – would both make it to the legislative agenda in US states, and be acted on. While individual entrepreneurs were also notable in state healthcare reform (Oliver and Shaheen 1997). When policy entrepreneurs are advocates they typically rely on research-based information to press their case but, not surprisingly, they use that research selectively. Increasingly, 'blockers' play a pivotal role in the development of policies (see also Chapter 8). Here an individual or group organizes to ensure that some volatile and even popular issues never make it onto the final policy issue table (Santoro 1999).

Changing sources

The increasing diversity of electronic information networks presents a challenge for managing complex change across national and state or province boundaries. More information is available, but it often arrives from sources that are not well known or trustworthy. The more diverse and detached the voices, the less likely that groups and individuals will share common assumptions about how to approach complex problems. It is possible that the electronic information age will result in even greater difficulty in reaching agreement about policies, as a consequence of information overload and the presence of more electronic 'issue networks' (Kirst and Neister 1984).

The contested nature of policy options is central for Carol Weiss, who was among the first to propose that knowledge needs to pass two types of tests before it is used. First, a *truth test*, which helps the individual or group looking at the information to decide whether it is a reasonable approximation of 'reality'. Second, a *utility test*, by which the same groups determine whether or not it can be applied, given a set of constraints. The latter could range from financial stringencies to potential unintended consequences not considered in the research (Weiss and Buculvalas 1980). Weiss contends that policy decisions are rarely distinct from ongoing organizational and administrative events. Policy choices rely on custom and implicit rules, mutual adjustment, accretion and negotiations in which expert knowledge is often viewed as a 'device of control' rather than a help. In other words, the process of incorporating knowledge into policy is 'unorganized, slow, wasteful, and sloppy' (Weiss 1982: 35–6).

Other studies indicate the need for some caution in generalizing this conclusion. Weiss studied mental health, but policy-makers in other fields may conform to the more rational, instrumental decision process that Weiss discards (Beyer and Trice 1982). Another challenge comes from an analysis of Australian educational policy (Vickers 1994), which showed that even while some uses of research may appear rational, others do not. Vickers points out that the meaning of knowledge use is not simple and that power can take on different forms, not all of which involve imposing one worldview upon another.

Creating Policy Coherence at Multiple Levels

The difficulty in understanding how specific decisions are affected by, and use, knowledge is compounded when we remember that decisions about policy are made at many levels. If the top officials studied by Weiss describe a lumpy, non-linear decision path, the information they deliver to policy-makers at the next level in the public service setting also necessitates a similar decision process. National policies and their associated rules, regulations, inducements and programme criteria are rarely, at least in the social service sector, fully fleshed out models for action. Instead, they need interpreting before being put into practice. To give just one example, England's National Literacy and Numeracy Strategy is a very detailed educational initiative designed to improve the performance of all teachers in all grades. Yet during the first four years there were serious problems of implementation, none of which appeared to involve resistance or lack of willingness to cooperate. Rather, there were issues within schools that caused them not to 'take an overview of all the elements' (Office for Standards in Education 2004). School staff interpreted the mandates differently, and did not respond in a coherent systemic way. An analysis of the 'literacy hour', a centrepiece of the programme, points out that even within this highly detailed policy, accompanied by vast stockpiles of information and extensive professional development, school staffs and individual teachers made decisions about how to introduce the programme into the ongoing life of their institutions. For example, they might consider how much emphasis to put on writing or reading. Their local decisions may have actually increased the variability between schools and classrooms (Miller 2003).

These contrasting perspectives – *central* policy as a lever for creating and managing complex system change and *local* policy as the more proximate factor affecting change – are central to educational improvement today (Hopkins and Levin 2000). In some countries we observe decentralization policies that place the responsibility for knowledge utilization and change in the hands of schools. In these countries, teachers and school leaders struggle together to create better learning conditions while remaining accountable for students' learning. Recent policies in New Zealand, which devolved most policy decisions to individual school boards, are a case in point (Gordon 1995). The assumption that localized decision processes can contribute to educational improvement is a distinct paradigm shift that has occurred on an international basis, supported by increasing consensus among teacher associations, politicians and parents in countries as diverse in educational tradition as Sweden, the Netherlands and the US.

On the other hand, political actors, even in these settings, continue to utilize, in part, more centralized, hegemonic decisions that are intended to shock parts of the system into change. In the US and the Netherlands, standards-based reforms have been adopted at the national level, while Sweden has faced pressures to exert central control over a high-stakes examination system. Ideas about effective schools and effective teaching that have been widely diffused through international research networks, and later, within countries, have been influential in affecting policy discourse (Firestone, Fitz and Broadfoot 1999). These and other examples suggest that international exchanges create an epistemic community of people who are not formally linked, but who nevertheless interact with each other and share a set of beliefs (Haas 1992).

The notion that 'you can't mandate what matters', first voiced by Milbrey McLaughlin and later popularized by Michael Fullan, continues to remind us of the limits of vertically integrated policy. Probably the single most researched policy initiative in history – fertility control in China – reveals that in spite of policy consistency that is unheard of in western countries, and an ability to orchestrate inducements at all levels, implementation is uneven (Hardee-Cleaveland and Banister 1988; Li 1995; Merli and Raftery 2000).

Some policies are more amenable to orchestration by formal leaders than others. Policies that require smaller schools to merge are, for example, successful in most settings, largely because of the ability of policy-makers to keep tabs on 'exit' and 'entry' of units (Wholey and Sanchez, 1991). Other policies are harder to monitor, either because counting the results is more difficult, or because the government's control over alternative inducements and competing pressures is limited.

The policy field for a given public sector is often rife with contradictory initiatives, each of which has its own set of both formal and informal orchestrators. For instance, merger or closure policies that are triggered by poor student achievement results or declining enrolments are intended to affect the 'population density' and quality of schools. At the same time, however, policies that encourage opening new schools under the rubric of 'privatization' and 'competition' increase the number of small, untested schools, and place policy development into the hands of parent boards. There is increasing evidence that, in spite of some successes, many of these new schools struggle with quality (Walsh 2004). Competing policies are therefore, in part, the consequences of political opportunism among competing 'movements', 'issue networks' and 'policy entrepreneurs' (Meyer and Staggenborg 1996).

Even when a new policy falls on uncontested ground (relatively rare in education), we still find that there is a lot of mutual adjustment (Mills 1998). A state policy regulating remedial education in public higher education in Oklahoma was perceived as clear in intent, met with no significant opponents, was publicly supported and adequately funded and was not in conflict with other existing policies. Yet it still required a complex meshing of institutional policies and cultures with the goals and expectations set forth by the state's higher education coordinating board (Mazzeo 2002). Another study of public sector response to new regulations suggests that prior organizational performance may condition how well an agency is able to respond. Poorly performing agencies tend to respond in a 'rule-bound' way, adhering strictly to the policy – while not improving their performance. More highly performing agencies, on the other hand, are more flexible in their implementation, and increase their performance (Marcus 1988). If this is the case in education, formal effort to orchestrate may have the least impact where improvement is most needed.

Finally, recent research applying rational-choice theory to the general problem of government control emphasizes the variety of layers and levels that make the command-and-control objective problematic (Kiser 1999). While in theory the top policy-maker relies on the civil service to regulate, oversee and implement, recent studies in the US indicate that state governors are increasingly relying on oversight of the overseer – but then who oversees the overseers?

Divergent value systems are almost always at work whenever there is role differentiation within a policy system, which increases opportunities for local interpretation by the actors in each subculture. This is often the case when the implementers actively, but informally, orchestrate their own reactions to the policies. They respond to efforts to constrain their autonomy or change their practice by strategically manoeuvring, sometimes in partnership with other stakeholders, to resist or reverse implementation by blaming the policy itself (Astley 1984). Collective strategy can be played at multiple levels as the interests of the actors compete with and complement each other.

Influence, Knowledge, Agendas and Complex Change: Some Implications for Research

The main point of this chapter has been to challenge what it means to 'manage complex change'. I chose policy making rather than policy implementation as my primary focus because if there is incoherence at the beginning of the process of change, it is unrealistic to assume that the implementation can be managed – at least in the conventional sense.

Three perspectives are reflected in this analysis: technical, political and practitioner. The first is based on my assumption that better knowledge will improve the development of policies that will be implementable and have the desired effects, even in a world that is characterized by 'wicked problems'. The second is articulated in my choice of Kingdon's (2003) streams model as a vehicle for arguing that our ability is constrained to ensure that better knowledge and policy options will be given due consideration. The final perspective corresponds to the underlying theme of incorporating diverse voices into the agenda-setting process. Each of these themes reminds policy-makers (as does Wallace in Chapter 1) that the real job of orchestrating complex change occurs informally on the shop floor as well as in the halls of power.

But the use of three perspectives, derived from a literature review rather than from empirical work, suggests the need for additional research. In particular, two questions stand out. First, we know very little about the way in which knowledge enters the policy formulation process. In other words, the intersection between 'streams' and formal and informal knowledge sources remains an important but under-investigated topic in an era where 'knowledge production' is often viewed as the salvation of modern (and even post-modern) social structures. Second, although I have argued that diversity is important in agenda setting, a careful reader of this chapter will see that there are surprisingly few empirical studies in education that investigate, in detail, how different voices enter the policy mêlée. I have argued elsewhere that it is critical to build a strong democratic base in education (Louis 2002), but in order to do so we need comparative studies about how alternative voices affect policy discussions at the local and national levels.

In emphasizing the messy nature of policy formulation, I do not intend to imply that the process of intentional social change is directionless. Even Margaret Wheatley, a prominent thinker in the application of chaos theory to human institutions, affirms the goal of direction, but argues for a non-authoritative approach:

> To step aside from aggressive responses to problem-solving requires using some little-used skills: *humility, curiosity, and a willingness to listen*. Humility is a brave act – we have to admit that we don't (know) enough to solve the problem, that our approaches aren't working and never will. Even our own treasured answers are insufficient – if everyone bowed to our demands and did what we asked, the problem still would not be solved. We need more information, more insight. This kind of humility is rare in competitive, embattled organizations and communities, but it is the door we must walk through to find the place of true solutions (Wheatley and Crinean 2004).

While Wheatley works primarily with smaller groups (organizations), some of her recommendations for direction setting are applicable to agenda setting as well: *cooling* (cultivating a belief in the need for patience and curiosity about different solutions), sustaining *fruitful opposition* (creating organized settings for what political scientist Benjamin Barbour calls 'strong democracy'), and *precise destroying* (looking for specific impediments to the desired change rather than enacting wholesale replacement of previous policies). Following the organizational and business analogies further, managing complex social change may turn out to resemble 'continuous improvement' and 'total quality management' more than the more dramatic but less effective 'reengineering' and 'restructuring'. The former require thoughtful, data-based reflection on regular policy improvements (including precise destruction of impediments) rather than bold initiatives. Bold is not necessarily bad, but it is too often a reaction of frustration and lack of patience.

This perspective stands in contrast to most thinking, which looks at chaos as a condition to be managed. Current emphases on 'comprehensive' educational policies are an example of the latter. A clear researchable question that emerges is:

- Do policy formation events that are more managed and less chaotic produce more durable, effective results (using a variety of outcome measures) than those that are less organized, address smaller issues, and are more targeted in their focus?

Research of this type would require comparative analyses of the evolution and impact of policies using historical research that better incorporates implementation and policy analysis perspectives. This volume, as a whole, sets out a clear call for this type of research.

Wheatley's work, like agenda-setting theories, tends to place issues of power in the background. It is interesting to note that the concept of power is rarely used by political scientists to explain the policy process. To give one example, neither Kingdon (2003), nor Sabatier (1999), nor Weimer and Vining (1999) have power or influence as entries in their book index. The view I have outlined here affirms the limited utility of traditional concepts of power in engineering complex social change.

Still, it is difficult to discuss how the policy process influences complex change initiatives in the social sector without addressing power, and nearly everyone acknowledges that it affects both agenda setting and policy implementation. The issue is not whether power can be avoided, but how it can be harnessed to improve complex social change. The main problem that emerges from my analysis is that the workings of power are covert during the very stage of policymaking – agenda setting – in which plans and processes begin to gel.

Power continues to be an often ignored feature of educational policy research. The notion of 'micro-politics' is accepted, but the kind of macro-politics that I point to has been of concern primarily to a few critical theorists. The issue of power in policy formulation is important, and connected with the research question posed above, which points to the need for empirical work on how diverse voices are treated or excluded. Investigations of power and policy should look outside the traditional legislative studies, which emphasize lobbying and party politics, and incorporate community power studies that may account for the often unexpected outcomes of policy formulation.

In order to make access to power more generally available, hopefully to improve policies for complex change, the agenda-setting process must become more transparent and open to ideas from alternative sources. In addition, any consideration of the evolution of policy needs to include the influences of new epistemic and electronically based networks as sources of democratic or elite influence over ideas related to solving 'wicked problems'. Policy coherence is enhanced when agenda setting is open to those who best understand the realities of implementation (Elmore 1979; Chrispeels 1996). This early influence can anticipate some of the adaptation and resistance that degrades policy coherence both as it evolves and as it is implemented. Without additional research that puts educational policy at the forefront of empirical investigations, we will have little chance of understanding how to link policy to desired outcomes for children.

REFERENCES

Allington, R.L. (1999) Crafting state educational policy: the slippery role of research and researchers. *Journal of Literacy Research*, **31**(4), 457–82.

Astley, W.G. (1984) Toward an appreciation of collective strategy. *Academy of Management Review*, **9**(3), 526–35.

Basu, O.N., Dirsmith, M.W. and Gupta, P.P. (1999) The coupling of the symbolic and the technical in an institutionalized context: the negotiated order of the GAO's audit reporting process. *American Sociological Review*, **64**(4), 506–26.

Beard, R. (2000) Long overdue? Another look at the National Literacy Strategy. *Journal of Research in Reading*, **23**(3), 245–55.

Berry, F.S. and Berry, W.D. (1999) Innovation and diffusion models in policy research. In P.A. Sabatier (ed.), *Theories of the Policy Process*. Boulder, CO: Westview Press, pp. 169–200.

Beyer, J.M. and Trice, H.M. (1982) The utilization process: a conceptual framework and synthesis of empirical findings. *Administrative Science Quarterly*, **27**(4), 591–622.

Brandon, D.P. and Hollingshead, A.B. (2004) Transactive memory systems in organizations: matching tasks, expertise, and people. *Organization Science*, **15**(6), 633–44.

Campbell, J. (2002) Ideas, politics, and public policy. *Annual Review of Sociology*, **28**, 21–38.

Chrispeels, J.H. (1996) Evaluating teachers' relationships with families: a case study of one district. *Elementary School Journal*, **97**(2), 179–200.

Cobb, R. and Elder, C.D. (1971) The politics of agenda-building: an alternative perspective for modern democratic theory. *Journal of Politics*, **33**(4), 892–915.

Easton, D. (1969) The new revolution in political science. *American Political Science Review*, **63**(4), 1051–61.

Edmondson, J. (2005) Policymaking in education: understanding influences on the Reading Excellence Act. *Education Policy Analysis Archives*, **13**(11), 1–18.

Elmore, R.F. (1979) Backward mapping: implementation research and policy decisions. *Political Science Quarterly*, **94**(4), 601–16.

Firestone, W.A., Fitz, J. and Broadfoot, P. (1999) Power, learning, and legitimation: assessment implementation across levels in the United States and the United Kingdom. *American Educational Research Journal*, **36**(4), 759–93.

Forrester, J.P. and Adams, G.B. (1997) Budgetary reform through organizational learning – toward an organizational theory of budgeting. *Administration and Society*, **28**(4), 466–88.

Gordon, L. (1995) Controlling education: agency theory and the reformation of New Zealand Schools. *Educational Policy*, **9**(1), 54–74.

Granovetter, M. (1973) The strength of weak ties. *American Journal of Sociology*, **6**(6), 1360–80.

Haas, P.M. (1992) Introduction: epistemic communities and international policy coordination. *International Organization*, **46**(1), 1–35.

Hansen, M.T. (1999) The search-transfer problem: the role of weak ties in sharing knowledge across organizational subunits. *Administrative Science Quarterly*, **44**(1), 82–111.

Hardee-Cleaveland, K. and Banister, J. (1988) Fertility policy and implementation in China, 1986–88. *Population and Development Review*, **14**(2), 245–86.

Honig, M. and Hatch, T. (2004) Crafting coherence: how schools strategically manage multiple, conflicting demands. *Educational Researcher*, **33**(8), 16–30.

Hopkins, D. and Levin, B. (2000) Government policy and school development. *School Leadership and Management*, **20**(1), 15–30.

Huberman, M. (1999) The mind is its own place: the influence of sustained interactivity with practitioners on educational researchers. *Harvard Educational Review*, **69**(3), 289–319.

John, P. (2001) Policy networks. In K. Nash (ed.), *The Blackwell Companion to Political Sociology*. Oxford: Blackwell Publishing.

Kaboolian, L. (1998) The new public management: challenging the boundaries of the management vs. administration debate. *Public Administration Review*, **58**(3), 189–93.

Kato, J. (1996) Institutions and rationality in politics – three varieties of neo-institutionalists. *British Journal of Political Science*, **26**(4), 553–82.

Kingdon, J.W. (1995) *Agendas, Alternatives, and Public Policies*, 2nd edn. New York: Harper Collins.

Kingdon, J.W. (2003) *Agendas, Alternatives and Public Policies*. New York: Longman.

Kirst, M. and Neister, G. (1984) Policy issue networks: their influence on state policy-making. *Policy Studies Journal*, **13**(3), 247–63.

Kiser, E. (1999) Comparing varieties of agency theory in economics, political science, and sociology: an illustration from state policy implementation. *Sociological Theory*, **17**(2), 146–70.

Li, J. (1995) China's one-child policy: how and how well has it worked? A case study of Hebei Province, 1979–88. *Population and Development Review*, **21**(3), 563–85.

Louis, K.S. (2002) Democratic values and schooling: reflections in an international context. In L. Moos (ed.), *Democratic Schooling in an International Context*. London: Routledge and Kegan Paul.

Louis, K.S., Febey, K., Gordon, M., Meath, J. and Thomas, E. (2005) Educational leadership from the States: a cultural analysis. Paper presented at the University Council for Educational Administration, November, Nashville, TN.

Louis, K.S., Rosenblum, S., Bingham-Catri, D. and Jones, L. (2003) *Dissemination Systems in Vocational Education: Observations across Three Cases*. University of Minnesota, Minneapolis: National Center for Career and Vocational Education.

Lupia, A. and McCubbins, M.D. (1994) Who controls? Information and the structure of legislative decision making. *Legislative Studies Quarterly*, **19**(3), 361–84.

Marcus, A.A. (1988) Implementing externally induced innovations: a comparison of rule-bound and autonomous approaches. *Academy of Management Journal*, **31**(2), 235–56.

Mazzeo, C. (2002) Stakes for students: agenda-setting and remedial education. *Review of Higher Education*, **26**(1), 19–39.

Mazzoni, T. (1993) The changing politics of state education policy-making: A twenty-year Minnesota perspective. *Educational Evaluation and Policy Analysis*, **15**(4), 357–79.

Merli, M.G. and Raftery, A.E. (2000) Are births under-reported in rural China? Manipulation of statistical records in response to China's population policies. *Demography*, **37**(1), 109–26.

Meyer, D.S. and Staggenborg, S. (1996) Movements, countermovements, and the structure of political opportunity. *American Journal of Sociology*, **101**(6), 1628–60.

Miller, P.C. (2003) Review of Fisher, R. (2002) *Inside the Literacy Hour: Learning from Classroom Experience*. Routledge Falmer: London. Available at http://edrev.asu.edu/reviews/rev220.htm (accessed February 2005).

Mills, M. (1998) From coordinating board to campus: implementation of a policy mandate on remedial education. *Journal of Higher Education*, **69**(6), 672–97.

Mintrom, M. (1997) Policy entrepreneurs and the diffusion of innovation. *American Journal of Political Science*, **41**(3), 738–70.

Mintrom, M. and Vergari, S. (2003) Policy networks and innovation diffusion: the case of state education reforms. *Journal of Politics*, **60**(1), 299–318.

Mishra, P. and Brewer, W.F. (2003) Theories as a form of mental representation and their role in the recall of text information. *Contemporary Educational Psychology*, **28**(3), 277–303.

Office for Standards in Education (2004) *The National Literacy Strategy: the First Four Years*. OFSTED. http://www.standards.dfes.gov.uk/literacy/publications/ofsted/63649/nls_4thyear.PDF (accessed February 2005).

Oliver, T.R. and Shaheen, P. (1997) Translating ideas into actions: entrepreneurial leadership in state health care reforms. *Journal of Health Politics, Policy and Law*, **22**(3), 721–88.

Ostrom, E. (1999) Institutional rational choice: an assessment of the institutional analysis and development framework. In P.A. Sabatier (ed.), *Theories of the Policy Process*. Boulder, CO: Westview Press, pp. 35–71.

Putnam, R. (1976) *The Comparative Study of Policy Elites*. Englewood Cliffs, NJ: Prentice Hall.

Rittel, H. and Webber, M. (1973) Dilemmas in a general theory of planning. *Policy Sciences*, **4**(2), 155–69.

Rosenbaum, J. (1996) Policy uses of research on the high school-to-work transition. *Sociology of Education* (extra issue), 102–22.

Ryan, R. (1999) How TAFE became 'unresponsive': a study of rhetoric as a tool of educational policy. *Australian and New Zealand Journal of Vocational Education Research*, **7**(2), 105–26.

Sabatier, P. (1991) Political science and public policy. *PS: Political Science and Politics*, **24**(2), 144–7.

Sabatier, P.A. and Jenkins-Smith, H.C. (1993) *Policy Change and Learning: An Advocacy Coalition Approach*. Boulder, CO: Westview Press.

Salisbury, R.H., Johnson, P., Heinz, J.P., Laumann, E.O. and Nelson, R.L. (1989) Who you know versus what you know: the uses of government experience for Washington lobbyists. *American Journal of Political Science*, **33**(1), 175–95.

Santoro, W.A. (1999) Conventional politics takes center stage: the Latino struggle against English-only laws. *Social Forces*, **77**(3), 887–909.

Soule, S. and Zylan, Y. (1997) Runaway train? The diffusion of state-level reform in ADC/AFDC eligibility requirements, 1950–1967. *American Journal of Sociology*, **103**(3), 733–62.

Stokey, E. and Zeckhauser, R. (1978) *A Primer for Policy Analysis*. New York: Norton.

Symes, C., Boud, D., McIntyre, J., Solomon, N. and Tennant, M. (2000) Working knowledge: Australian universities and 'real world' education. *International Review of Education*, **46**(6), 565–79.

Vickers, M. (1994) Cross-national exchange, the OECD and Australian education policy. *Knowledge and Policy*, **7**(1), 24–47.

Wallace, M. (2003) Managing the unmanageable? Coping with complex educational change. *Educational Management and Administration*, **31**(1), 9–29.

Wallace, M. (2004) Orchestrating complex educational change: local reorganization of schools in England. *Journal of Educational Change*, **5**(1), 57–78.

Walsh, J. (2004) State charter results mirror poor performance nationally. *Star Tribune*, 18 August.

Weatherly, R. and Lipsky, M. (1977) Street level bureaucrats and institutional innovation: implementing special education reform. *Harvard Educational Review*, **47**(2), 171–97.

Weimer, D. and Vining, A. (1999) *Policy Analysis: Concepts and Practice*. Upper Saddle River, NJ: Prentice Hall.

Weiss, C. (1982) Policy research in the context of diffuse decision making. *Policy Studies Review*, **6**, 19–36.

Weiss, C. and Buculvalas, M. (1980) *Social Science Research and Decision Making*. New York: Columbia University Press.

Wejnart, B. (2002) Integrating models of diffusion and innovation: a conceptual framework. *Annual Review of Sociology*, **23**, 297–326.

Wheatley, M. (1999) *Leadership and the New Science: Discovering Order in a Chaotic World*. San Francisco: Berrett-Koehler.

Wheatley, M. and Crinean, G. (2004) Solving, not attacking, complex problems. A five-state approach based on an ancient practice. http://www.margaretwheatley.com/articles/solvingnotattacking.html (accessed November 2005).

Wholey, D.R. and Sanchez, S.M. (1991) The effects of regulatory tools on organizational populations. *Academy of Management Review*, **16**(4), 743–67.

Wilson, L.J. and Al-Muinhanna, I. (1985) The political economy of information: the impact of transborder data flows. *Journal of Peace Research*, **22**(4), 289–301.

CHAPTER 6

THE CHALLENGES OF GOVERNANCE, LEADERSHIP AND ACCOUNTABILITY IN THE PUBLIC SERVICES

Paul Thomas

This chapter examines further complexities of public service reform connected with the plurality of interests that play a part in policy decision making and mobilizing implementation activity. The interplay of governance and risk-taking leadership expressed by politicians and senior civil servants frames the operational practices to implement change that were explored in earlier chapters. Paul Thomas argues for a more sophisticated typification of the multiple aspects of context that affect both policy making and implementation (significantly elaborating the context-dependence characteristic of complex change discussed in Chapter 1). His analysis implies that generalization between public services and public service systems is, at most, insightful at only a high level of abstraction. Further, any such generalization must indicate sensitivity to the range of contextual variables that he identifies.

Thomas is interested in developing knowledge-for-action, advancing a normative account of the role of governance in mobilizing diverse groups with an interest in the direction of public policy, the shared leadership of policy making and oversight of reform programmes needed from policy-makers and public servants, and the significance of multiple forms of accountability requirements that influence implementation. The analysis is grounded in an extended discussion of the complexities of reforming health care across Canada (consistent with the account in Chapter 3 of unintended hybridization within the networked services initiative in Quebec). A key policy initiative examined here is the regionalization of health care within this largely province-driven healthcare system. (The problematic nature of regionalization – leading to ameliorative re-regionalization – in the province of Alberta is also discussed by Ann Casebeer in Chapter 10.)

Introduction

Change is supposedly a defining feature of today's public sector in all countries. There are different types of changes taking place or being contemplated on different levels throughout a diverse array of public sector organizations. The complexity of the change process can vary significantly depending upon the field of activity and service administrative levels most centrally implicated. The interdependence among these different levels of change adds to the complications of orchestrating the process.

This chapter examines the complexities of recent attempts to undertake major policy and programme reforms to Canada's healthcare policy system. The analysis focuses on the broad contours of policy making and implementation, not on the substance of healthcare reform at an operational level. It is recognized, of course, that the two levels of decision making and activity are highly interdependent. Using healthcare policy making in Canada as an illustrative case can contribute to the refinement of theoretical models of complex and programmatic change. It can also provide insights into the practical constraints and requirements for successful change.

Three themes are central to the analysis. First is the challenge of how to activate and accommodate diverse interests and voices with a legitimate claim to contribute to setting directions for change (as also explored in Chapter 5) within and between different political and administrative levels of a multi-tiered healthcare system. The notion of governance is employed here to address this theme. Second, leadership counts for much in the change process. There is a requirement for shared leadership between politicians and public servants in setting the change agenda and putting it into practice across policy, organizational, programme and service provision levels. Third, (as heralded in Chapter 4) any significant change in the public sector involves uncertainty and risk. This is especially so in the contemporary political environment of declining public trust and confidence, leading to an insistence on more collaborative forms of policy making and greater accountability for all parties involved with healthcare provision.

The next section will examine the meaning and relevance of three key analytical concepts: the context for change; the orchestration of change; and the implementation stage of the policy cycle. Subsequent sections will explore the contextual complexity of the Canadian healthcare policy system; its exposure to pressures for change; complications and constraints rendering sweeping, planned changes almost impossible; and the implications of these conditions for future policy.

The importance of context

This volume is focused on complex change, which Wallace (Chapter 1) suggests may possess five characteristics: it is large-scale, componential, systemic, differentially impacting and contextually dependent. *Context* is often mentioned as a dependent variable that significantly shapes the change process, though fewer writers actually define context and identify its key components in a specific change situation.

There is a general recognition in the public administration literature that the management of change within public sector organizations involves a distinctive context which is different from the private sector. Significant components include the:

- nature of the tasks assigned to different public organizations;
- emergence of policies and programmes to meet those tasks out of the political process;
- openness of public organizations to outside influences and criticism flowing through the political and media processes;
- manner in which revenues and human resources are acquired and allocated;
- requirement to reconcile competing values and interests, leading to more complicated and slower decision making;
- greater insistence on transparency and accountability;
- need to respect the history, traditions, values and norms of behaviour of the public sector.

To these general characteristics may be added more specific aspects of the Canadian health policy system:

- the inherent qualities of health policy and of the task of delivering healthcare services compared to the tasks of other organizations;
- related to task, the degree of knowledge and observability about what works in terms of improving healthcare outputs and health outcomes;
- the changing technology which drives, enables and complicates the change process;
- the constitutional, legal and regulatory rules which condition behaviour;
- the scope, visibility and nature of the impacts of health policy and programme decisions;
- the political salience of health policy, the politics of policy formulation and implementation, and shifts in public opinion on health issues;
- wider changes in the economy (such as economic downturns) and in society (such as the ageing demographic);
- relationships of power between different actors and institutions.

In stressing the importance of context, it is not implied that political, administrative and professional leaders in the health fields are completely captives of circumstance, lack choice or any control over a system which is complex and unpredictable. To accept a model of the system as chaotic and uncontrollable implies that no one can be held accountable for unwanted events, a situation which is inaccurate and which the public would find unacceptable.

Orchestration and governance

A key concept of the complex change planning framework put forward by Wallace in Chapter 1 is orchestration. The concept refers to a network of senior leaders implicated in a complex change. Each works to initiate, organize, monitor and consolidate change across part or all of a multi-organizational system, according to pluralistic beliefs and values connected with interests which may or may not coincide. Orchestrators of complex and programmatic change, therefore, do not necessarily operate with collective purpose.

Insofar as orchestration encompasses collaboration within and among organizations, the concept is related to the concept of governance. Both terms emphasize pluralistic, dispersed, interdependent decision making within or across organizational boundaries. Governance diverges from orchestration, however, in emphasizing the reduced reliance upon hierarchy in favour of informal processes of communication and coordination to achieve shared goals. (With orchestration, it is not assumed that orchestrators' goals are fully shared at any time.) Further, orchestration does not extend to the activation and articulation of the interests of various stakeholders (organizations and individuals who can affect or are affected by proposed changes) within the policy process.

Governance and government are not the same, although both involve the idea of direction setting within society. Government occurs when political institutions with formal authority, including ultimate coercive powers, take actions. In contrast, governance refers to the creation and execution of activities based upon the complex mechanisms, processes and relationships through which citizens, groups and organizations articulate their interests, exercise their rights, meet their obligations and reconcile their differences. Governments are no longer, if they ever were, completely in charge of this process, although they continue to play a crucial role. But governments can no longer rely upon unilateral, hierarchical, top-down direction for change within society. Increasingly they share the initiation and formulation of policies with outside organizations and they deliver policies, programmes and services through private firms, not-for-profit agencies and other orders of government.

The inter-organizational and dispersed character of governance requires elected politicians and public managers to develop improved skills in activation, communication, persuasion, mediation, negotiation, collaboration, coordination and implementation. The definition of governance by Hult and Walcott (1990: 36) emphasizes the crucial role that power and politics play:

> . . . governance structures emerge as people in organizations strive to develop patterned ways in which to discover and articulate goals, select among means, cope with uncertainty and controversy generated both within and outside of the organization and foster legitimacy and commitment inside and outside of the organizations.

Different types of governance structures (persistent patterns of decision making) exist within individual organizations over time, and governance networks among organizations also emerge and evolve. Increasingly, governments find themselves entangled, constrained, but also empowered by a web of relationships and obligations. Decisions are rarely one-time, discrete events involving a single actor or institution. Instead they are the product of long chains of events, including responses to the consequences of past policy choices, and involve multiple actors and institutions, making bargaining and the accommodation of competing values and interests central to the process.

In the dynamic context of the Canadian health policy system, the new preferred governance paradigm is based upon networks rather than the more traditional, hierarchical jurisdiction-specific model (Tuohy 2003). The new paradigm is held to describe and explain governance as an adaptive process involving uncertainty, risk and controversy, taking place on multiple levels and consisting of the coordinated and uncoordinated actions of multiple organizations. No one set of institutions or actors has the authority to govern through command and control. Instead there are shared authority, shared financing and shared risks. The sharing takes place across orders of government within the Canadian federal system, between provincial governments and regional health authorities in all but one province, across domains of the healthcare system, with adjacent policy fields, with major stakeholders within society (particularly the self-regulating health professions), and increasingly across borders with other national governments and international institutions. The kaleidoscopic and demanding conditions of health policy making pose enormous challenges for goal setting, control and the management of change.

As Rhodes (2002) puts it, people matter in how policy networks are constructed, operated and change over time. Prevailing approaches to network analysis emphasize the interplay of interests, the creation of routines and the prevalence of certain patterns of change. This approach leads to a mechanistic understanding of networks. Rhodes calls for a constructivist alternative, positing that networks cannot be understood apart from tradition: the changing values, beliefs and norms of behaviour which are embedded in institutions and processes. He writes: 'Because a constructivist approach decentres networks, by exploring how individual actors enact them, it encourages us to look for the origins of change in the contingent responses of individuals to new ideas and problems' (Rhodes 2002: 400). This approach calls attention to the way that meaning is socially constructed and sense making takes place within networks. It also counters managerial models of governance and networks which ignore the public sector requirement to uphold fundamental values like legitimacy, representation, equity and support.

The characteristics of people involved with networks clearly affects which changes are made, how they are made and how successful they are. Leadership is therefore significant, interpreted here as processual: 'a group process in which individuals motivate and influence others to work towards a shared purpose' (Rost 1991: 3). Under this definition, the distinction between leaders and followers becomes blurred. Leadership is not limited to people with formal authority and status; it can be found at all levels within particular organizations and across organizational boundaries.

Compared with the heroic stereotype of popular best-sellers, rigorous studies suggest that leadership is more dispersed, collective or shared, and relies on the talents and support of others to achieve strategic goals. Lipman-Blumen (1996) calls this 'connective leadership', involving long-term strategies, common purposes, an emphasis on collaboration and an ethical approach to the exercise of power. As will be discussed, in the networked world of health policy and programme change, new kinds of leadership knowledge and skills become requirements for success.

The complexities of implementation

In simple terms, implementation means to carry out, accomplish or to complete. However, it is not an automatic or straightforward stage between the adoption of a new policy idea and opening the door to provide a public service. Implementation in the 'real world' involves a multitude of institutions and actors and therefore inevitably leads to its own form of 'politics'. Generally, it is assumed that successful implementation depends upon clear goals, appropriate instruments to achieve those goals and adequate resources (financial and personnel). Explanations for implementation difficulties or failures have been varied (Hill and Hupe 2002): poorly articulated or conflicting goals; flawed policy designs, particularly the lack of a causal model of how policies will produce change in the 'real world'; inadequate resources; the capacity for bureaucracies and interest groups to resist change; the failure to maintain coalitions of support beyond the point of policy choice; and breakdowns in communications and monitoring by authorities through the implementation phase.

The central ideas of two recent case studies of the British health system have relevance for the Canadian situation. Schofield (2004) examines the introduction of capital investment appraisal into the National Health Service (NHS), demonstrating the importance of individual and organizational learning to the enactment of new policy initiatives. Earlier implementation studies had tended to assume that public managers already had the technical knowledge and skills needed to carry out policy, but the NHS case study suggests they must learn new techniques to implement what are often ambiguous policy directives.

Exworthy and Powell (2004) argue for the need to revise models of policy implementation in the era of the 'congested state', with multiple institutions 'bumping into one another' in the crowded policy spaces of the British healthcare system. Their case study focuses on policies to deal with health inequalities. Their theoretical framework fuses Kingdon's (1995) notion of the problem, policy and politics streams (discussed in Chapter 5) converging to push issues on to the policy agenda with Wolman's model of policy failure. The latter comprises policy formulation and policy implementation. According to Kingdon, at critical junctures when the three streams come together, major policy changes are more likely to occur. However, implementing rapid changes in multi-levelled policy systems is difficult. Typically, implementation studies have focused on the vertical relationship between central and local authorities.

The case study highlights also the horizontal relationships within the central policy machinery and within local health authorities, indicating that there are both 'big' windows of policy opportunity at the national level and 'little' windows at the local level. The recognition that significant divisions of power can be non-territorial and that there are limited windows of opportunity for radical policy changes have implications for interpreting the Canadian health policy system.

The Context of the Canadian Healthcare System

Primary responsibility for health care under Canada's constitution resides with the 10 provincial and three territorial governments. However, the healthcare system in practice is multi-tiered, with important policy leadership and financial support for health care coming from the national government and most of the operational side of healthcare delivery taking place below the provincial level on a regional and local basis. The certification of doctors, nurses, therapists and other health professions involves a combination of professional self-regulation and provincial regulation.

The government of Canada plays no direct role in the delivery of health services and the regulation of health professionals (except for aboriginals living on reserves or in the northern territories, and for the armed forces). The national government indirectly affects health care both through its legislation and spending decisions. Its authority over immigration gives it an important role in admitting doctors and other health practitioners.

The major role of the national government since the 1960s has been in setting the policy framework for health care. The Medical Care Act set down the principles that provincial healthcare systems had to respect in order to qualify for federal cost sharing on a 50/50 basis. To qualify for federal financial assistance, provincial health systems had to exhibit public administration, universal access, comprehensive coverage and portability among jurisdictions. The ambiguity of these principles became a political problem during the 1970s when Ottawa 'capped' its financial contributions to the provinces and some provincial governments allowed the practices of 'extra billing' by physicians and 'per diems' for hospital stays to emerge.

The Canada Health Act of 1984 enabled the national government to penalize provinces which allowed such practices. National government intrusion into an area of provincial responsibility reflected the fact that the principles of medicare had become sacrosanct in Canadian politics. What Ottawa lacked in terms of constitutional legitimacy was more than compensated for by public support for the idea that the national government should establish and protect national standards of health care.

National policy leadership during earlier decades was also supported by the fact that Ottawa had money, whereas the poorer provinces had difficulty in meeting rising health costs. Most provinces were prepared to sacrifice some degree of policy independence in return for federal financial support. Nevertheless, from the late 1970s, the national government's share of public spending has fallen. To the extent that the national government's influence on provincial health policy depends on withholding federal transfer payments, such influence may appear to have weakened. However, this ignores the politics of health care in which the public insists on universality and provincial governments (especially the more dependent ones) annually demand more federal money.

Health care is expensive. Canada's total healthcare spending amounts to about $130 billion, representing 10 per cent of the gross domestic product. About 70 per cent of this expenditure is financed by the public sector. While hospitals remain the largest expenditure category – 30 per cent of the total – this proportion has declined steadily from a high of 45 per cent in 1976. Drugs represent one of the fastest growing components of health spending, along with capital expenditures on high-tech equipment.

Since the late 1970s, federal and provincial governments have disputed the size of their respective contributions to the total health spending. During 2001–2 provincial premiers launched an advertising campaign claiming that the government of Canada was contributing only 14 cents of every health dollar spent. The national government responded that the figure was closer to 50 cents. Determining the percentage contributions of each order of government is probably impossible. Federal financial support is provided in the form of cash and tax points, and not all of the money is earmarked for health. The tangled system of federal financial transfers to provincial governments complicates the search for accountability within the health system, but without such financial support the range and quality of health services would be reduced, especially in the poorer provinces.

As a result of provincial pressure and public concern, in 2004 the government of Canada announced a 10-year action plan on health involving $41 billion in federal transfers tied to reforms in waiting time, human resource planning, home care, primary care reform, a pharmaceuticals strategy, prevention and promotion in public health, and accountability to citizens. It remains to be seen how much progress this ambitious and rather general 'game plan' will achieve.

Four broad sets of forces are particularly important in prompting change in health care: demographic shifts, particularly ageing populations; technological innovations; economic conditions and the strained financial circumstances of governments; and political factors, such as shifts in ideological and policy thinking among elites and the public. The resulting healthcare reform agenda has parallels with other OECD countries (Tuohy 1999). Common elements include:

- slowing the rate of spending increases;
- moving away from reliance upon expensive institutions like hospitals and making greater use of community-based delivery;
- improving the incentives embedded in the programmes and financing arrangements;
- shifting away from a curative to a preventative model of health care by integrating health policy concerns into other policy fields and improving the effectiveness of health programmes;
- improving the responsiveness and accountability of the healthcare system to meet the demands of a more knowledgeable and less deferential public.

A key contextual factor affecting the reform strategy adopted is the power relationships between actors in a complex policy system. Tuohy identified three broad
strategies of reform in a comparison of six OECD countries including Canada:

- big bang reform – comprehensive and fundamental changes rapidly forced
  through;
- blueprint reform – the presentation of a 'game plan' to be implemented in phases;
- incremental reform – gradual, marginal changes as resources, agreements and
  political support permit.

Canada followed mainly an incremental approach. There was no political will
to undertake more fundamental changes, which would require overcoming resistance in numerous locations and would involve risks, not least losing political support (Naylor 1999).

Characterizing Canada's health policy pattern as incremental hides the fact that
contextual factors can align in particular ways to generate the potential for other
strategies. For example, the adoption of medicare in 1964 – a national policy of
universal, pre-paid access to health services – represents a fundamental shift. It
reflected earlier incremental decisions, like federal financial transfers to support
the construction of hospitals. After medicare was adopted nationally, it took
several years for all provincial governments to sign up and numerous smaller
policy steps to implement it across the country.

In the health field, it is artificial to think of change like a switch which is either
off or on. There will always be changes taking place. Part of the leadership
challenge is to recognize and to coordinate the interactions among decisions on
different levels, as well as horizontally within health and with other policy fields.
Changes that are narrower, more operational and technical in nature are generally easier to adopt and implement. But the constraints become more numerous
and more difficult when higher level policy changes are involved.

Regionalization of health care

A major policy change of the 1990s was regionalization (see also Chapter 10).
Eventually all provincial governments created an intermediary level of governance for health care residing between the provincial and the local level. Official
and unofficial aims of regionalization (e.g. Rasmussen 2001; Casebeer 2004;
Contandriopoulos *et al.* 2004) included to:

- promote coordination by reducing the number of health-related decision-
  making bodies;
- curtail spending increases by promoting greater efficiency and effectiveness;
- increase responsiveness to the needs and wishes of the local community;
- encourage the integration of services, particularly linking prevention and
  treatment;

• improve accountability to regional populations and insulate healthcare decisions from partisan controversies.

Critics of regionalization have accused financially stressed provincial governments of 'off-loading' difficult budgetary choices to the regional level and arranging for themselves a kind of 'discretionary' accountability. Others took the blame
for bad news, allowing them to take credit for good news over allocating scarce
health resources.

The regionalization process across the 10 provinces has been varied and
incomplete (Lewis and Kouri 2004). Regional health authorities (RHAs) have been
defined territorially, but there is no common approach to designating regions. Within
individual provinces, RHAs vary in terms of geography, regional populations served
and organizational capability. There are 10 regions in rural Manitoba, ranging
in size from 25,000 to 98,000 residents, and one RHA for the capital city of Winnipeg
representing over 600,000 people. The Winnipeg RHA is a large organization. It
has a deep reservoir of expertise compared with small RHAs like Churchill in the
far north, which services a largely First Nations population. Differences in their
societal contexts and in their organizational capabilities mean that RHAs' capacity
to influence provincial authorities and to respond to provincial policy directions
varies enormously.

Provincial governments brought RHAs into existence, but generally RHAs have
struggled to find an autonomous place within the wider governance network in
which to operate (Contandriopoulos *et al.* 2004). Provincial ministers of health
appoint and remove members of the boards of RHAs, issue province-wide, bind-
ing policy directives, allocate global budgets and exercise informal influence over
RHAs. Boards of RHAs are thus obliged to look in two directions: they must work
within the policy and budgetary parameters set by the provincial government and
they must be responsive to the needs and demands of the communities they serve.

Regionalization represented a qualified form of decentralization that involved
consolidation at the local level. Prior to regionalization, provincial ministries of
health dealt directly with hospitals and other facilities, each typically with its own
governing board. Creating RHA boards was meant to streamline this fragmented
governance structure by bringing all institutions and services under one umbrella
organization. However, many provinces stopped short of complete regionalization. In terms of governance structures, some provincial governments allowed
hospital boards (especially for faith-based institutions) to continue. For service
provision, RHAs in most provinces rely on religious organizations, non-profit
and commercial firms, rendering coordination and integration of services more
challenging. Also, regions are rarely employers of physicians, and remuneration arrangements (mainly fee-for-service) are in the hands of the provincial
government.

The provincial–regional relationship has lacked stability. Some provinces have
changed their minds on elected versus appointed boards. The number and the
boundaries of RHAs have been changed. Ministries of health have, in effect, placed
individual RHAs in 'trusteeship' when problems have arisen (or appear to have

happened). The same ministries have struggled to move towards a more 'strategic' orientation, which emphasizes provincial policy leadership, system-wide planning, the promotion of standards and monitoring, periodic in-depth evaluations of progress, and a more constructive approach to accountability. There have been recent attempts to establish a more long-term approach through requirements that RHAs produce strategic plans, develop multi-year budgets, sign performance contracts, issue annual performance reports and regularly evaluate their own governance procedures. But these accountability devices have their limits, in practice.

Governance rhetoric in most provinces implies 'steering by remote control', with less resort to direct provincial intervention in regional matters. However, the reality is that the public in the regional communities will ultimately blame the provincial government when their health needs are not met. This is mainly because health policy is the main focus of political debate at the provincial level. Also, because RHA boards are appointed, not elected, it is unclear whether members are 'agents' of the provincial government or 'trustees' of the long-term interests of the community. If provincial politicians feel they will ultimately be blamed, they will continue to insist on control. Lewis and Kouri (2004: 26–7) conclude that: 'Regionalization cannot hope to succeed unless provincial governments provide more long-term stability to RHAs, and authority commensurate with accountability'. Once principles, plans and rules are established, 'provinces should avoid ad hoc interventions and micromanagement'. This recommendation reflects a widespread desire in the professional community 'to take the politics out of health policy-making', something which is not likely to happen under whatever structural and procedural arrangements are adopted.

Representing stakeholder interests

Federal–provincial and provincial–local relations are a big part of the health governance environment, but there are other influential actors and institutions. For actual provision of medical services, the healthcare system has always relied upon 'indirect governance' through individual physicians and the organizations which represent them: the medical colleges for professional self-regulation, and the medical associations for lobbying and fee negotiations with provincial governments. Physicians have traditionally been influential in healthcare policy making and decision making on all levels. Deference to their expert knowledge and skills and the serious nature of the consequences of their clinical decisions caused governments to delegate extensive authority to physicians. They were trusted to ensure quality and safe care, and to put the interests of patients first. This thinking has been increasingly challenged over recent decades as elected politicians, reflecting shifts in public opinion, no longer assumed that a highly autonomous medical profession would always act in 'the public interest'.

Growing 'politicization' of healthcare issues has caused governments to insist on stricter professional self-regulation, mechanisms to strengthen patients' voice, and greater monitoring of professional performance (Tuohy 2003). The dominance

of the medical profession has also been challenged by the greater political asser-
tiveness of established health professions (like nurses and pharmacists) and by
the emergence of new occupational groupings within the health field (a US parallel is discussed in Chapter 8). Management in the health field has also become
much more important. At the institutional level, tensions have grown between
clinical and administrative perspectives on issues, particularly related to the
application of budgetary restraints. Despite these trends, physicians still remain
the single most powerful stakeholder group within health policy networks. Their
support remains crucial for the success of most major initiatives.

Royal commissions, task forces and permanent advisory committees have
become prominent components of the health governance network. Typically,
these institutions are used to undertake more fundamental policy reviews. Given
the political salience of health issues and the sense of crisis which pervades the
field, it is not surprising that beleaguered governments have turned to outside
bodies for policy advice and to help with the promotion of consensus and political support for reforms. Since 2000 there have been at least four provincial health
commissions, plus the Romanow Commission on the Future of Health Care in
Canada (2002). The reports from these commissions reflected many common themes
(Carson 2003). They all found continued majority support for a public model of
health care. But they also identified anxiety about its long-term viability, and a
growing willingness to extend the use of the private sector.

Other institutions and actors who are part of the governance environment of
the healthcare system include medical, nursing, pharmacy and other educational
institutions, research foundations, 'think tanks', advocacy groups, unions, the media
and a fledgling patients' rights movement. Gradually courts are becoming more
involved through the Charter of Rights and Freedoms in reviewing the allocation
of scarce health resources (Scheldrick 2003). There are also bilateral and international health law issues which impact on Canada. Globalization in the form of
liberalized trade agreements, multinational firms providing healthcare technology and products, new threats of disease transmission across national borders, the
intersection of public health concerns with the terrorism threat and the impacts
of rising health costs on the competitiveness of domestic firms, all add to the swirl
of forces operating in and around the health policy system.

In summary, governance structures and networks in health care have become
complex, dynamic, pluralistic, multi-tiered and cross-sectoral in character. It
becomes compelling to think of governments as simply one set of actors among
others in a complex web of relationships and interactions taking place from the
local to the global level. This raises questions about what changes governments
are prepared to attempt and what capacity and instruments they have to effect
desired changes. Obviously there are no quick policy, organizational and managerial 'fixes' to the challenges facing Canada's healthcare system.

In practice, most change to health policy and programmes will continue to resemble strategic improvisation more than strategic planning. Consistent with the
current mood of disenchantment with governments, there is in the health reform
literature a thinly disguised desire to 'take the politics out of health care',

supposedly to allow for long-term planning and to grant professionals more freedom to make decisions on an objective basis. Such an approach would not eliminate 'politics'. There would still be the need to accommodate competing needs and values, and new problems of accountability would be created.

Leadership and Change

Leadership in the public sector is affected by the contextual components listed earlier (see also Rainey 2003). An important feature is its dual nature within government. Successful performance depends on a close working relationship between elected politicians and appointed public servants. Political and administrative leaders occupy different, but overlapping worlds. They engage continuously in what Alex Matheson calls a 'strategic conversation' (quoted in Shergold 1997) concerning the external and internal environments of the organizations they lead, the issues likely to affect them, and the need for changes to policies and programmes to meet anticipated future conditions (see Chapter 7). In such conversations, political and managerial concerns merge as the broad goals of government are integrated with the operational realities of departments. However, the strategic conversation is not exclusively two-way. Many voices representing other stakeholders, both inside and outside of government, must be taken into account.

Both politicians and public servants have a legitimate role to play in policy formulation and implementation of public policy. Elected ministers can claim democratic legitimacy; they are usually not policy experts, but they have obtained the support of the public. In contrast, public servants have professional legitimacy based on their technical knowledge of programmes and administrative matters. Finding the most appropriate balance between the political values of representation, responsiveness and democratic accountability and the management values of expertise, effectiveness, efficiency and professional responsibility is a central challenge of governance under modern conditions.

Politicians and public servants may occupy a shared space in the policy process, but they contribute different perspectives and skills. Often this difference is described as passion versus reason. It is true that political life is driven significantly by emotions, but it does not follow that it is always irrational. Politics follows its own type of rationality. Usually this rationality is assumed to consist of doing whatever must be done to get re-elected. This interpretation fits with the prevailing cynical view of the political process. However, politicians are correct to worry about their re-election prospects if they believe in the programmes they are sponsoring and wish to continue in office to see them implemented. In political life, making the 'right' decision in terms of the available evidence is not a sufficient basis for success. There is also the requirement to mobilize political support and to diffuse opposition. In managing their policy agendas, governments strive to govern, and appear to govern, on the basis of a widespread consensus and low levels of conflict.

Ideally, political leaders should have the skills to read public opinion, to present issues in ways that the public understands, to promote debate and to mobilize political support for actions. In contrast, administrative leaders have skills in gathering information, analysing issues and presenting options. Political leaders, because of the nature of their occupation and the requirements for getting elected, are obliged to consider a wider range of interests and values than do administrative leaders. Politicians are expected to be skilful as 'brokers' of competing interests and values. In contrast, the professionalism and expertise of public servants inclines them to search for the optimal policy solution. In the processes of their analysis, administrative leaders are expected to be aware of the political feasibility of their advice but not the point where they abandon completely their professional objectivity and judgement.

Governance involves calculation in two directions: the strength of political commitment to particular policy goals, and the probability of accomplishing those goals given environmental conditions and available knowledge. Rose (1987: 413) describes how both types of calculation involve imperfect knowledge, uncertainty, and therefore risk:

> ... politicians want to discriminate between more or less risky options, and civil servants to discriminate between goals to which ministers are more or less strongly attached. The greatest uncertainties in policy analysis are not measurement problems, but substantive: politicians are often uncertain about what they want to risk doing, and civil servants are often uncertain about whether the policy instruments that they devise will succeed as intended.

In terms of the changing healthcare environment, interdependence and the dispersal of power means that the activities and skills required of politicians and public servants are converging rather than diverging. Both must learn how to lead and manage horizontally across organizational boundaries rather than just vertically within individual organizations. Formal authority counts for less in such relationships which involve peers rather than subordinates. The leaders of collaborative undertakings must understand the nature and the limits of different kinds of power. They must use this understanding to manage conflict, to deal with resistance and to ensure that desired actions take place. They must use power in an enabling and ethical manner. Skills in encouraging, motivating and persuading people are important, as are skills in negotiation and compromise. Such activities depend greatly upon effective communication skills.

The Changing Meanings of Accountability in Health Care

Another challenge for leaders of healthcare institutions is an insistence on stricter and new forms of accountability – essentially the flip side of leadership. With the exercise of responsibility and authority comes the obligation to answer for performance. In the Canadian healthcare system, which has incorporated new public management ideas from the broader public sector, the meanings and practices of accountability have become multiple and contradictory. This adds to the complications and risks of change. (For a contrasting discussion of accountability from a service organization perspective, see Chapter 11.)

For our purposes, accountability will be understood as an authoritative relationship supported by a process. Components of an accountability relationship are the:

- assignment or negotiation of responsibilities along with the provision of commensurate authority and resources to carry out those responsibilities, within a generally supportive environment;
- duty on the part of the accountable institution or individual to answer for the performance of responsibilities, especially through the provision of valid, reliable and timely information;
- duty of the authorizing institution or individual to monitor the performance of the agents acting on their behalf and to insist on corrections to performance when deficient;
- potential use of sanctions and rewards to promote responsible behaviour and to recognize inferior and superior performance.

Accountability processes can operate both within the boundaries of organizations and between organizations. Accountability processes are meant to set limits on freedom of action and to require justification for behaviour as a way to prevent abuses of public power, to encourage responsiveness to others and to promote improved performance.

Formal accountability along the lines described above should be distinguished from an informal, subjective sense of responsibility: a self-imposed duty to do what is right based on prevailing standards or an individual's sense of moral obligation. The notion of professional responsibility plays a key role in the allocation of authority within the healthcare system. Given the extensive training and expert knowledge involved with the various health professions, they have been granted on the basis of trust considerable autonomy to licence and to regulate their members (O'Reilly 2000). The normative model of the self-regulating professional presumes that individuals are committed to the highest professional standards and to meeting the needs of their clients. Ongoing educational processes, disciplinary procedures and codes of ethics are among the devices used by the self-regulating health professions to promote responsible behaviour.

Accountability should also be distinguished from 'responsiveness', although the two concepts are clearly related. Responsiveness refers to the inclination and capacity of health institutions and healthcare providers to recognize and to reflect in their actions the needs and the wishes of the individuals and communities they serve. Prior to the 1960s, responsiveness of healthcare system was left largely to the professionals who operated the system, particularly the physicians. They have since faced a mounting challenge to their trust-based autonomy and the closed nature of the policy system, in the form of public demands for greater openness, participation, consent, responsiveness and accountability.

As a result, there has been limited 'democratization' of the structures and processes of self-governing control by various health professionals. Ministers and departments of health have stepped up requirements for accountability and public input, and steps to improve responsiveness to the community have been implemented, such as regionalization discussed earlier, and use of the courts to promote access to health care and patient rights.

It is difficult to identify who is responsible and accountable for what within Canada's healthcare system. Traditional approaches to accountability in the public sector emphasize unified direction and control. However, the reality here is shared and devolved authority, joint financing and shared power – making the traditional approach to accountability unrealistic. Recognizing the complexity of the system and responding to crises, governments have imposed new and strengthened existing mechanisms of accountability. There are now at least five types of accountability within the system.

Table 6.1 summarizes each type, the mechanisms for enforcement and potential sanctions which are designed to promote safe, high-quality and efficient health care, including the correction of problems when they arise. Each type of accountability has its own content, dynamics of enforcement and criteria of successful or satisfactory performance.

Political accountability involves the requirement that governments and, more specifically health ministers, defend their actions and inactions before their legislatures on an ongoing basis. This accountability process is mainly adversarial and blaming in character (Thomas 1998). In theory, governments could be defeated or ministers of health forced to resign, but in practice the real sanction is loss of political reputation.

Institutional/hierarchical accountability involves the setting of policy parameters by government and the downward delegation of authority and resources to RHAs and devolved institutions within them. Reporting and other monitoring requirements are intended to generate the flow of accountability back to the ministry of health, which can order corrective action when problems arise.

Financial and results-based types of accountability are meant to ensure the efficient, effective and equitable use of resources within the health policy field. With healthcare consuming 40 per cent of most provincial budgets, there have been many attempts to curtail spending increases and to demonstrate that value is being obtained through better performance of the system and the health statistics of the populations served.

Legal/professional accountability refers to the role of the approximately 20 self-regulating health professions which set educational standards, licence professionals, handle complaints, discipline members and order remedial actions.

Customer accountability reflects the rise of consumerism in the health field. It has led to such innovations as patients' bills of rights, health ombudsmen, physician profiles and hospital report cards.

In summary, the accountability environment in health has become increasingly complicated and more demanding. As new clinical and managerial problems have arisen, new accountability mechanisms have been added. Thus healthcare

Table 6.1 Five types of accountability in the Canadian healthcare system

Type of accountability	Mechanisms of enforcement	Consequences
Political	Collective and individual ministerial responsibility involving the parliamentary process and media coverage	Potential defeat of a government or resignation of a minister, and loss of reputation
Legal/professional	More than 20 self-regulating health professions ensure professional competence and deal with misconduct	Investigate complaints, discipline members and order remedial action
Institutional/ hierarchical	The setting of policy direction and the downward flow of authority and funds to regional health authorities and devolved institutions, and the requirement for such institutions to report back to ministers of health	Corrective actions ordered by ministers of health and discipline within the administrative hierarchy
Financial	Resource allocation by ministries of health, requirements to demonstrate efficiency and effectiveness	Changes to annual funding levels, prohibition of deficits
Results-based	Performance framework for regional health authorities, performance reporting and indicators of health status	Promotes public understanding and pressures for improvement
'Customer'	Health quality councils, patient bills of rights, physician profiles, hospital report cards, health ombudsmen	Encourages responsiveness but does not constitute formal accountability

providers will at times face conflicting accountability requirements. However, the essence of accountability in practice has not changed all that much: the focus remains on retrospective blaming for mistakes. Given the challenges of the new governance environment involving the need for greater foresight and collaboration, there are pressures to redefine accountability in broader, more prospective terms. Also there is a perceived need to develop theories and mechanisms of collective accountability to reflect the new realities of governance in the health policy field. This will not be an easy achievement because of the adversarial nature of political accountability, and public insistence when something goes seriously wrong that an identifiable individual or institution pay a significant price. It is not good enough to say that 'the system' failed us.

Conclusion

The pace of change within the Canadian healthcare system has been intense and shows little sign of abating in the future. Yet we should not assume that all changes are sweeping in their scope and consequences. Fundamental decisions (like the adoption of universal health care) set the policy context for more incremental decisions at other levels of policy and management. Narrow, technical changes are more easily accomplished than sweeping policy change involving complex networks of institutions and actors. Hyperbole from the change literature is that all organizations must transform themselves rapidly and constantly or they will fail. If true for some private firms, it is far less true of public organizations. Here many policies persist, there is considerable continuity in managerial activities even when the issues of the day change, and the prospect of 'failure' (depending upon how the concept is defined) is not an immediate reality.

In its popular usage, the term 'governance' in the health policy field has mechanistic and managerial overtones. Properly understood, however, governance involves the changing role of governments and other sectors in setting policy directions and delivering programmes in the health field. Governance inevitably involves politics and power. It involves considerations of public trust and confidence, representation, responsiveness, ethics, legitimacy and accountability. Consequently, governance arrangements and processes cannot be judged on narrowly managerial criteria.

Governance processes in health are deeply affected by their context. They operate across organizational to international levels and within a variety of specialized policy domains. The role of powerful national and multinational corporations within the health policy field must also be recognized. Federal–provincial negotiations are probably the most visible dimension of the health policy process because of the political controversy and the extensive media coverage involved. But lower profile forms of policy making probably have more direct immediate impact on the health care available to individual Canadians.

Leadership of change is increasingly shared and collective, reflecting the fact that government actors lead change not through command and control but on the basis of influence, negotiation and persuasion. The leadership skills required in the new governance environment are not strictly 'managerial'. They are more 'political', bringing stakeholders together to pursue common ends in a situation of increased interdependence.

Governments have been unable to ignore the growing public demand for accountability within the healthcare system, resulting in the proliferation of types of accountability and mechanisms for enforcement. But accountability is still couched primarily in terms of blame. Concepts and mechanisms for a more constructive, collective approach to accountability need to be developed. In a decentralized healthcare system involving diffused power, improved legal, structural and procedural mechanisms can make an important, albeit limited, contribution to current accountability challenges. Ultimately, Canadians most rely greatly upon a collective culture of responsibility, where all significant actors agree to act on the basis of a subjective, internalized sense of legal and moral obligation to provide efficient, effective, safe and ethical healthcare services.

Healthcare policy making in Canada provides a useful illustrative case study of the complex and problematic nature of contemporary, indirect approaches to governance based upon inter-organizational networks of dispersed actors and institutions. Future comparative research in different policy fields could contribute to greater theoretical and practical understanding of the paradoxes and methods of large-scale change processes. For example, it could identify the relative importance of international pressures and constraints, the constellation of domestic forces and the power structures within particular countries and the challenges these conditions present in terms of leadership, coordination and management of the change process.

There is a strong recognition in the literature that process affects the substance of policy and that the reverse can also be true: that what is at stake in policy terms affects the type of involvements and processes which occur. Healthcare policy is a highly complex, visible and politicized field; other policy fields are more operational, technical and less 'political' in content. This implies the need for a contingency model of policy making which develops theoretical perspectives on how policy content affects policy processes and policy outcomes. To be useful in the world of practice, such theoretical perspectives must pay more attention to the policy context in terms of which situational trends and factors matter most to the formulation and implementation of successful policies.

On both the theoretical and practical level, simplified and mechanistic models of successful governance must be avoided in favour of more complex understandings based upon recognition of ambiguity, uncertainty, risk and the need to develop support and legitimacy for different types of changes. Academics should strive to develop new vocabulary and analytical tools to help public officials – both elected and appointed – to diagnose and map external and internal environments, and to develop new strategies for 'working' these environments to achieve broad societal goals. This process is inherently 'political' in the sense that it involves the accommodation of competing interests and values. Therefore, values like representation, legitimacy, responsiveness, consensus, fairness, transparency and accountability must be factored into policy making, along with the more traditional emphasis on economy, efficiency and effectiveness. There is a large and daunting research agenda before us.

REFERENCES

Carson, M. (2003) What happened to health care reform? *Commentary*, December, 193. Canada: C.D. Howe Institute.

Casebeer, A. (2004) Regionalizing Canadian health care: the good – the bad – the ugly. *Health Care Papers*, **5**(1), 88–93.

Contandriopoulos, D., Denis, J-L., Langley. A. and Valette, A. (2004) Governance structures and political processes in a public system: lessons from Quebec. *Public Administration*, **82**(3), 627–55.

Exworthy, M. and Powell, M. (2004) Big windows and little windows: implementation in the 'congested state'. *Public Administration*, **82**(2), 263–81.

Hill, M. and Hupe, P. (2002) *Implementing Public Policy: Governance in Theory and Practice*. London: Sage.

Hult, K. and Walcott, C. (1990) *Governing Public Organizations: Politics, Structures and Institutional Design*. Pacific Grove, CA: Brooks.

Kingdon, J.W. (1995) *Agendas, Alternatives, and Public Policies*, 2nd edn. New York: Harper Collins.

Lewis, S. and Kouri, D. (2004) Regionalization: making sense of the Canadian experience. *Healthcare Papers*, **5**(1), 12–31.

Lipman-Blumen, J. (1996) *Connective Leadership: Managing in a Changing World*. Oxford: Oxford University Press.

Naylor, D. (1999) Health care in Canada: incrementalism under fiscal duress. *Health Affairs*, **18**(3), 9–26.

O'Reilly, P. (2000) *Health Care Practitioners: an Ontario Case Study in Policy Making*. Toronto: University of Toronto Press.

Rainey, H. (2003) *Understanding and Managing Public Organizations*, 3rd edn. San Francisco: Jossey-Bass.

Rasmussen, K. (2001) Regionalization and collaborative government: a new direction for health care governance. In D. Adams (ed.), *Federalism, Democracy and Health Policy in Canada*. Kingston: McGill-Queen's University Press, pp. 239–70.

Rhodes, R. (2002) Putting people back into networks. *Australian Journal of Political Science*, **37**(3), 399–416.

Romanow Commission on the Future of Health Care in Canada (2002) *Final Report*. Ottawa, Canada.

Rose, R. (1987) Steering the ship of state: one tiller but two pairs of hands. *British Journal of Political Science*, **17**(4), 409–34.

Rost, J. (1991) *Leadership for the Twenty-First Century*. New York: Praeger.

Scheldrick, B. (2003) Judicial review and the allocation of health care resources in Canada and the United Kingdom. *Journal of Comparative Policy Analysis: Research and Practice*, **5**, 149–66.

Schofield, J. (2004) A model of learned implementation. *Public Administration*, **82**(2), 283–308.

Shergold, P. (1997) The colour purple: perceptions of accountability across the Tasman. *Public Administration and Development*, **17**(3), 293–306.

Thomas, P. (1998) The changing nature of accountability. In G. Peters and J. Savoie (eds), *Taking Stock: Assessing Public Sector Reforms*. Ottawa: Canadian Centre for Management Development.

Tuohy, C. (1999) *Accidental Logics: The Dynamics of Change in the Health Care Arena in the United States, Britain and Canada*. New York: Oxford University Press.

Tuohy, C. (2003) Agency, contract and governance: shifting shapes of accountability in the health care arena. *Journal of Health Politics, Policy and Law*, **28**(2–3), 195–215.

CHAPTER 7

INEVITABLE TENSIONS IN MANAGING LARGE-SCALE PUBLIC SERVICE REFORM

Ben Levin

It is not unknown for practitioners involved in implementing government-driven public service reform to blame government policy-makers for creating the complexities with which they have to cope. Implicit in this view is the assumption that policy-makers have sufficient agency to control the form that reform policies take and the means and timetable for their implementation. Therefore they should know better and could do better. Ben Levin's account in this chapter, pursuing knowledge-for-understanding, suggests that this common assumption is not entirely valid. In especially turbulent political contexts, it is largely false. Uncontrollable things make public policy making happen, just as policy making makes uncontrollable things happen in public service organizations.

The discussion centres on major factors that intrinsically limit the manageability of government-driven public service reform. They must be lived with because they cannot be eliminated. His analysis carries the authority of his 'insider' experience within the Manitoba government as deputy minister (in Canadian provinces the senior civil servant) responsible for education (Levin 2005), and his international comparative research in education as an academic (Levin 2001). He points to broad constraints imposed by democratic political systems and international political trends that combine to delimit the room for expression of agency, even among politicians. Their electoral mandate may give them unrivalled legislative authority to reform public services, but it does not give them exclusive control in the face of pressures from a plurality of stakeholders within and beyond their jurisdiction. Diverse contextual factors also make any large public service system structurally complex, and so complex to change (echoing the analysis in Chapter 6). Most fundamentally, Levin points to a series of endemic tensions that policy-makers and senior civil servants endeavouring to bring about reform both contribute to and are compelled to cope with (consistent with the notion of endemic dilemmas discussed in connection with the ironic perspective in Chapter 4).

Introduction

Most public service reforms are predicated on a straightforward rationalist model in which the introduction of a given set of policies is supposed to lead inevitably to a set of desired results. In line with the contrary emphasis of other contributors to this book on the non-rational (for example, Chapters 1, 4 and 5), the present chapter takes the view that reforms designed or understood in that way are unlikely to succeed. Substantial reform of a public service always involves a set of tensions and trade-offs. These tensions arise from the fundamental characteristics of politics, government and institutional practice. The early sections of this chapter set the scene, indicating why it is that policy-makers simply do not have the level of control over the change process that the rationalist model would assume. First, the multiplicity of constraints is discussed that governments in western democracies are compelled to operate under. Second, several international political trends are noted which serve to render these constraints even tighter. Third, aspects of complex public service systems are considered which militate against policy-makers achieving a strong and predictable impact on service practice. The fourth section outlines four generic tensions that public service reform efforts inevitably embody: top-down vision versus bottom-up responsiveness, planning versus coping with the unexpected, short-term versus long-term attention and political versus administrative requirements. Although the discussion is based primarily on my experience in the field of education, as other chapters in this volume illustrate, similar dynamics occur in other areas of public service as well (see Chapters 6 and 10).

Characteristics of Public Policy

Any significant public policy effort is likely to be subject to several significant constraints that make both policy development and implementation particularly challenging. The most important such constraints are conflicting goals, lack of time in the policy process and sudden changes in context. (I provide here only a very brief discussion of some features of government. A fuller discussion can be found in Levin 2005.)

Governments do as they do for what they consider to be good reasons. They don't set out to make a mess of things any more than schools set out to have high numbers of dropouts or unhappy parents, even though the latter is sometimes the result. In my experience governments generally try to do what they think most voters want. Since that is why we vote for them, it is hard to object to this approach – though people sometimes do. Would we like governments better if they had the so-called courage to do what is unpopular? The British cabinet minister in the TV series *Yes Minister* always reacted with dismay when his chief civil servant, Sir Humphrey, called for taking a courageous stand, since this meant doing something that would get him into serious trouble. When people talk about governments having 'political will' what they usually mean is that the government should do what they want, even though it is not popular. That is precisely how you get defeated in the next election.

Of course each government is more attuned to some voters than to others, and each starts with some predispositions about the kinds of policies that seem attractive. But many commentators overestimate the importance of ideology and underestimate the power of practical politics. The problem is that pleasing voters is very hard to do, because voters do not need to be reasonable or consistent in their views. They can insist on 'six impossible things before breakfast' if they wish, and they frequently do. The political world is characterized by Arrow's (1970) 'impossibility theorem' – that preferences cannot be aggregated. Voters can and do demand more accountability but less bureaucracy, uniformity of treatment but special consideration for their own circumstances, protecting children at risk but not disrupting families, and so on. Polling (COMPAS 2001) has shown that people want schools to give more emphasis to every subject – clearly impossible unless the school day or year is to be made longer, which people do not favour.

For politicians, what people believe to be true is much more important than what may actually be true. I have had a number of politicians tell me on various occasions that while the evidence I was presenting for a particular policy might be correct, the policy was not what people would accept. Nor are voters' views necessarily amenable to change either through persuasion or evidence. As Marcel Proust put it,

> The facts of life do not penetrate to the sphere in which our beliefs are cherished . . . they can aim at them continual blows of contradiction and disproof without weakening them; and an avalanche of miseries and maladies coming, one after another, without interruption into the bosom of a family, will not make it lose faith in either the clemency of its God or the capacity of its physician (Proust, *Swann's Way*).

No wonder governments try to do everything all at once – that is what we ask them to do. The presence of diverse and conflicting goals means that governments are pulled, often strongly, in different directions at the same time. That is one reason policies may be contradictory or incoherent. In these circumstances clarity of purpose is not necessarily a virtue. Governments may try to maintain political credibility and social harmony by softening the edges of what they do, or by giving a little bit to many different, and even competing, agendas.

At the same time as they face multiple, conflicting pressures on a given issue, governments are also dealing with a huge array of issues and never have enough time to give them the attention they deserve. A myriad of decisions, many of them quite difficult, end up in the hands of a relatively small number of politicians and senior managers, not all of whom have backgrounds that give them a good sense of the issues. A minister has to deal not only with her or his own department – which, in a case like education, is already large and complex – but also with the whole range of substantive issues from other parts of government as well as with all the demands of political work and life. Ministers are under enormous pressure almost all the time: to meet with people, to respond to demands, to attend events, to visit places. Nor can many decisions be put off for further study. As discussed further below, some issues arise suddenly and require immediate response. Even where this is not the case, the political pressure is often such that to take time for further study is seen as evidence of incompetence. Moreover, every issue that is deferred has to be decided at some point, and since new issues are constantly emerging, delay can have the result of creating impossible pressures later. The reality is that many decisions, even important ones, have to be made without adequate study or consideration of knowledge and evidence. During my time in government I have often been amazed not by how many things went wrong, but by how many decisions turned out reasonably well, considering how quickly they were made.

A further implication of the huge number of issues and lack of time is that questions of implementation tend to get short shrift. In situations where there is not even enough time to work through the alternatives with any degree of care, discussions of what might happen later or of how policies will be taken up in various contexts, tend to sink to the bottom of the agenda. The kinds of practical concerns around implementation described in chapters in Part I are rarely at the forefront when important policy decisions are made. Moreover, the political focus is more often on showing that government is responding to an issue than it is on whether policies are implemented or succeed (Hopkins and Levin 2000). Once a policy is announced and initial implementation has occurred, there tends to be little attention from the media or the public as to its long-term effects.

The pressures of multiple issues and lack of time are accompanied by the possibility – even the probability – of changing circumstances, unexpected events and crises. If the economy turns sour and revenues drop, if natural disasters occur, if new domestic developments take place, governments must respond in some way, even if that means taking attention and resources away from other activities that were high on the priority list. As Dror (1986: 186) puts it, there is 'at any given moment a high probability of low probability events occurring. In other words, surprise dominates'. As a new issue comes to be highly salient, other important issues inevitably drop out of sight. It is easy to think of examples of unexpected events that created many changes in plans.

While some political pressures relate to very important, long-term issues, others may concern small short-term details. One cannot assume that the former will always be more important than the latter. Sometimes very small items can turn into huge political events (Bovens and t'Hart 1994). For example, a single untoward event can undermine an entire system that may actually be working reasonably well, as those involved in health care or child welfare know only too well. Ninety-nine per cent of children may be receiving wonderful care, but if one dies or is abused the entire system will be under scrutiny. Just imagine the public and media response to a minister who reacted to the death of a patient in a hospital waiting room by pointing out that nothing is perfect and the vast majority of patients were well looked after.

Governments are particularly susceptible to issues that take on public salience through the media. Because most people get their information about public events this way, an issue that is played up in the media often – though not always (the media does not have unlimited impact, see Levin 2004a) – becomes something that a government must respond to, even if the issue was no part of the government's policy or plan. Media coverage is itself motivated by a number of considerations, but long-term importance for public welfare is not necessarily one of them. Stories often focus on the situations of individuals, even where these are not at all typical (Neuman, Just and Crigler 1992). Novelty is also an important requisite for the media in order to sustain reader or viewer interest, so that governments are likely to be faced with an ever-changing array of issues supposedly requiring immediate attention.

All of this means that issues go in and out of public attention and therefore in and out of political favour. Almost any important policy commitment or reform requires sustained attention over several years, yet the chances of maintaining political and public interest over that long a time frame are very small. People go on to other things.

Increasing Constraints on Public Policy

These constraints or pressures are inevitable features of the political environment of any modern democratic state. Moreover, changing political dynamics in contemporary societies are making the constraints tougher. An extensive discussion of the changing context of politics and public policy is beyond the scope of this chapter, but a few trends can be noted. One important change is that conflict over public policy appears to have sharpened in recent decades, with more interest groups pursuing their agendas more actively than ever before – perhaps in part because people are better educated than ever before. At one time in many jurisdictions education policy was made through discussion between a few key organizations of those directly involved, such as teachers and administrators. Today, governments are unlikely to embark on significant change in education policy without some kind of broad public consultation involving parents, employers, community groups and many others. A more consultative policy process inevitably has the effect of introducing more conflict into the policy process. As Heath (2001: 35) puts it, 'The exercise of human reason, under conditions of freedom and equality, tends to generate more – not less – disagreement about the ultimate aims of life'.

Greater population diversity in many countries, coupled with an increasing view that diversity has to be accommodated if not respected, have rendered the problem of policy making more difficult. It is not only the case that more people and groups want to have a say in public policy, but that those groups represent a wider range of views than used to be the case, and that minority groups are less willing to accept that they should adjust to the majority.

At the same time as policy making is more open to a variety of influences, governments have been under pressure to shrink the public sector and to provide greater accountability for their efforts. This means that increasing pressure runs up against fewer resources and therefore often less ability to respond. At the same time, the accountability pressures put greater focus on process questions – not so much whether policies have achieved their goals (about which more below), but whether all the procedures were correctly followed. Governments can land in a great deal of political trouble if, for example, records of expenditure are inadequate, regardless of the merits or success of the programme in question.

Public Service Systems

The systems that public policy is trying to affect in areas such as education and health are themselves very hard to change. They are large, diverse and substantially decentralized. Let us take the Canadian public education system as an example. Canada has 13 provinces and territories, approximately 500 school districts, 16,000 schools, 5.6 million students and about 275,000 teachers (Canadian Education Statistics Council 2003). A reasonable guess would be that more than 10 million Canadians – about a third of the population – have a very direct connection to public schools as parents, teachers or the immediate family of parents or teachers. Canada spends about $37 billion per year on public education, among the higher proportions in the OECD.

The school system in Canada has two official layers of governance. Provinces have constitutional authority and all provinces have, through legislation, created local elected school districts with important management functions. Canadian school districts range in size from a few hundred students in one or two schools to some 250,000 students in hundreds of schools. The largest districts have substantially greater student populations than several of the provinces. The federal government plays a minor role in limited areas of education. First Nations (Aboriginal communities) largely run and control their own school systems with federal funding, but independent of provincial regulations. Teachers are unionized on a district and provincial basis. In most, but not all, provinces school administrators are part of the teachers' unions. Parents are increasingly well organized, with most provinces having some kind of provincial parent organization and some provinces having several such organizations with quite different positions on the political spectrum. The picture is equally complex in other countries and in other fields of public service.

Not only are politics and governance in education quite decentralized, so is control over many practices. A very large body of research shows clearly that most practices in schools and classrooms are highly resistant to changes in policy from upper levels of the hierarchy (Fullan 1991). When I became Deputy Minister of Education in Manitoba, I was well aware that although the Manitoba Department of Education had produced a large amount of high-quality curricula, much of it was not being used by many teachers. (Since we had produced something like 6000 pages of material for the primary grades, it's hardly surprising that teachers had not fully assimilated all of it!) The joke was that curriculum documents were sitting on teachers' shelves in the original shrink-wrapping. I promised to put an end to this situation – by ceasing to shrink-wrap the documents.

Many similar examples could be cited where pronouncements made with good intentions and in good faith by provincial governments or school districts, or even principals of schools, had little or no result in terms of the daily experience of students and teachers. And even where honest efforts are made to implement new policies, we know that they are adapted and modified to suit people's perceptions of their own needs and conditions. McLaughlin's (1990: 12) statement that 'policy cannot mandate what matters' is perhaps too strong, but it is an accurate recognition of the limitations of any policy pronouncement.

Local adaptation or modification of policy is not necessarily a bad thing. As already noted, many policies are drafted far too quickly and with too little attention to implementation. Moreover, circumstances do alter cases. The diversity in the situations of schools, even in relatively small and homogeneous countries, is still likely to be quite considerable. As several chapters in this volume show, the way in which a particular policy plays out can vary considerably from one setting to another.

The issue of implementation is especially difficult because in most public services the reforms that are likely to produce real results require changes in the actual delivery of services, meaning that a very large number of people have to change their behaviour. While many articles are written about how schooling can be reformed through some simple step such as introducing choice, creating school governing bodies or giving school head teachers more autonomy, the reality is that there is no credible evidence to support this view and much that contradicts it. Student outcomes, such as secondary school completion or skills in reading or writing are largely shaped by factors outside the school. Whatever contribution schools make does not happen because of the way schools are organized or governed or financed, but as a result of the learning and teaching practices that go on every day. This means that a reform that is intended to improve student outcomes must address how teachers and students do their work, something that is much harder to accomplish than is a change in structure or finance.

Further, although policies and reforms are usually designed one by one, they are experienced by those subject to them as interacting. Wallace and Pocklington (2002) make the case that policies in different areas may actually contradict each other – as was the case in England when policies promoting school choice ran up against policies seeking to remove excess capacity from the system. Similarly, calls for greater decentralization may contradict requirements for greater accountability. Governments may talk about 'joined-up thinking', but in practice this is very difficult to do. In large part policy incoherence is inevitable, given the political dynamics described at the outset of this chapter: the attempt to meet multiple and diverse goals all at the same time, sudden shifts in the context and the lack of attention to implementation issues. In part it can also be seen as an inevitable characteristic of large human organizations. Dror (1986) describes magnificently the gap between our aspirations and what we are usually capable of achieving. As examples from climate change, through security, through energy management, to public health show us over and over, the world is often more complex than we can comprehend, let alone control.

At a more mundane level, another reason why policy change does not have more impact on practice is the lack of capacity in most public systems to manage complex change. Wallace and Pocklington (2002) show how local authorities and schools had to struggle and improvise to put the systems and resources in place to manage reorganization and consolidation of schools. People lacked background and skills for the tasks they now had to take on. The organizations did not have adequate systems to produce the required information, to organize the necessary consultation processes or to deal with all the various fallouts. The result was a tremendous amount of scrambling around and improvisation, often at great cost to the individuals assigned to look after the task.

This lack of capacity has been exacerbated in recent years by some of the macro-political trends mentioned earlier. Pressure on resources has led service delivery organizations such as school systems to reduce central operations in favour of focusing resources in classrooms. For example, research capacity in many school systems has been essentially eliminated. Moreover, accountability pressures have meant that more support time is taken to check and double check on a variety of administrative functions, which may actually reduce productivity. At one level it is a perfectly reasonable strategy to focus resources on the core mission of the organization, and it is certainly true that central bureaucracies are not always helpful or productive. Yet organizations under stress, as most public services today are, do require some central organizational capacity to manage the pressures and need the analytic capacity to ascertain whether current policies and practices are successful.

The Tensions

With that background, let us return to the four tensions described at the beginning of this chapter and look at how they are manifest in the management of large-scale change. The empirical basis for the following analysis is drawn from four main sources: the general research literature on large-scale change in education; my study of large-scale education reform in four countries in the 1980s and 1990s (Levin 2001); my work with colleagues evaluating the implementation of the National Literacy and Numeracy Strategies in England from 1998 to 2002 (Earl *et al.* 2002, 2003), and my experience as a senior civil servant, including serving as Deputy Minister (chief civil servant) for Education for the Province of Manitoba from 1999 to 2002 (Levin 2005).

Top-down vision versus bottom-up responsiveness

Large-scale reform must, by definition, come from a central authority of some kind. Reform often begins with the enunciation of a vision or perceived future benefit that will arise from the actions being taken. But as already noted, the implementation of many reforms must be put into place at the local level, in individual schools and by individual teachers. This is especially so for reforms that go beyond changes in structure to affect teaching and learning practices, and so rely on the skills and commitment of individual educators. The same would be true of changes in health care involving physician or nursing practice, or changes in child welfare that require new practices by social workers. Efforts can be made to increase fidelity of implementation – say, through testing or inspection systems – but these may be expensive and still have only limited impact. It is especially difficult to increase skills or performance levels through mandates (Elmore 1995). You cannot make people better at things by ordering them to improve. You must have people's active engagement, but skilled people will not engage in a practice unless it makes sense to them and gives them some scope to exercise their skills in ways that make sense to them. The more prescriptive a central direction, the less likely it is to build commitment to implementation. This means that any reform programme faces the requirement to balance central direction with the possibility of local decision making.

Moreover, context matters, so that slavish adherence to a central mandate can produce bizarre and undesired results. In the late 1980s Chicago brought in school governing councils with the authority to hire and fire principals and to develop school plans. In many schools these bodies worked quite well. Yet in others they were entirely unproductive, as strong disagreements among participants led to conflict and sometimes stalemate (Hess 1995). The Chicago initiative did give some training to the members of the new councils, but a few days of training will not eliminate massive levels of distrust or even active dislike built up over many years.

The National Literacy and Numeracy Strategies in Britain provide a very interesting case of the limits of central reform efforts, even when they are very well organized and supported (which, as noted earlier, is not often the case). When the Strategies were implemented in 1998 and thereafter, the Department for Education and Employment (now Department for Education and Skills) took seriously the research on large-scale reform. An implementation strategy was designed that involved substantial resources for teacher training, high-quality materials and extensive consultant support services. At the same time, the results of the Strategies in terms of student test scores were very high profile. The Office for Standards in Education (OFSTED) put considerable additional pressure on schools to implement the Strategies through its regular and special inspections. Overall the Strategies represent the most extensive effort by any government to implement a classroom-based change in teaching and learning that we know about.

Our team's evaluations (Earl *et al.* 2002, 2003) showed that the supports, resources and pressures all played a very important role in increasing the attention teachers and schools paid to implementing the Strategies. Staff in all schools took the Strategies seriously and made considerable efforts to put them into action, often at the expense of other areas of school operations. Yet after two or three years of significant improvement in student test results, the gains levelled off and were static for several years. Our analysis of actual teaching practices showed that the Strategies resulted in significant improvement in some classrooms and were of some value in many classrooms. But on the whole, teaching practice – even with this considerable level of pressure and support – did not change all that much. Some teachers saw themselves as implementing the Strategies where observers felt that they were far from doing so. Some teachers deliberately modified the Strategies, which were quite prescriptive in many ways, to accord with their own teaching preferences. Quite a few teachers did not have, even with the additional training, the skill to implement some of the high-level teaching practices being called for.

Central policy-makers must recognize that they cannot determine school practice through central direction, but must find the right balance between central direction and local autonomy. Like many virtues, balance is much easier to advocate than to achieve, leaving the dilemma of how much room any reform must give to local desires.

Planning versus coping with the unexpected

Many a reform has been scuppered because something unexpected came along that cut its legs out, or because some other policy made it impossible for the planned change to succeed. A prime example is a change in political power as a result of an election. The Labour government in New Zealand embarked in 1987 on a very ambitious set of reforms of the organization of schooling, moving from a highly centralized system to one in which each school would be self-governing. However, just as the change was being put into place, Labour was defeated by the National Party. The new government took the reforms in some quite different directions and also reduced significantly the funding that was supposed to be available for the newly autonomous schools (Levin 2001; Butterworth and Butterworth 1998).

Even a change of the minister in charge or of a key senior manager can send a reform in quite a different direction, as can be seen in the interviews by Ribbins and Sherratt (1997) with the various education ministers in the Thatcher and Major governments in the UK. As senior civil servants recognize, the personality of the minister is often more important than her or his political party affiliation.

Another common change is in funding levels. California implemented limits on class size and ambitious new curricula in many areas in the 1990s, only to face a budget crisis that took so much money out of the system that effective implementation became impossible. As an aside, the class size initiative in California had already produced some side effects that should have been anticipated but were not, and made implementation exceedingly difficult. They included a shortage of classroom space, shortages of qualified teachers, and, due to the shortage, extensive movement of teachers from less attractive to more attractive jobs and districts, creating significant disruption for students (Biddle and Berliner 2002).

A third kind of change involves distraction. Everyone may be facing in the same direction, ready to go (more or less, one has to add) with a reform, when something else happens that causes everyone to turn around and forget all about the line of march. Something happens due to some accident, or a media story appears and suddenly time and attention, especially of leaders, is entirely taken over by new concerns.

One of my main interests while Deputy Minister was to develop a positive agenda for school improvement in Manitoba. We did develop what we called the K-S4 Agenda (Levin and Wiens 2003; see also www.edu.gov.mb.ca/ks4/agenda). But it took at least twice as long as it should have because so much time was taken up with other issues and crises. In autumn 2001 about two months of my time and the minister's time, as well as that of many other staff, was almost entirely preoccupied by a scandal around falsified enrolments in adult learning in a small school district that was trying to be entrepreneurial (Levin 2005). Many other issues simply had to be put aside.

Unexpected changes are normal, even inevitable, as noted earlier. One cannot, by definition, get ready for big surprises. The challenge for reformers is to figure out how much flex to leave in the plan to accommodate the inevitable surprises. Governments typically are already trying to do more things than they can manage, so there is considerable resistance to providing extra time or money to a given initiative 'just in case'. More often, because of limited resources plans move ahead without even the minimum level of support that is required. Yet a plan that assumes everything will go smoothly and on time is a plan that is almost certainly destined for failure.

Short-term versus long-term attention

Politics is largely concerned with the short term, while reform requires long-term commitment. Governments have to produce a steady stream of announcements and initiatives because that is how they communicate their ideas and priorities to voters. It is very difficult to get media coverage or other attention for something that has been ongoing for some time, even if it is very important. The political adage that 'voters have short memories' reflects what politicians see as their reality.

Almost any significant educational reform, on the other hand, will take years to put into place and show meaningful results. Teaching and learning practices, which are key to any real improvement in student learning outcomes, are very difficult to change even with substantial pressure and support, as the example of the National Literacy and Numeracy Strategies shows. When the Strategies were announced in 1998, the Secretary of State, David Blunkett, said he would resign if the government's targets for 2002 were not met. Blunkett remained as Secretary for four years, much longer than the normal span for a minister. But by 2002 he was in a new portfolio, so his promise no longer mattered.

To its credit, the British government has continued to provide substantial support – and pressure – for the Strategies for over seven years after their announcement, a very rare level of commitment. On the other hand, New Labour has issued a huge array of policy changes and reforms in education and other related fields in Britain during its time in office – a veritable deluge of new programmes, funding schemes and policies – especially in the first few years. Even where schools and school systems welcomed many (though certainly not all) of the new policies, they felt overwhelmed by the sheer number of initiatives to which they were supposed to attend.

The United States provides some especially poignant examples of short-term approaches. Some US states have implemented a major new reform programme every three or four years for decades. I can recall a colleague pointing to one state that had had six new comprehensive education reform strategies in 10 years. From the standpoint of schools, this kind of change followed by change makes it impossible to respond and leads to a weary 'this too shall pass' stance, in which no new policy is taken seriously.

The dichotomy between the short-term demands of electoral politics and the long-term requirements for system change is exactly why there is such a strong political predisposition to prefer reforms that have a shorter time line. Results of some kind can be shown quickly. Even relatively short-term structural changes, such as reducing the number of school districts (something that all Canadian provinces have done over the last decade or so), take years to work through. Insofar as voters – and the media that provides information to voters – are not interested in what might happen in three or four years, or what happened three or four years ago, politicians cannot be too interested in it either.

Political versus administrative requirements

Some of the elements of this tension have been raised already. But there are other ways in which political dynamics work against the real requirements of lasting reform in public services. At one point in the 1980s I was responsible for policy and the funding of universities for the Manitoba government. The president of one of our universities complained to me one day that a new library had been promised for his university in the last three elections but had still not been built. 'But', I responded, 'if we build it, we would spend quite a bit of money only to lose a really good election announcement'.

There are several ways in which political and administrative realities clash (Levin 2005). Politicians want to do things quickly, but many important changes take time, as already discussed. Politicians want to do things relatively cheaply, especially in these days of huge pressures to reduce the size of the public sector, while administrators are acutely aware of how much easier change is when the gears are lubricated with additional money. Politicians want to keep things simple so that they can be explained publicly in the time that people are willing to spend to understand them, while managers are always stressing the complexities. Politicians want to announce things now, while managers want time to figure out how the new policy will actually work. Politicians want to keep things under wraps until they are announced, while managers often want to explore ideas with others to see what complications might arise. Politicians are concerned with how things look to voters – who cannot give much attention to most public issues even if they want to, because there are simply more issues than they have time or interest to engage with – while managers are focused on how the system will behave under reform.

The Literacy and Numeracy Strategies in England again provide a good example, even though they were reforms that had much more substance to them than do many education reforms. When the Strategies were announced, the Secretary of State set targets, as noted earlier, promising that 80 per cent of students at age 11 would reach the desired level in literacy, and 75 per cent in numeracy. These targets were no doubt set in order to give a strong and easily understood public commitment. They were very ambitious, given performance levels at the time. However as we noted in our reports (Earl *et al.* 2002, 2003) setting a single target had the effect of distracting attention from other important goals in literacy and numeracy, such as reducing gaps between the top and bottom of the performance range both among individuals and among schools. The irony was that in 2002, when performance did not quite reach the targets, the public story was 'government fails to achieve goal' when it could more accurately have been 'substantial improvements in literacy and numeracy'.

These differences in the political and bureaucratic views of the world result in tensions between those who decide on reforms and those who implement them. As Fitz and Halpin (1991) put it, bureaucrats see their task as going from 'a fuzzy policy to a workable scheme', which inevitably means rounding off some of what was intended in favour of what is seen as workable. Politicians feel, not without reason, that their goals are being subverted in an effort to reduce pressure on the system. Thus politicians tend to see the bureaucracy as self-serving and unwilling to change, while administrators tend to see politicians as lacking understanding of how complex systems actually work. A vicious circle results in which politicians look for more secrecy in policy design and even more mandatory provisions, while managers look for ways of evading disliked aspects of the policy while still seeming to comply. Effective reform requires a strong partnership between policy-makers and managers at all levels, but the dynamics just described make it very hard to build and sustain those partnerships.

Implications for Practice and Research

This analysis might seem very pessimistic to some. It suggests that grand policy reforms are always likely to encounter very serious if not fatal weaknesses in the way they are developed and implemented. Further, that these limitations are built into the dynamics of politics, government and large organizations. In large measure I believe that such an analysis is correct. Large-scale reform always has unintended consequences, but whether it yields the hoped-for results is always contingent.

Does this mean that large-scale reform is impossible? Certainly not; there is no sign that governments are wavering in their commitment to big changes. If anything, governments in many countries over recent years have been prepared to try to implement even bigger changes than in the past.

The dilemmas and tensions illustrated here cannot be wished away or designed around. However, to the extent that various actors are aware of them, there could be modifications around the edges that would be improvements. Political leaders cannot get away from making commitments in simple language that communicate to the public. But they could perhaps be a little more cautious in their promises, and they could pay more attention to issues of implementation. Managers cannot avoid the need to match goals to the real possibilities of their organizations. But they could perhaps be a little more understanding of the requirements that politics bring, and a little more open to doing things differently. Most of all, ongoing debate and dialogue among the parties could help everyone understand the overall dynamics of reform more fully. Other developments, such as the growing interest in research and evidence (Levin 2004b), the growing public pressure for participation in decisions, or the growing awareness that policies and initiatives have an interconnected or even ecological nature to them, might help move these processes along in productive ways. That is a main purpose of this book, to which I hope this chapter makes some contribution.

My analysis also poses some challenges for researchers. A great deal of research on education policy seems to aim at showing how changes have not worked or have been ill conceived. Yet it does so without adequate acknowledgement of the dilemmas governments face in organizing and supporting large-scale change. The cause of knowledge might be better served if more research agendas were sensitive to trade-offs and constraints, and tried to understand how the various actors – politicians, senior civil servants and the 'recipients' of policy in public organizations – tried to understand and cope with the multiple pressures and limitations on them. It is particularly important to avoid focusing on only one policy at a time in a world in which multiple pressures operate simultaneously.

Part of the mission of research in the area of public policy should be to help build understanding, hence improving practice. To advance that purpose researchers will have to manage their own dilemmas, such as combining scepticism about claims with empathy for the realities of various actors. Researchers should also think carefully about how their accounts serve the purpose of building public engagement rather than cynicism, and how to help people remain optimistic about what they can do rather than focusing on what has gone wrong or failed to work.

None of this means that researchers should relinquish efforts to be objective or should relax standards of what is good public policy. However research also needs to reflect in a thoughtful way what it really means to live and work in a world of contradictions and dilemmas.

REFERENCES

Arrow, K. (1970) *Social Choice and Individual Values*, 3rd edn. New Haven, CT: Yale University Press.

Biddle, B. and Berliner, D. (2002) Small class size and its effects. *Educational Leadership*, **59**(5), 12–23.

Bovens, M. and t'Hart, P. (1994) *Understanding Policy Fiascos*. New Brunswick, NJ: Transaction Books.

Butterworth, G. and Butterworth, S. (1998) *Reforming education: the New Zealand Experience 1984–1996*. Palmerston: The Dunmore Press.

Canadian Education Statistics Council (2003) *Pan-Canadian Educational Indicators*. Ottawa: Canadian Education Statistics Council, Ottawa. http://www.cmec.ca (accessed February 2006).

COMPAS (2001) *The Educational Experience: State of the Nation*. Poll for the National Post and Global TV. 26 August.

Dror, Y. (1986) *Policy-Making under Adversity*. New Brunswick, NJ: Transaction Books.

Earl, L., Levin, B., Leithwood, K., Fullan, M. and Watson, N. (2002) *Watching and Learning 2: OISE/UT Evaluation of the Implementation of the National Literacy and Numeracy Strategies*. Prepared for the Department for Education and Skills, England. Toronto: OISE/University of Toronto. http://www.standards.dfes.gov.uk/primary/publications/literacy/ (accessed February 2006).

Earl, L., Watson, N., Levin, B., Leithwood, K., Fullan, M. and Torrance, N. (2003) *Watching and Learning 3: Final Report of the OISE/UT Evaluation of the Implementation of the National Literacy and Numeracy Strategies*. Prepared for the Department for Education and Skills, England. Toronto: OISE/University of Toronto. http://www.standards.dfes.gov.uk/primary/publications/literacy/ (accessed February 2006).

Elmore, R. (1995) Structural reform in educational practice. *Educational Researcher*, **24**(9), 23–6.

Fitz, J. and Halpin, D. (1991) From a 'sketchy policy' to a 'workable scheme': the DES and grant-maintained schools. *International Studies in Sociology of Education*, **1**, 129–51.

Fullan, M. (1991) *The New Meaning of Educational Change*, 2nd edn. New York: Teachers College Press/OISE Press.

Heath, J. (2001) *The Efficient Society: Why Canada is as Good as it Gets*. Toronto: Viking.

Hess, G.A., Jr. (1995) *Restructuring Urban Schools: a Chicago Perspective*. New York: Teachers College Press.

Hopkins, D. and Levin, B. (2000) Government policy and school improvement. *School Leadership and Management*, **20**(1), 15–30.

Levin, B. (2001) *Reforming Education: From Origins to Outcomes*. London: RoutledgeFalmer.

Levin, B. (2004a) Media–government relations in education. *Journal of Education Policy*, **19**(3), 271–84.

Levin, B. (2004b) Making research matter more. *Education Policy Analysis Archives*, **12**(56). http://epaa.asu.edu/epaa/v12n56/ (accessed February 2006).

Levin, B. (2005) *Governing Education*. Toronto: University of Toronto Press.

Levin, B. and Wiens, J. (2003) There is another way. *Phi Delta Kappan*, **84**(9), 658–64.

McLaughlin M. (1990) The Rand Change Agent Study revisited: macro perspectives, micro realities. *Educational Researcher*, **19**(9), 11–16.

Neuman, R., Just, M. and Crigler, A. (1992) *Common Knowledge: News and the Construction of Political Meaning*. Chicago: University of Chicago Press.

Ribbins, P. and Sherratt, B. (1997) *Radical Educational Policies and Conservative Secretaries of State*. London: Cassell.

Wallace, M. and Pocklington, K. (2002) *Managing Complex Educational Change: Large-Scale Reorganization of Schooling*. London: RoutledgeFalmer.

PART

III

EXPLORING THE COMPLEXITY OF FACILITATING PUBLIC SERVICE IMPROVEMENT

CHAPTER 8

UNSYSTEMATIC RESPONSES TO A CHAOTIC SERVICE ENVIRONMENT: SHAPING THE DIVISION OF LABOUR IN PATIENT CARE

Eugene Schneller and Mike Wallace

This chapter is concerned with the evolving complexity of change affecting service organizations which originates not with reforming politicians but with service providers. Eugene Schneller and Mike Wallace are concerned to develop knowledge-for-understanding by exploring the extent to which Wallace's conception of orchestration (Chapter 1) may be applicable to two very different coping strategies: to preserve present practice in the face of the perceived threat of unwanted change; and to add positive momentum and unity to disparately emerging and moderately diverse practices.

Orchestration is linked with Abbott's (1988) notion of 'extensive organization' of professions. These ideas are used as heuristic tools for analysing two starkly contrasting cases of change affecting the division of medical and nursing labour in US health care – one conflictual, the other collaborative. Key national contextual factors are the far-reaching involvement of the private sector and widely distributed governance of health services. They militate against national or even regional politically driven reform programmes. Change therefore tends to be more distributed and emergent.

The first case entails orchestration by nursing professional association representatives to stop an unacceptable change proposed by the medical professional association. The account draws on past research carried out by Schneller. The concept of a 'counter-policy', previously developed by Wallace (1998), is employed as a frame for exploring how one medical profession manoeuvred to kill off the proposal for change put forward by another.

The second case tracks the emergence and coalescing of the 'hospitalist' movement. Hospitalists are doctors who coordinate the care of acutely ill patients during their stay in hospital. Evidence from the authors' small-scale case study research shows how this movement has gradually taken on characteristics of complexity articulated in Chapter 1. Diverse hospitalist arrangements have come to be conceived as a single 'movement' as a result of orchestration by academic medical researchers, culminating in the establishment of a national professional association.

Introduction

The nature of change in the delivery of different public services and its complexity vary between different countries for historical, political, economic and social reasons. The US and the UK both feature extensive service provision for the delivery of health care. Change in the UK, where healthcare provision is principally a public service, is frequently engineered by central government and carried out on a grand scale.

In the US, where there is a robust mix (almost 50–50) between public and private financing of care, innovations usually evolve more gradually. Change is frequently associated with service professions themselves. In many instances reaction to altered economic incentives, from either government or private financing, drives change. This is not to say that broader government-led policy or research revelations fail to influence action. The US government has influenced the emergence of entirely new medical specialties such as family medicine. But action in the US is much less centrally orchestrated. As demonstrated below, locally emergent changes that become routinized and coalesce to become more systemic may be more likely to gain national traction than centrally planned innovations. Thus the US is much like the UK – but it is also very different. We will explore some complexities of change processes in this national context by focusing on the division of labour in US health care.

Not only national context but also service-sector specific factors affect service change and its complexity. The degree of diversity prevailing over the content and methods of public education is scarcely tolerable in health care. Here interventions that fail can be life threatening, and the consequences of change can frequently be assessed in a relatively short period of time. Adults generally 'know' at first hand about formal education, having been to school in childhood, and they tend to refer back to their own experience of being educated when dealing with education for their children. They have much more varied first-hand knowledge of health care, and older people generally welcome technological advances rather than looking back to their healthcare treatment in the past.

To deepen our understanding of what makes public service change complex to manage, it is important to analyse the context in which change processes occur. The precise combination of detailed factors affecting any individual change is likely to be unique. Yet change can be characterized by patterns that allow the analyst to strike a productive balance between such context sensitivity and features across different instances of change. The conceptual framing of any empirical study of a change process can direct attention towards patterns, and provide a basis for comparison between cases. As revealed below, comparative generalization draws attention to patterns and commonalities affecting different changes at some level of abstraction from the contextual detail.

This chapter is based on observations of two contrasting cases relating to changes in the delivery of US health care. One is a story of success in resisting a proposed change in a confrontation between the principal national professional associations representing medicine and nursing (Feldstein 1988). The other is a story of success in pre-empting potential resistance and fostering acceptance of a new emergent professional role that would minimize past failures of inefficient and fragmented practice.

We focus primarily on how key players orchestrated organized resistance in one case and a climate for successful change and innovation in the other. Our eclectic analysis is aimed at revealing what made for success or failure from the orchestrators' different perspectives. In particular, we will concentrate on the change management theme of *culture building and communication* (Chapter 1). Through the management of their affairs and their environment, professions become characterized by what Abbott (1988: 82–3) has termed the 'extensive organization' which enables them to claim jurisdiction, the (mostly exclusive) right to practise in a particular service realm:

> ... the more strongly organized a profession is, the more effective its claims to jurisdiction ... The organized profession can better mobilize its members, can better direct media support of its position, and above all, can better support the effective academic work that generates cultural legitimacy for jurisdiction ... In contests between professions, the profession with more extensive organization usually wins.

Abbott's depiction of professions as engaged in competitive contests for position in a system of professions provides a robust lens for assessing the emergent, sustained and changed patterns of separate (and sometimes overlapping) *intra-professional* jurisdictions of different specialties inside the same profession. We will also supplement his ideas to operationalize the notion of extensive organization. We wish to allow for the possibilities that:

* Power may be used collaboratively to achieve shared goals, as well as conflictually to achieve one set of goals at the expense of another.
* The notion of orchestrating change may be extended to encompass mobilizing support for resisting or subverting the perceived external threat posed by an undesired move to transgress established jurisdictional boundaries.
* Boundary spanning may lead to a new settlement over intra-professional jurisdictions without necessarily precipitating conflict.
* One stakeholder group may use power to try and shape other groups' culture to gain their acceptance for change.

The first case concerns the effort of the American Nurses Association (ANA) to block a unilateral attempt by the American Medical Association (AMA), the US's strongest healthcare professional association, to introduce the new bedside

care role of 'registered care technician' (RCT). Succinctly, the RCT was proffered
as assuming routine aspects of care provided by nursing at the bedside, enabling
nursing to concentrate on more complex tasks. The case reveals that a professional
association, even when it possesses great authority within the sector it serves
(coupled with extensive economic and political influence), cannot necessarily impose
its will on what many have seen as a subordinate profession (Freidson 1970). Indeed,
nursing was able to marshal extensive organization by bringing together a diversity of stakeholders to defeat the AMA proposal. They significantly reduced organized medicine's longstanding power to shape jurisdictions in the hospital.

The second case scrutinizes the emergence of the 'hospitalist' as a hospital-based
care-giving medical management role, initially designed to replace a patient's
community-based primary care physician as the physician of record during the
patient's hospitalization. The hospitalist, serving as the agent of both the patient
and the primary care physician (Schneller and Epstein 2005), is dramatically shifting the relationship between community and hospital care in the US. Hospital
consultants in the UK have long been separated from their community-based
general practitioner (GP) counterparts. But for the US, the hospitalist idea portends
major changes in the doctor–patient relationship, and in the accountability of
different physicians for the care of their patients.

The remainder of the chapter falls into three parts. First, we set out our conceptual framework for analysing the dynamics of public service change, linking
Abbott's ideas with selected concepts underlying Mike Wallace's framework
for analysing the complexity of change. Second, we recount how the AMA's
registered care technician proposal, designed to ameliorate a chronic shortage of
nursing staff, was defeated at the national level. Third, we examine how the
hospitalist movement has gradually emerged from diverse local origins and is now
being actively unified, at least to an extent, across the US. Finally, we conclude
by considering the implications of our analysis for the nature of change in the US
division of labour in health care, for understanding and coping with the complexity of change that may emerge from any realm of practice at any system level,
and for working towards a model of change in US health professions that fits the
contemporary complexity of this change process. The discussion is consistent,
as we shall demonstrate, with the contention of Schneller and Ott (1996) that new
modes of change characterize the medical division of labour and that such
change may well prevail in the twenty-first century.

Power and Culture in Orchestrating Change within the System of Professions

Much analytic power of Abbott's perspective on the evolution of professions derives
from conceiving them as a *system* of inter-professional competition for exclusive
jurisdiction over domains of practice. Following Bucher and Strauss (1961), we
would add that jurisdictional competition in the health sector, as in education (Jarvis,

Holford and Griffin 2000), may also occur intra-professionally between different specialties of the same profession. The resultant division of labour is perennially in flux. Change is stimulated by a variety of relatively uncontrollable factors. They include knowledge expansion and technological advances, imbalance in the supply of trained professionals, transgression of jurisdictional boundaries by other professions or specialties within a profession, and quality concerns ranging from client safety to professionals' work–life balance. The case of the RCT and the hospitalist show how the division of labour is changing, not through the emergence of new knowledge or the abandonment of an area of knowledge by a profession, but as the result of a detected need for the enhancement of care and the purposive design of roles to meet such needs (Schneller 1978).

For Abbott, jurisdictional boundary maintenance entails claiming and attempting to legitimate exclusive entitlement to practise on the basis of a unique body of formal knowledge, which is separate from professional tasks themselves. This knowledge base is drawn upon selectively when carrying out tasks that entail making inferential diagnoses and formulating treatments in the contingent circumstances of particular practice settings. Esoteric knowledge acquisition is controlled through training and associated credentials that qualify professionals to practise within a jurisdiction. Abbott notes that publicly proclaimed jurisdictional exclusivity is not necessarily enforced in the workplace. Local factors such as staff shortages and negotiated informal arrangements may result in *workplace assimilation*, with tasks being shared privately between professions across publicly proclaimed jurisdictional boundaries.

Protective maintenance of one profession may involve impinging on the jurisdiction of related and potentially competing professions. Forms of new jurisdictional *settlement* emerging from such inter-professional challenges identified by Abbott (1988) (which we would extend to intra-professional negotiations) include:

- *full* – transfer of tasks from one profession/specialty to another;
- *subordination* – transfer or tasks from a dominant to a subordinate profession/specialty;
- *intellectual* – one profession/specialty retains control of knowledge in an area but permits practice by other professions/specialties;
- *divided* – two professions/specialties share tasks;
- *advisory* – one profession/specialty offers input to the activities of another.

The inter- and intra-professional division of labour represented by public settlements may be blurred inside organizations. Jurisdictional tasks may become shared out among professionals, paraprofessionals or untrained personel through workplace assimilation. The latter may learn a craft version of practices, without much of the esoteric knowledge base of the parent profession. In health care, the advent of large institutions, proliferating specialization and multi-specialist teams all render the traditional domination of the medical profession vulnerable to jurisdictional erosion by other groups. The strict boundaries of the past between dominant and subordinate professions are becoming blurred. This shift is a result of increasing flexibility and teamworking that imply some sharing across hitherto separate jurisdictions (Schneller and Ott 1996). Similarly, the exponential growth of specialties within the medical profession offers scope for new boundary-spanning roles, which help further to blur specialty jurisdictional domains.

Perhaps it is overly restrictive to follow Abbott's assumption that the process of inter-professional change (or, by extrapolation, intra-professional change) is necessarily competitive and conflictual. In some instances, erosion of the one-time dominant status of particular professions across the sector is giving way to synergistic alliances, partnerships and collaborations – as well as power struggles. Boundaries are changing. The ascendancy of osteopathic medicine in many parts of the US to equal status with allopathic medicine is one signal of such change. Yet power to change the division of labour is unevenly distributed across the system of professions, and attempts to do so are not always accepted as legitimate. Each stakeholder group has recourse to some leverage over public claims and work-place assimilation. None are all-powerful. To the extent that multiple professional jurisdictions are implicated in contributing to a particular service (whether as formal equals or in a hierarchical dominant–subordinate relationship) contributors are interdependent. Physicians are widely accepted as playing the leading role in treating patients on the basis of their formal medical knowledge. But the power of the medical profession over the subordinate nursing profession is tempered by physicians' dependence on nurses to carry out bedside care. Within the medical profession, every new specialty creates new intra-professional boundaries. They generate potential for inconsistencies or gaps between parts of the service offered by different specialties, and so conditions favouring boundary-spanning roles to coordinate multiple specialist contributions.

Stakeholders use whatever resources they can and deem appropriate (at minimum, their capacity for contributing or withholding their labour) to realize their perceived *interests* – contributing to the fulfilment of their jurisdictional purposes. *Power* may be conceived as 'transformative capacity' (Giddens 1984): by providing the currency to intervene in events so as to alter their course. In this sense, power allows both for synergy to realize shared interests and for conflict to achieve one incompatible interest at the expense of another. Bacharach and Lawler (1980) distinguish two forms of power: *authority* implies the use of resources to achieve interests which are legitimated by beliefs and values associated with status, including the entitlement to apply sanctions. Whereas *influence* implies the informal use of resources to achieve interests without recourse to sanctions connected with authority, though other sanctions (especially withholding labour) may be available. It is within the context of these ideas regarding power that we can better understand jurisdictional contests.

Orchestration in jurisdiction contests

Stakeholder groups, such as professions, may share an *ideology*. The term is used neutrally here to describe a set of beliefs and values shaping a group interest and guiding action to realize it. Such an ideology, together with more subliminal norms and codes of behaviour (Firestone and Louis 1999), constitute the professional *culture* of each group. The complex change management theme of culture building and communication (subordinate to orchestration) implies that one group uses power in attempting to shape the culture of another group. It becomes especially significant where power is widely distributed between interdependent stakeholder groups.

Orchestrators are then reliant on securing the acquiescence or endorsement of another group whose members might otherwise successfully resist a proposed change. But (as discussed in Chapter 1) culture cannot be directly manipulated with reliable results. The response of those who are the target of culture building may depend on the degree of congruence or contradiction between the beliefs and values underlying their current practice and their perceived interests, and those reflected by the change being advocated. Where the existing professional culture is challenged, one response is to engage in extensive organization to block this perceived threat through a *counter-policy*, defined by Wallace and Pocklington (2002: 66) as:

> a proactive response by powerful actors in a locality to a policy initiated elsewhere that they perceive to threaten their beliefs and values, where they harness their institutional resources in a coordinated manner to mediate implementation of this external policy in ways that challenge or subvert the initiators' aims.

One possibility is for orchestrators to try pre-empting such concerted resistance by seeking some *confluence of interests* between themselves and the target group so that both groups cooperate in implementing the change, possibly in an adapted form that maximizes the overlap of interests that has been found. Our two contrasting cases portray how the dynamics of professional change may play out in radically different ways, depending on the degree of culture building and communication activity and the degree of success in reconciling the self-interests of the stakeholder groups implicated.

Upsetting the Inter-Professional System: the Registered Care Technician Proposal

The advent of a chronic nursing shortage in US health care by the mid-1980s led to much debate about the division of labour in US hospitals. It centred on the supply and role of nurses. The stance of the primary nursing professional association, the ANA, was to increase recruitment into nurse training programmes and to improve retention through enhancing nurses' salary and occupational benefits. Healthcare managers actively recruited from within the US and abroad to shore-up the provision of in-patient services reliant on nursing support. The interests of the medical profession came under threat since physicians were so dependent on nurses, as a subordinate profession, to provide bedside care.

In 1987 the AMA, the leading physician professional association, launched a proposal to solve the nursing shortage. A key characteristic of the complexity of this centrally initiated change by a national professional association was its systemic implications. Implementation would depend on nationwide acceptance and support among multiple groups of stakeholders, over whom the AMA did not have jurisdictional authority. One of us (Eugene Schneller) investigated what subsequently happened, through a document survey and a postal questionnaire. The latter was administered to representatives of the various healthcare professional associations, and it explored their response to the AMA proposal (Schneller and Taylor 1990).

The AMA proposal immediately disturbed the uneasy historical settlement between the medical and nursing professions. Consistent with the unique level of authority over health care long claimed by the medical profession (and widely accepted by the general public), AMA officials developed their proposal without consulting other stakeholder groups whose members' interests would be affected, especially the ANA.

The content of the AMA proposal was to create a new occupation, the 'registered care technologist' (a term which was soon changed to 'technician'). RCTs would be non-nurse care workers who would work under the supervision of nurses and report to physicians. They would carry out routine tasks connected with montoring patients and implementing the orders of physicians at the bedside, 'a resource for nurses but not a direct substitute for nurses in long-term care institutions and in acute care hospitals' (AMA 1987). The proposal thus originated with a dominant profession and was designed to reshape the jurisdiction of the subordinate profession, on which the former depended. The proposers sought a new jurisdictional settlement for nursing that meant further subordination of routine tasks to trained RCTs. In Abbott's terms, it would represent an *intellectual* settlement. RCTs would be permitted to practise, while control of nursing knowledge would be retained by the nursing profession.

The absence of consultation suggests that orchestrators of the RCT proposal were concerned more with communicating their solution to the nursing shortage problem than with culture building, perhaps because officials assumed that the authority of the AMA would be sufficient to secure acquiescence from nurses. Not so. Abbott's dictum that 'in contests between professions, the profession with more extensive organization usually wins' was soon borne out. Elaborate orchestration efforts by ANA officials – to block a proposed change rather than to implement one – embodied extensive organization. Orchestration was directed towards developing and implementing a sophisticated counter-policy, designed to defeat the AMA proposal threatening their jurisdiction. It is important to note that the primary ANA goal was to counter this external threat, rather than to address the underlying chronic nursing shortage as such.

Culture building and communication featured centrally in the extensive organization of the ANA. Officials' response was founded on a well-articulated and widely accepted ideology that had contributed to consolidating the existing settlement, positioning qualified nurses as the sole providers of bedside care. The ideology was founded on a 'primary care' nursing model embracing the concept of a 'nursing diagnosis', supported in the nursing literature by considerable research. The primary care nursing model protected nurses' jurisdictional interest through the idea that only professional nursing staff should be involved in bedside care – even for non-technical skills (Manthey 1980). Nurses alone were capable of making a nursing diagnosis, distinguished from that associated with medicine and drawing on a partially distinct knowledge base. Bedside care was the critical locus of activity for nurses holistically to gather information and so fully to understand the complexities of individual patients' diverse needs.

The ANA counter-argument to the RCT proposal rested on the claim that patients would be short-changed of the full value that nurses bring to the bedside if RCTs took on some of their care tasks. Such inroads into the qualified nursing effort would deprive nurses of information which was critical to carrying out their holistic professional nursing role. The proposal would undermine current standards of patient care and safety achieved by nurses. Thus ANA officials readily conceded that RCTs, who would have less formal education than professional nurses, could carry out some bedside care tasks competently. But they would then deprive nurses of information that only they were trained to use in making their nursing diagnosis. Officials asserted that the RCT proposal demonstrated a lack of understanding within the medical profession of the factors associated with high-quality nursing care, and of the consequences for patient safety and healthcare outcomes.

Using influence to isolate the AMA

To increase the chances of the ANA counter-policy working, culture-building and communication efforts were targeted at persuading stakeholder groups other than the medical profession that the proposal to alter the division of labour would be detrimental to their interests. They should therefore support the ANA position. Key groups which must be influenced were healthcare professionals (managers and other professionals in organizations where nursing care was provided) and the wider public – patients, their relatives and others who might need health care in the future. Culture building with these groups focused not only on what would be in their direct interests. It also focused on persuading them that the AMA had stepped beyond the bounds of its legitimate jurisdiction: in acting unilaterally as the change agent for remodelling the nursing profession in particular, and for reconfiguring the division of healthcare labour in general.

ANA activities amounted to very extensive organization to articulate the ANA stance and persuade other stakeholder groups to support their ideology, so isolating the AMA as an inappropriate change agent for nursing. These activities included:

- Gathering information on the nature and scope of the RCT proposal.
- Interpreting the meaning of the proposal for organized nursing.
- Studying current strategies and theories of nursing care.

- Developing a clear and coherent policy concerning the RCT proposal.
- Educating the ANA membership and staff in other healthcare organizations about the RCT proposal.
- Providing occasions for representatives of different organizations to come together in opposition to the RCT.
- Utilizing the RCT issue to reiterate its own pre-existing solution to the nursing crisis outlined earlier.

Since ANA officials had no way of assessing the strength of AMA commitment to implementing the RCT proposal, they assumed that the AMA was serious, committed and could utilize its full resources to achieve its goals. Huckabay (1989: 518) provides a succinct statement of the position emerging in the ANA and nursing educational arena:

> The sooner the nurses face the professional imperative that only they deliver nursing care and establish appropriate levels of quality of care, the sooner the public's confusion will be eliminated, and nurses can assume control over their practice. Nursing directors should support this stand and require the baccalaureate degree to be the minimum requirement for entry into practice.

ANA officials soon built up a focused public relations campaign. Their media blitz reached a variety of national newspapers including the *Wall Street Journal*, *New York Times*, *Chicago Tribune* and *Healthweek*. Television appearances by ANA staff included *CBS Evening News*, ABC's *The Health Show* and *Good Morning America*. Editorials in papers such as the *Boston Globe* came out in strong opposition to the RCT. ANA literature was produced to alert other healthcare professions that the AMA had overstepped the mark. This literature asserted that the AMA was acting independently of nursing and other healthcare delivery occupations, and that failure to consult was an example of the continuing insensitivity of physicians to other health professions.

Support of the physician specialty and state medical associations was also sought in order to harness their anticipated resistance to the AMA proposal, since their consent had not been gained by the AMA in advance of the RCT proposal announcement. The everyday work of physicians is affected by state and local intra-professional politics and labour shortages. Local physicians had witnessed workplace assimilation, with nurses experiencing job expansion and maintaining control over bedside care. These physicians, in attempting to ensure top quality care of their patients, had often encouraged nurses to take on specialty tasks and to participate in a flexible intra-organizational division of labour. ANA officials believed that physicians would not welcome RCTs, with little formal education, as a key bedside care provider for whom physicians would shoulder responsibility. The emerging division of labour increasingly emphasizes physicians and nurses working as a team. Implementing the RCT proposal would ill suit physicians' interest. It would place them in a new and perhaps unwanted supervisory role at the bedside, which could destroy local collaborative physician–nurse relationships. Thus the AMA design of the RCT role violated both emergent and long-accepted principles framing the social organization of the workplace.

Hospital managers were another group that ANA officials targeted, to persuade them that the RCT proposal was not in their interest either. The AMA had not consulted with those associations and individuals involved in managing US hospitals. Yet the American Hospital Association and state hospital associations had been at the forefront of documenting the nursing shortage. And hospital administrators throughout the nation had spent the preceding years working to market their hospitals as attractive environments for nursing. If hospital managers backed the AMA, they risked compromising their workforce interest. They stood to lose potential recruits if their organization was perceived as no longer supportive of a strong nursing staff. As nurses became more militant, the ANA suggested in print that the introduction of a non-nurse caregiver at the bedside could lead to strikes and the inability of hospitals to recruit nurses. Building extensive organization entailed a 'divide and rule' approach to culture building among the health professions and service organizations where practice would be most changed by the introduction of the RCT role.

Nurses were also targeted. A pamphlet distributed by the ANA (1989) to its members contained a list of 'warning signs' associated with any attempt to introduce the RCT role in a given facility. Advice on resistance strategies included:

- Organizing nursing staff to defeat any attempt to bring in RCTs.
- Seeking the cooperation and support of physicians and other healthcare personnel.
- Gaining the assistance of nursing administration to communicate to boards of hospital trustees.
- Increasing nurse representation on appropriate hospital bodies.
- Using collective bargaining processes.
- Examining personnel policies.
- Urging staff development educators to refuse to participate in activity related to introducing the RCT role.
- Direct action (which might extend to strikes) at the 'first sign of activity'.

The AMA proposal had soon been followed up with an associated curriculum for training of RCTs. While AMA officials claimed that they had identified sites for RCTs to be introduced, none were ever publicly announced. Capitulation came in 1990 when the AMA House of Delegates voted to 'cease the Association's activities to recruit Registered Care Technician program sites'. The traditionally accepted authority of the AMA had been challenged, and the extensive organization of the ANA, maximizing the use of influence in culture building and communication, had triumphed in protecting the jurisdiction of a subordinate profession. The existing jurisdictional settlement remained in place, but the nursing shortage remained unresolved.

Reshaping Intra-Professional Jurisdictions: Emergence of the Hospitalist Movement

Let us now shift focus towards a contrasting change in the medical division of labour, which no one initially proposed. Moreover, it has been achieved without attempting either to capture another profession's body of knowledge or to secure exclusive intra-professional dominion over a new body of knowledge. The hospitalist movement emerged at the local level during the 1990s, gradually becoming conceived as a single entity and spreading across the US healthcare system without significant conflict.

Hospitalists are a new specialty within the medical profession. They take over responsibility for the care of acutely ill patients during their stay in hospital from the primary care physician or non-hospital-based specialist who may have admitted them to hospital. They liaise with medical specialists who treat these patients' illness, and with nursing staff, patients' families and their primary care physician, acting as physician of record. Hospitalists take responsibility for discharging patients when they have sufficiently recovered, normally returning them to the care of the primary care physician. They therefore act as the agent of acutely ill patients while they are largely incapacitated from making their own medical decisions, and of patients' primary care physician.

Experiments with new boundary-spanning roles for coordinating hospitalized patient care have been tried sporadically in individual hospitals since the 1980s. Not until much later was the label 'hospitalist' coined by Wachter and Goldman (1996), who are leading university medical school advocates of more coordinated provision for hospitalized patients. The label was quickly adopted as the umbrella term for moderately diverse roles in what became conceived as an expanding movement. By 2004, hospitalists were being employed to care for an estimated 60 per cent of hospitalized patients in the US. The Society of Hospital Medicine (SHM), a nationwide professional association for hospitalists launched in 1997, had become firmly established as the leading national organization providing resources and a collective voice for hospitalists with 4000 members. An SHM (2004) estimate puts the number of hospitalists at 10,000 and offers a projection of some 25,000 by the year 2010.

This change emerged as dispersed and unrelated responses among healthcare professionals to local patient care coordination problems in particular hospitals. It gradually diffused across the country without significant government involvement or regulation, but with local and eventually national orchestration. There is not a strong federal policy framework driving US healthcare reform, and we have noted how change rarely originates with government. Change tends to follow revelations that the system is failing: whether in terms of the chronic nursing shortage that featured in our first case, variable healthcare performance, the high cost of diagnosis and treatment, or patient safety. Varied adaptive innovations tend to be developed locally, reflecting diverse circumstances. But dissemination of information across the healthcare professions is rapid. Disparate innovations may become labelled as local instances of a more systemic and routinized innovation – as with the hospitalist movement – that is eventually accepted as the new norm.

It is questionable how system-like US health care really is, having been described as 'an enormously complex, trillion dollar industry . . . the US health care system is the world's eighth largest economy, second to that of France, and larger than the total economy of Italy' (Sultz and Young 2004). This 'industry' is founded on a diversity of local private sector insurance and entrepreneurial service provision, philanthropic not-for-profit services and arrangements to manage regional provision of health care while containing costs. Limited state and federal government funding exists primarily to ensure that elderly, disabled and poor citizens receive baseline care. Some 25 per cent of the population has no health insurance, the basis of citizens' entitlement to healthcare services.

We undertook a small-scale investigation of the hospitalist movement in 2004, interviewing an opportunity sample of 13 informants and scrutinizing relevant literature and websites. Our aim was to gather information from occupants of different hospitalist and related managerial and educator roles. We chose contrasting organizational settings, which might affect informants' motivation for involvement in the emergence and expansion of the hospitalist movement:

- A private not-for-profit *elite hospital and ambulatory care clinic* employing its own hospitalists, belonging to a charitable foundation set up at the end of the nineteenth century.
- A *physician health organization* located within a private not-for-profit system of healthcare facilities servicing subscribers to a health insurance company plan, which outsourced the services of self-employed hospitalists.
- A private for-profit *hospitalist company*, employing and training its own hospitalists who were contracted to provide services in various hospitals.
- A hospital linked to a university *medical school* at the forefront of the hospitalist movement, whose staff practised as hospitalists.
- A university *medical education consortium* providing initial education for medical doctors.

As already indicated, there is no unequivocal point where the hospitalist movement can be said to have begun. According to the medical educator we interviewed, it had been quite common over the years for medical staff in particular hospitals to negotiate some kind of coordination responsibility for acute patient care, instead of the more typical involvement of patients' primary care physician. A recent survey of hospitalists indicated that many actually began their inpatient practices in the 1980s (Wachter 1999). This finding suggests that workplace assimilation had long occurred whereby specific, mutually acceptable arrangements for inpatient care were negotiated locally. Within the system of professions, this change in practice might represent a threat to the entrenched interests of physicians occupying different roles inside the medical profession. It had the potential to create conditions for intra-professional conflict.

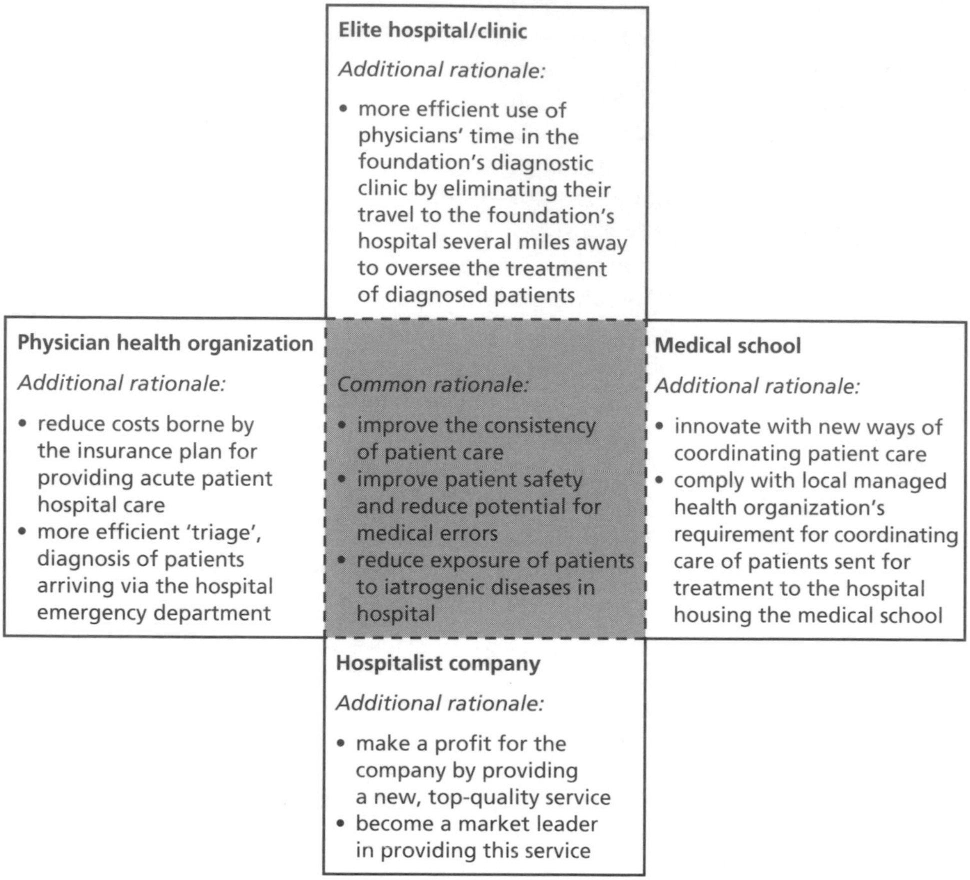

Elite hospital/clinic

Additional rationale:

- more efficient use of
  physicians' time in the
  foundation's diagnostic
  clinic by eliminating their
  travel to the foundation's
  hospital several miles away
  to oversee the treatment
  of diagnosed patients

Physician health organization	Common rationale:	Medical school
Additional rationale:		*Additional rationale:*
• reduce costs borne by the insurance plan for providing acute patient hospital care • more efficient 'triage', diagnosis of patients arriving via the hospital emergency department	• improve the consistency of patient care • improve patient safety and reduce potential for medical errors • reduce exposure of patients to iatrogenic diseases in hospital	• innovate with new ways of coordinating patient care • comply with local managed health organization's requirement for coordinating care of patients sent for treatment to the hospital housing the medical school

Hospitalist company

Additional rationale:

- make a profit for the
  company by providing
  a new, top-quality service
- become a market leader
  in providing this service

Figure 8.1 Rationales for developing hospitalist practices in different organizational settings

Such local arrangements were straightforward in terms of the medical coordination tasks involved. They were conducted by a few individuals in any hospital, unrelated to what might be happening in other hospitals, unregulated beyond extant requirements for medical practice, and unidentified with any new label. What came to be denoted as the 'hospitalist' role began with disparate practices. They entailed different forms of employment, depending on the organizational base. Contrasting origins of the hospitalist practices in four informants' organizational bases illustrate how a common interest in maintaining or improving the quality of acute patient care accompanied diverse additional motivations (Figure 8.1). The shared concern with quality, coupled with the fact that the change was taking place within the medical profession (widely viewed by patients as authoritative in medical matters), favoured ready acceptance of the new role.

A full jurisdictional settlement within the medical profession is accreting in hospitals up and down the country. Various medical personnel, and especially primary care physicians, have stood to lose not only control over the hospital care of their patients but also the remuneration they hitherto received for assuming this responsibility themselves. But sufficient confluence of interests appears to have been achieved among key stakeholders affected by the employment of hospitalists (and who could have resisted this move) to bring about their cooperation and endorsement.

For the *elite hospital/ambulatory care clinic*, employing hospitalists in its newly built hospital solved a local problem, which was to the advantage of diagnostic physicians based at the foundation's clinic. (Primary care physicians were not directly affected here, as the foundation took formal responsibility for diagnosis and treatment.) An unintended consequence of a decision to build the hospital several miles from the clinic was to soak up a significant proportion of diagnostic physicians' time each week. They had to travel between the clinic and the hospital to supervise hospital treatment for patients whose illness they had previously diagnosed. Handing over responsibility for managing treatment to hospitalists enabled the diagnostic physicians to make more efficient use of their time by remaining in the clinic, so catering for a larger number of patients. A new intra-professional division of medical labour could thus be smoothly implemented, since it suited the interests of hospitalists and diagnostic physicians alike. As with all hospitalist arrangements, its effectiveness relied on accurate communication of medical information between hospitalists and other physicians involved.

For the *physician health organization* (PHO), contracting hospitalists to manage acute patient care saved money for the insurance plan paying for this care. The hospitalists built up 'triage' expertise, diagnosing whether patients who turned up in the emergency department actually needed treatment. They then saw to hospital care for those who required it, but determined the earliest point when they could be discharged safely afterwards. The fewer patients who were hospitalized and the less time they spent in the hospital, the less the insurance plan paid out. The financial cost to the PHO of paying for the hospitalists' service was demonstrated to be less than the money saved. Here the new arrangement had proved to suit the financial efficiency interest of hospital managers and the employment interest of hospitalists. Records soon demonstrated that patient safety had not been compromised. Primary care physicians associated with the plan were paid on a capitated basis. So they experienced no loss of income with contracted hospitalists assuming care of their capitated patients. On the contrary, they were free to see a larger number of patients in their offices (surgeries), thus increasing their incomes.

The *hospitalist company* was the brainchild of a medical doctor who judged that market conditions were favourable for a new approach to managing inpatient care. Hospitalists could take over responsibility for patients referred by their primary care physician while in hospital. This arrangement would save primary care physicians from having to travel to the hospital to visit their patients. He secured venture capital to set up a company employing hospitalists, contracting to provide a service which would be financially attractive to hospital staff and primary care physicians. The envisioned role of hospitalists would be in the interests of the other key stakeholder groups. Hospitalists could save hospitals and insurers money by discharging patients promptly. They could also enable primary care physicians to make more money by seeing more patients in their office, because they no longer travelled so frequently to the hospital. The rapid expansion of the company, soon providing services in cities across several states, testified to his business acumen and the confluence of interests he had perhaps foreseen.

Experimentation with new technology, treatments and the management of care was integral to the work of academics in the *medical school*. Very able beginning practitioners were trained here and some were subsequently appointed to medical posts. They were encouraged to innovate and to disseminate good practice. A local factor also featured. The managers of a local community hospital organization applied pressure for a coordinated approach to the care of acutely ill patients whom they referred to the medical school hospital for treatment. The medical school academics perceived that it would not be in their interest to lose control over the hospital care of these patients, with community hospital physicians visiting instead to care for them during their treatment in the medical school's hospital. The academics therefore engaged in local protective maintenance to retain their existing intra-professional jurisdiction over such patients.

Nurturing intra-professional acceptance of the hospitalist movement

Culture building and communication played an increasingly important part as the hospitalist movement gathered momentum. Wachter and Goldman were senior academics in this medical school who became national orchestrators of the movement, employing extensive organization appropriate to the circumstances. Their coining in 1996 of the unificatory term of 'hospitalist' was instrumental in generating a sense of diverse inpatient medical care practices being, nevertheless, of a kind. These practices now became increasingly perceived as different expressions of the same phenomenon. Publication of Wachter and Goldman's paper raised medical and wider public awareness across the country, creating conditions for the diffusion of ideas and active networking between organizations. They ensured that their medical school became a hub of this network, reinforcing the shift of perception through unificatory culture-building activities. These efforts included consulting, negotiating and establishing continuing medical education programmes for hospitalists, and helping to found and promote the growth of the national professional association, SHM.

Time was also a contributory cultural factor. Gradually, increasing numbers of experienced hospitalists moved on in their careers, spreading the word and experimenting in their new organizational settings. Some agencies providing hospitalist services expanded to cover multiple hospitals in different states, as with the hospitalist company referred to earlier.

But overall the hospitalist movement remains an emergent and widely dispersed change. Central culture building and communication through SHM activity continues to be significant. It includes providing an annual national conference and regular regional forums for hospitalists, liaising with politicians and representatives of powerful stakeholder groups (an early success for SHM was affiliation with the American College of Physicians), articulating quality standards, and promoting national certification for hospitalists. But it is weak compared with the decentralized drivers of hospitalist medicine, operating in different locations, and for partially divergent healthcare and economic reasons (Figure 8.1). There seems little prospect of the specialty carving out an exclusive jurisdiction as a new profession, since hospitalists command no unique knowledge base. But they span the intra-professional boundary between longer established medical specialties. Their knowledge base brings together as the basis for inference what would otherwise be distributed among specialists and the primary care physician, and so more prone to failures of communication which might compromise patient safety. The confluence of interests between hospitalists, clients, other medical professions, managers and payers seems sufficient to underpin further expansion and consolidation of the hospitalist movement.

Conclusion

Our two cases of attempted and actual change in the US division of labour in health care illustrate how the nature of professions and their interrelationships are not only in continual flux but are also becoming more complex. Jurisdictional boundaries are becoming fuzzier with the advent of multiple roles – sometimes purposively boundary spanning – that contribute to healthcare practice. Advances in ever more differentiated medical knowledge and technology, coupled with imperatives for workplace assimilation (whether driven by labour shortages or the synergy of complementary craft expertise) are undermining the old healthcare hierarchy topped by the medical profession.

One case documents how a change was stopped; the other documents how a change was made to happen in this context of increasing ambiguity and accelerating evolution. Both portray some of the complexities of the change process in a technologically advanced but organizationally distributed healthcare system. The importance of national context for understanding and managing change is underscored, as is the need for caution in generalizing across systems and services beyond a fairly high level of abstraction. The capacity for non-governmental initiation of change by professional associations and the potential for emergence exist in US health care for contextual reasons: its historically determined configuration as a diverse and distributed system, the pattern of inter- and intra-professional jurisdictions, the diverse sources of resourcing and extensive access to high technology. The 'tax and spend' economic orientation allowing UK central government ministers to conceive of a single strategy for programmatically modernizing all public services scarcely occurs in the US.

Aspects of Mike Wallace's practical planning framework for addressing the complexity of public service change (Chapter 1) have a moderate degree of applicability for interpreting our cases, at a high level of abstraction. The framework centres on the complexity of change. So it offers analytical purchase only insofar as a change expresses the characteristics of complexity to a significant degree.

The 'context-dependence' characteristic of complexity allows for the possibility that the nature of change may be affected by economic, social and political factors. The RCT proposal had the potential to become quite complex to manage: it was conceived on a national scale, and its implementation would have required extensive training arrangements and workplace assimilation. Perhaps, as with other innovations (Schneller 1978) it would have become institutionalized and elevated to a field where there was universalistic certification and licensure. But this, of course, did not happen.

The emergent and locally driven hospitalist movement did not possess the entitiness of a single, complex change until it gained a central advocacy and a facilitatory organization. Even then the degree of centralization remains modest in comparison with the expansion of locally determined arrangements. This case suggests that the framework only begins to have strong application if and when an emergent change coalesces to become reasonably systemic across a public service. More obviously applicable is the subordinate change management theme of culture building and communication, crucial to the ANA orchestration of its counter-policy at the national level. It was equally crucial to pre-empting resistance and gaining support for hospitalists to carve out their role at the local level, later augmented nationally by the founding of its professional association.

Our account testifies to Abbott's insightfulness in asserting that analysis should not bracket individual professions. Rather, they should be examined as an interacting system, where each profession is part of the context for others. Thus, each healthcare occupation is part of the context for others, and change in the division of labour implies some form of mutual adjustment in professional cultures supporting whatever inter- and intra-professional settlement exists. Abbott's notion of 'extensive organization' captures how the formal ordering of power associated with the medical division of labour can be 'trumped' through influence that mobilizes resistance, or incrementally reordered through influence that mobilizes acceptance through securing a confluence of interests.

On the other hand, Abbott's conception underplays the possibility that such interaction might be collaborative for mutual advantage in terms of perceived interests, so not necessarily competitive. Any theory inevitably reflects the milieu in which it was generated. Changes over the last decade or so run to the nature of professional work, its knowledge base, perceptions of the legitimacy of exclusive jurisdictions, laws affecting professions' capacity for protective maintenance (Jost 1997), the emphasis on performance measurement, concern for patient safety and sanctions for malpractice. The system of professions, with their exclusive jurisdictions, is no longer what it used to be. Further theoretical development is therefore required to understand and explain the way things are changing now.

Schneller and Ott (1996) predicted that many of the future changes in the US medical division of labour would be brought about by individual and frequently isolated workplace settlements – rather than the result of large-scale changes in licensure or certification of new kinds of practitioners. Since that time, it has become clear that local settlements reflecting workplace assimilation are indeed the norm. But as these settlements prove to solve problems related to either the delivery of care or to extra-clinical issues including cost and access, workplace innovations may become memorialized and transformed into formal movements, as with hospitalists. A stronger theoretical focus is therefore needed on the negotiation of workplace practices linked to the potential for their incorporation into larger-scale movements. This theoretical development should take into account the context of expanding ambiguity (as conceptualized in Chapter 4). It should also embrace how the division of labour is rendered increasingly diverse and fluid within structural limits, due to external factors beyond professional control and the multiplicity of contributions to the provision of public services.

REFERENCES

Abbott, A. (1988) *The System of Professions: an Essay on the Division of Labor*. Chicago: University of Chicago Press.

AMA (1987) *Report SS: Registered Care Technologist*. Chicago: American Medical Association.

ANA (1989) *Defeating the RCT Proposal and Similar Workplace Strategies*. Kansas City, MO: American Nurses Association.

Bacharach, S. and Lawler, E. (1980) *Power and Politics in Organizations*. San Francisco: Jossey-Bass.

Bucher, R. and Strauss, A. (1961) Professions in process. *American Journal of Sociology*, **65**, 325–34.

Feldstein, P. (1988) *The Politics of Health Legislation*. Ann Arbor, MI: Health Administration Press.

Firestone, W. and Louis, K.S. (1999) Schools as cultures. In J. Murphy and K.S. Louis (eds), *Handbook of Research on Educational Administration*, 2nd edn. San Francisco: Jossey-Bass, pp. 297–322.

Freidson, E. (1970) *The Profession of Medicine*. New York: Dodd Mead.

Giddens, A. (1984) *The Constitution of Society*. Cambridge: Polity Press.

Huckabay, L. (1989) Professional issues facing the field of nursing services. In B. Henry, C. Arndt, M. DiVincenti and A. Marriner-Tomey (eds), *Dimensions of Nursing Administration: Theory, Research, Education and Practice*. Cambridge, MA: Blackwell Scientific Publications, pp. 515–35.

Jarvis, P., Holford, J. and Griffin, C. (2000) *Problems of Mapping the Field of Education for Adults through the Literature*. AERC Proceedings. http://www.edst.educ.ubc.ca/aerc/2000/jarvispandetal-web.htm (accessed April 2005).

Jost, T. (ed.) (1997) *Regulation of the Health Care Professions*. Chicago: Health Administration Press.

Manthey, M. (1980) *The Practice of Primary Nursing*. Boston: Blackwell Scientific Publications.

Schneller, E. (1978) *The Physician's Assistant: Innovation in the Medical Division of Labor*. Lanham, MD: Lexington Books.

Schneller, E. and Epstein, K. (2005) The hospitalist movement in the United States: agency and common agency issues. Unpublished manuscript, Arizona State University, Phoenix AZ.

Schneller, E. and Ott, J.A. (1996) Contemporary models of change in the health professions. *Hospitals and Health Services Administration*, **41**(1), 121–36.

Schneller, E. and Taylor, M. (1990) Affirming jurisdiction: response to the AMA proposal to establish the registered care technologist. Paper presented at meetings of the American Sociological Association, Washington DC.

Society of Hospital Medicine (2004) Growth of hospital medicine nationwide. www.hospitalmedicine.com (accessed June 2004).

Sultz, H. and Young, K. (2004) *Health Care USA*, 4th edn. Sudbury, MA: Jones and Bartlett.

Wachter, R. (1999) The hospitalist movement: ten issues to consider. *Hospital Practice*, **34**, 95–111.

Wachter, R. and Goldman, L. (1996) The emerging role of 'hospitalists' in the American health care system. *New England Journal of Medicine*, **335**, 514–17.

Wallace, M. (1998) A counter-policy to subvert education reform? Collaboration among schools and colleges in a competitive climate. *British Educational Research Journal*, **24**(2), 195–215.

Wallace, M. and Pocklington, K. (2002) *Managing Complex Educational Change: Large-Scale Reorganization of Schools*. London: RoutledgeFalmer.

CHAPTER 9

HOW IS KNOWLEDGE TRANSFERRED BETWEEN ORGANIZATIONS INVOLVED IN CHANGE?

Jean Hartley and Lyndsay Rashman

The promotion of knowledge transfer between public service organizations is explored in this chapter, as a way of orchestrating the spread of good practice and encouraging the creative adaptation of what works in one setting to other organizational contexts. Jean Hartley and Lyndsay Rashman pursue a knowledge-for-action intellectual project. They draw on their research into a UK central government scheme for fostering knowledge transfer between local government organizations with a view to conceptualizing more generically how inter-organizational knowledge transfer may be brought about.

This national scheme represents quite a complex change in itself, enacted on a large scale, and involving multiple components. It entails the prior evaluation and public identification of good practice in service provision, coupled with an obligation to 'disseminate' that good practice. Other organizations in the same institutional field are encouraged to learn from this good practice, and to try new and improved ways of doing things.

Hartley and Rashman reject the assumption underlying the framing of this scheme that there can be a simple transfer of 'best' practice knowledge, since what can be made to work is often heavily dependent on the organizational and local context. Stress is also placed on the learning that is integral to changing practice (discussed also in Chapter 4). Transfer of knowledge implies learning to make that knowledge useful in contingent circumstances. Doing so, they argue, requires the flexibility to adapt – rather than merely adopt – others' good practice.

They derive a model which may have broader applicability for nurturing the conditions and capabilities needed for effective diffusion, through adaptation, of local innovations and good practice. It is based not on 'dissemination' of existing knowledge but on the interactions between the source and recipient organization, and the characteristics of these organizations which, from the research evidence, facilitate both knowledge creation and transfer for the new context. Their focus on enhancing emergent inter-organizational learning is complemented by Casebeer in Chapter 10.

Introduction

Knowledge creation and transfer is particularly valuable for public service organizations but is poorly understood. Our purpose, therefore, is to examine the concepts of knowledge and knowledge transfer to underpin theory building and practical action in the diffusion of changes across public service organizations. Significantly, we propose a model of inter-organizational knowledge creation and transfer. The model is based on research evidence from national surveys and case studies of English local authorities. (Local government in England takes the form of local authorities, run by local councils whose political members are regularly elected. Executive functions carried out by local authority officials relate to local provision of school education, social services and other public services.) Implications for knowledge transfer in other sectors and contexts, and the implications for influencing complex change, are examined.

The value of knowledge as an asset for organizations has been well established. Firms can achieve strategic advantage over competitors by developing and leveraging organizational knowledge (Nahapiet and Ghoshal 1988; Nonaka 1994). Knowledge has become as important as financial, physical, technological or human assets across all sectors. Knowledge can be used to generate and support change (both planned and emergent), to implement value-creating strategies and to increase organizational performance. Globalization of manufacturing and services, the application of information and communication technologies, and restructuring to achieve more distributed modes of organizing work have increased the importance of knowledge acquisition and transfer for firms (Argote, McEvily and Reagans 2003).

Competition has not traditionally been the engine of innovation and change for public service organizations (though this situation has been changing over the last two decades). However, the catalysts which influence the drive to gain and utilize knowledge are pervasive. Benington (2000) adds to the above factors additional forces such as the increasing role of the European Union, the changing demographic composition (an ageing population in European countries, more single-person households, the changing structures of families) and increasing needs, expectations and demands from service users. Finger and Brand (1999) also note the increasing pressures on governments across the world to do more with fewer financial and staffing resources. Some writers suggest that governments and public services are attempting to forge a shift to new political and organizational forms which are citizen-centred and based on networks across the public, private and voluntary sectors, and between levels of government (Benington 2000; Newman 2001). All require greater knowledge sharing and transfer.

In the public services, there are pressures not only to acquire and use knowledge, but also to share it with other organizations. Innovations in public services are often spread through open, collaborative networks, and between organizations, services and institutional fields. This contrasts with the deliberate protection of innovations in many parts of the private sector. Protective practices include patents and property rights, and limiting the sharing of knowledge either to benchmarking across dissimilar firms or industries or to strategic alliance partners. Sharing knowledge in public services is undertaken voluntarily in order to contribute to improving services; to try to develop and maintain standards across the nation; to achieve more integrated or 'joined-up' services; and to provide value for money by adapting existing practice rather than ploughing investment into reinventing the wheel. Some organizations in the public service sector have developed an enthusiasm for sharing their good practice with other organizations in part because this enhances their reputation, both within particular professional groups and also with central government. They hope that a strong reputation enhances influence with and resources from central government.

Improving public services is not just about each organization, or even a strategic alliance of organizations, but rather improvements in public services as a whole, and the public sphere more generally. Public service organizations are embedded in society. They produce not only benefits (and obligations) for individuals but also provide public goods and services, establishing collective efficiency, and constituting collective rules and purposes (such as human rights, justice and freedom) (Marquand 2004).

On the other hand, there are also pressures to avoid or restrict the sharing of knowledge, both within and between public service organizations. In the UK, the highly centralized national government has generated some competition for resources and reputation among local public service organizations. Its establishment of an elaborate and pervasive regime of inspection and audit of local public services has discouraged the sharing of and learning from mistakes and improvement journeys.

In addition, the increasing use of privatization, contracting out of services to the private sector, and market testing of service provision has increased competition. There is a danger that the narrowed sharing of innovation or good practice seen in the private sector may be an unintended consequence. Finally, sharing knowledge between individuals, teams and organizations can be complex and problematic, for cognitive, social and political reasons.

However, while knowledge transfer and its use in change and improvement initiatives has grown considerably in scale and importance over the last two decades, theory development lags behind practice. First, there are varying conceptions of what is understood by knowledge, and how knowledge is developed, used and acquired by individuals and organizations. Second, depending on the epistemological approach taken to knowledge, there are a variety of explanations of how, why and whether knowledge is transferred between organizations. Easterby-Smith and Lyles (2005) document the diversity of approaches and note four main areas of research and practice: organizational learning; the learning organization;

organizational knowledge; and knowledge management. This chapter is located particularly in understanding organizational knowledge and organizational learning. This requires an understanding of how organizational learning takes place.

Moreover, empirical research lags behind conceptual development (Bapuji and Crossan 2004). In particular, relatively few studies have examined whether the acquisition and use of organizational knowledge actually leads to improvements, either in organizational functioning or in outputs and outcomes (which include higher quality or more responsive services, or impacts on citizens and communities). Most of the literature focuses on the private sector, with theorizing about the processes and the competitive advantage for the individual firm (or with its subsidiaries, alliances and network members). Less attention has been paid to knowledge transfer by public service organizations, with their different goals, and policy and institutional context. It is widely recognized that context is critical to understanding organizational knowledge and knowledge transfer (e.g. Lave 1993; Tsoukas and Vladimirou 2001), but this acknowledgement has not been systematically used to analyse public service organizations, or the range of differences which can exist both within and between public and private organizations and their contexts. Bate and Robert (2002) note that, in contrast to the private sector, the conceptualization and practice of knowledge transfer to enhance organizational learning and performance in public service organizations is in its infancy. Contextual and strategic differences impose limitations in transferring theory and empirical findings about knowledge transfer from private firms to public services (Hartley 2005).

In policy terms, the last decade has seen considerable emphasis on the sharing and transfer of knowledge as a means to improve public services (Hartley and Benington 2006). National policy mechanisms, such as healthcare collaboratives and the Beacon Schemes in health, education, local government and other local public services, have built upon a tradition of local and informal practitioner networks and established practitioner benchmarking groups as a source of new ideas. The growth of local, regional and national networks and inter-agency partnerships has encouraged a more outward-looking approach and opportunities for increased interaction with others (Newman, Raine and Skelcher 2001). However, Hartley and Benington (2006: 102) note that:

> while central government has emphasized the importance of learning across organizations and between sectors, it has not developed any clear theory or strategy for knowledge transfer and application . . . There seems to be an underlying assumption that all and any sharing of knowledge is somehow beneficial for public service organizations, staff, users and citizens.

Knowledge Creation and Transfer

Dixon (2000) makes a helpful distinction between information and knowledge, noting that information is data that has been sorted, ordered and displayed (e.g.

in books, databases and standard operating procedure manuals). It exists separately from the individual, team or organization that created it. Knowledge, by contrast, is concerned with the understandings which people create or develop – and is inextricably linked to human functioning. Others also make this distinction. For example, Nonaka and Takeuchi (1995: 58–9) argue that: 'Information is a flow of messages, while knowledge is created by that very flow of information, anchored in the beliefs and commitment of its holder, which emphasizes that knowledge is physically and socially embedded.'

Not all knowledge researchers maintain this distinction. Some continue to treat knowledge as though it is a disembodied commodity, with the emphasis on organizational capture of individual knowledge in, for example, electronic forms. However, this chapter follows the line of argument taken by seminal writers such as Tsoukas and Vladimirou (2001), Nonaka (1994) and Blackler (1995) that knowledge is not something that people have but something they do. Knowledge is therefore intimately related to both context and practice.

This view of knowledge as socially constructed and embedded through praxis is underpinned by the conceptual distinction between tacit and explicit knowledge (Polanyi 1966), which has been elaborated by other writers (e.g. Nonaka 1994). Explicit knowledge can be articulated in formal systems (such as language and mathematics) and captured in language-based records (such as those in libraries, archives and databases).

Tacit knowledge cannot be precisely communicated through formal language systems: it cannot be written down. It has both cognitive and motor elements and forms the basis of individual skills. Cognitive elements 'centre on the working models of the world of human beings which are created and manipulated analogies in their minds' (Nonaka 1994: 16). These include schemata, paradigms, beliefs and viewpoints providing perspectives that help individuals to define and perceive their world. The technical or motor element of knowledge 'covers concrete know-how, crafts and skills that apply to specific contexts' (Nonaka 1994: 16). These can include a range of practical skills, political leadership skills and the skills and judgements of change management. Tacit knowledge underpins all explicit knowledge, as an understanding of how to use explicit knowledge generally requires an understanding of context and culture if it is to be effective.

Awareness of the tacit dimension of knowledge acquisition, transfer and use is evident in the research perspectives which see organizational knowledge as socially constructed. They build on the concept of communities of practice (Brown and Duguid 1991; Lave and Wenger 1991) to explain how fluid, self-organizing groups of individuals form knowledge networks and create new collective knowledge by sharing experiences of particular practices. Means of sharing include informal interaction, story telling and exchanging metaphors and anecdotes (Nonaka and Takeuchi 1995). This emphasis on knowledge creation through social practice appears to be particularly appropriate to the multiple actors, professional disciplines and co-production of services of public service organizations, in situations where complex and non-routine knowledge is required to bring about innovation and change. It is central to complex change and its orchestration (Wallace and Pocklington 2002).

In this chapter, we focus particularly on organizational knowledge creation as a social or collective practice, where individuals participate in networks of communication to share knowledge and generate shared meanings (Brown and Duguid 2001). In organizations undertaking or undergoing complex change and operating in a relatively turbulent environment, knowledge use entails both the creation of new knowledge and also its transfer through learning and praxis. The creation of new knowledge and its transfer between individuals, units and organizations do not occur independently. Therefore the processes of knowledge generation and its transfer are 'inexorably intertwined' (Newell *et al.* 2003).

Dissemination, Organizational Learning and Organizational Capacity

Traditional approaches to the diffusion of innovation, or the sharing of good or 'best' practices, focus on the transfer of knowledge through dissemination of information among a group of individuals concerned with the uptake of new ideas. Often, such approaches are based on the assumption that there is a (single) 'best practice' which can be transferred, wholesale, and in a single move, to a new site. Yet in practice, knowledge may be inherently difficult to transfer. Some characteristics of the transfer situation, as well as those of the knowledge being transferred may be said to be 'sticky' (Szulanski 2003), requiring considerable effort to produce transfer – even where individuals or teams are motivated to share ideas and practices.

The issue can be illustrated from research into sharing good practice through the Beacon Scheme in local government (Downe, Hartley and Rashman 2004; Rashman, Downe and Hartley 2005). In the 2004 national survey of local authority use of learning through the Beacon Scheme, 79 per cent of those elected members and managers who had visited a Beacon Council to gain new ideas and practices said they had made changes in their own organization which were wholly or mainly due to the visit. Interestingly, the transfer of learning was an active process of reading the context and culture, and modifying practices to fit the new context. Among those implementing changes, 63 per cent said that they had made a change through adapting a Beacon Council idea. Over a quarter (29 per cent) said that the visit had helped them to push through or accelerate an idea for change that they already had. Only 8 per cent said that they based their change closely on the Beacon Council.

These findings suggest that adaption rather than adoption is central to knowledge transfer: innovation continues to occur at all stages in the process, in response to particular circumstances and resources. They imply that 'replication' rarely takes place, and that we need therefore to reconsider ideas about 'dissemination' and 'adoption' of knowledge. Hartley and Benington (2006) have argued that 'graft and transplant' becomes a more appropriate metaphor than 'copy and paste' to understand inter-organizational knowledge transfer.

This active, socially constructed perspective on knowledge acquisition and transfer is reflected in recent interest both in absorptive capacity, and in public service organizational capacity. But the organization's ability to acquire, assimilate, transform and apply new knowledge for organizational purposes is far from straightforward. Cohen and Levinthal (1990) coined the term 'absorptive capacity' to describe the ability of organizations to recognize and use new knowledge based on their existing knowledge and experience. An organization needs to have sufficient absorptive capacity, the stock of prior knowledge which will make it able to recognize the value of new knowledge and to transfer and apply it successfully.

Internal organizational capacity is a major concern of UK policy-makers who have emphasized its importance for change and improvement of public service organizations. Organizational capacity, rather than motivation, is likely to support or prevent the transfer of knowledge to local public services (Greenhalgh *et al.* 2004). The organizational value depends on creating effective social interaction and network structures for inter- and intra-organizational transfer of knowledge. Research into local government organizations found a strong correlation between proactive, externally oriented leadership and organizational innovative capacity. An established tradition of participation in inter-organizational networks helped to create knowledge flows, structures and systems, as well as receptivity to change and a predisposition to adopt and adapt to new policy measures (Newman, Raine and Skelcher 2001). Organizational capacity involves not only the ability to assimilate new knowledge but also the ability to apply such knowledge to lead and manage complex organizational change and bring about improvements.

Inter-organizational relationships, networks and partnerships have been a key driver of innovation and change in public services, and for creating capacity through collaborative action. Networks, whether temporary or more longstanding, formal or informal, can be important catalysts and facilitators of sharing good practice across the public services (Hartley and Benington 2006; Rashman and Radnor 2005).

Testing a Framework of Knowledge Transfer through the Beacon Scheme

Many of these ideas are captured in the framework for understanding and developing knowledge transfer which we will present shortly. It has been developed from and tested through detailed empirical research with English local authorities in a large and longitudinal research programme. The research aimed to monitor and evaluate the impact of the Beacon Scheme on improvement in local government. The focus included examining the extent to which inter-organizational learning took place. The data drawn on for the present chapter include two national surveys and a set of 12 detailed and multi-respondent case studies. The first survey was sent to all English local authorities in 2001 and the second in 2004. The first included responses from both strategic and service managers, while the second included these and local politicians responsible for the leadership of the local authorities.

The first survey achieved a 47 per cent response rate, with 180 local authorities completing the survey. The second achieved a 49 per cent response rate, from 191 local authorities. Actual numbers of completed questionnaires were higher, reflecting the range of respondents in each local authority.

The Beacon Scheme was originally called the Beacon Council Scheme from its inception in 1999 to mid-2005. It has two main elements for improving the performance of English local government and other local public services (Rashman and Hartley 2002). First, the Beacon Scheme provides national recognition through a competitive application and award scheme. It is run annually by central government, with awards for local authorities which are judged to be models of excellence, of innovation, or both in specific service themes. Second, the Beacon Scheme aims to diffuse knowledge and application of good and excellent practice so that all councils can continuously improve. It has been widely perceived as succeeding in its aims of sharing good practice (Downe, Hartley and Rashman 2004) and contributing to service improvement (Rashman, Downe and Hartley 2005). The Scheme was extended to include police, fire, national park, waste management and passenger transport service organizations in 2003.

The four types of Beacon event designed to promote the sharing of good practice can be conceptualized in knowledge creation and transfer terms. National (and sometimes regional) learning exchange conference events include all award holders within an award scheme. Attendees are primarily managers, but there are also some local elected representatives and partner agencies. The conferences provide a broad presentation and information about each Beacon Council within the award theme, so that further learning opportunities can be selected. The second type consists of open day visits, hosted by a Beacon Council on site. This offers exchange of knowledge, information and ideas, based on more intensive learning. Third, resource packs and web-based materials are available through a national agency concerned with local government improvement. Fourth, a visitor may request tailored exchange of knowledge and experience with a Beacon authority, through means including peer support, mentoring, shadowing or partner agency staff exchange. Visits to individual Beacon authorities are seen to be the most productive of new knowledge.

By the sixth round of awards, there were or had been a total of 160 Beacons. Most of the 386 local authorities in England had participated in Beacon events as visitors and learners in one or more rounds (Rashman and Hartley 2004). Opportunities for inter-organizational knowledge transfer had thus been extensive across the national system of local government.

A Framework for Understanding Inter-Organizational Knowledge Transfer

A systematic review of the academic literature on sharing good practice found a number of factors which are important in understanding successful transfer between organizations (Greenhalgh *et al.* 2004). However, the review also noted the fragmented nature of much of the research, with many studies examining mono- rather than multi-causal influences on the diffusion of innovation. There were only 'a tiny proportion of empirical studies' (Greenhalgh *et al.* 2004: 322) which reflect the complexities of interactions between aspects of practices, innovation processes and context.

The model presented here represents, we hope, a step forward in several ways. First, it focuses specifically on knowledge creation and transfer as the means of understanding how practices are shared and spread between organizations (or fail to be shared and spread). Second, it examines multiple influences on these processes in interaction, specifically the four sets of factors outlined below. In particular, knowledge receptivity and absorptive capacity have received attention but the characteristics of the originating as well as the recipient organization are important for understanding knowledge transfer. Third, it treats the knowledge to be transferred as socially constructed and organizationally embedded rather than acontextual and ahistorical 'best practice'. Fourth, it highlights a range of approaches to sharing knowledge, in part based on the aims of the 'learner' and the types of knowledge to be transferred (e.g. tacit or explicit, complex or simple, routine or bespoke, strategic or operational). Fifth, there is little other relevant research focusing on the context of public service organizations.

The framework for sharing of knowledge between units within an organization and between organizations depends on four sets of factors: features of the source organization; features of the recipient organization; the enabling social conditions between organizations; and the environmental context. These are shown in Figure 9.1. Each factor will be discussed in turn.

The features of the source organization

Little attention has been paid in the literature to how source organizations (or teams and individuals within them) are motivated and sufficiently skilled to be able to share their knowledge. Traditionally, the assumption has been that an organization with good practice can both recognize and articulate to others what makes it interesting or unique to learn from. However, such an assumption is not warranted (Szulanski and Winter 2002) for a number of reasons. The expert source may not realize the extent to which its practice is innovative compared with others in similar circumstances. This happened to a local authority with a Beacon award for its partnership-based service to address community safety. The local authority had applied for and won the Beacon award. However, it was not until service managers had to give a presentation on their work, and had talked with other local authorities eager to learn from them, that they realized quite how innovative their own practices were.

Alternatively, those in the source organization may be aware of the extent of its excellent or innovative practices, but may not be able to articulate this clearly or accurately, due to the high levels of tacit knowledge and skills required to do

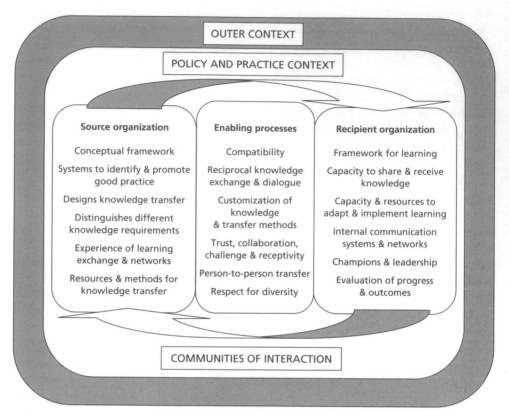

Figure 9.1 Key enablers of inter-organizational knowledge transfer

the job well or to design appropriate knowledge transfer systems. Or, they may have drawn inappropriate inferences as to *why* their practice is effective and therefore point learners in the wrong direction.

The research on Beacons enabled comparison of those local authorities which were skilled in sharing their knowledge with those Beacons which were less skilled (or which learned quickly). A number of influences may be identified that enable the source organization to recognize, articulate and communicate the value of knowledge resources and its expertise in the co-creation of knowledge. To transmit and share knowledge, the organization needs to have systems to identify, capture and promote good practice; capability to design forms of knowledge that others can use and interpret according to their knowledge requirements; expertise in social processes of learning exchange and collaborative networks; and resources for knowledge transfer. These are shown in the left-hand side of Figure 9.1.

Local authorities that were successful at sharing their practices with others had a conceptual framework to identify their own good practice. Officers at one council, an early Beacon in raising school standards, had a systematic approach to tackling school failure and our case study showed that they had a clear overview of the work still to be done. Research showed that education managers and staff had reflected on and discussed the lessons learnt from turning around failing schools. They also had expertise in sharing their analysis with their schools and with other local authorities. The education officers were able to recognize those aspects of good education service practice that had an impact on the local authority's wider organizational achievements within modernization, corporate performance and innovation (Rashman, Downe and Hartley 2005).

Systems and procedures to identify and promote good practice were also apparent in effective source organizations. Several local authorities had a policy and performance unit in the corporate centre that scrutinized performance data from a learning perspective, trying to work out the features which enabled a particular service to be effective. They engaged both local politicians and strategic and service managers in discussions about what were successful features and whether and why (or not) those successful features could be transferred to other services. One local authority held breakfast seminars with those services which had already gained a Beacon award. The purposes were to understand what features had contributed to the award, what other services could learn as they made an application, and what elements of the service might be of wider interest both within and beyond the local authority.

Those local authorities that gained more than one Beacon award over several years were particularly well placed to be able to reflect on how they designed and improved the learning processes for visitors. One local authority had used many PowerPoint presentations in a town hall setting, on its first Beacon open day concerned with public transport services. However, managers realized that they had not been able to get across to visitors the finer points of the innovative service (in theoretical terms, this was an over-reliance on explicit knowledge with little opportunity to share the tacit knowledge which underpinned the service). Later open days engaged visitors in both tacit and explicit knowledge. Means included taking visitors on local buses, showing them the new rail–bus interchange, and demonstrating traffic-light coordination for buses. Visitors also had opportunities to talk informally with local politicians and local users of services about the practicalities of planning, mobilizing support for the new services, delivery of changes and the actual use of services. Some local authorities surveyed their visitors by email or phone prior to arrival. In this way they could find out what kinds of practical experiences, access to information and opportunities to observe services and talk with service providers and users would be most valued by their visitors.

This also related to their competency in being able to distinguish different knowledge requirements according to type of visitor (see also Rashman and Hartley 2002). For example, a visiting local politician or chief executive might be particularly interested in strategic aspects of how change was orchestrated or sustained, especially where this involved either radical or complex change. By contrast, lower tier managers might be most interested in the practical aspects of benchmarking performance data that they could use to compare with their own service. The source organizations, where skilled at knowledge transfer design, would not only respond to the immediate and articulated needs of their visitors, but would also relate those needs to their own conceptual framework, thus helping visitors to pay attention to aspects of performance which might not immediately be seen as relevant, but which the experience of the source organization showed to be significant.

It helped if the source organization already had experience of participating in and learning from other local, regional or national networks. A Beacon council in community safety had established local and regional practitioner networks with colleagues in neighbouring councils and partner agencies, before it became a Beacon. This helped officers to create a trusting, informal environment. It enabled them to share learning from mistakes, identify key factors for success and demonstrate the importance of knowledge exchange between diverse actors (who included local politicians and representatives of partner agencies).

Features of the recipient organization

Knowledge take-up is not simply a feature of the attractiveness of the ideas or practices. Nor is knowledge transfer a simple, one-off process of relocating knowledge from one context to another. It typically involves a number of people engaged in a process of adaptation of ideas to the new context and culture, using sense making, experimentation and discussion to work out 'what works' and what does not in the new location. Szulanski (2003) has commented that 'stickiness' is a concept which stands for the amount of effort required to ensure that knowledge transfer takes root in the new location. He notes that stickiness is the rule rather than the exception: most knowledge transfer is effortful. The Beacon research shows that the majority of informants from visitor organizations say that they adapt ideas where they take them from Beacon authorities. This empirical evidence on the adaptation of Beacon ideas reinforces the view that adaptation of knowledge to local practices and context – not wholesale adoption – is central to knowledge transfer. Therefore it matters how organizations develop or enhance the organizational features which enable them to recognize, explain, use, integrate and adapt knowledge, and to align knowledge resources with organizational strategy.

The framework presented here has a number of features which interact to have an impact on whether, how far, how deeply and for how long new practices are taken up and used by the recipient organization. It includes motivation, capacity and the role of key agents in promoting and sustaining what is generally complex change. Even relatively straightforward service improvements will have to be interpreted for a new context, with perhaps a different set of demands and expectations from local politicians, managers and service users. The analysis of data from the 2001 survey, confirmed in the 2004 survey, shows that those organizations which have many or all of the features of the recipient organization listed in the framework are more likely to acquire and adapt new knowledge.

Visitors to Beacons (in both survey and interview data) reported that they were motivated to capture and assimilate knowledge by a combination of national policy imperatives to improve services, and internal organizational influences to acquire new knowledge from external sources. The case study research showed that those managers and organizations most skilled at gaining knowledge for practical service improvements reported that their own local authority had a framework of learning, which guided what they sought from the Beacons, and which linked to their organization's wider strategies.

Nearly all visitors prepared for a visit by accessing information about the Beacon Scheme or the particular Beacon service. Fewer, however, considered how their particular council could benefit from the Scheme by identifying aspects or areas to learn about or issues to explore at the event. Strategic managers were more likely to identify areas for organizational learning, while operational managers were more likely to be ready to collect comparative performance data. Elected members and managers of more effective recipient organizations had prepared carefully for the visit. They looked outside for new information and articulated the knowledge gaps and practice gaps in their own organization which they needed to learn more about. They also understood how the sought-after new ideas would fit within the broader picture of their own local authority's strategic efforts to improve, in the context of the wider central government agenda for local government.

Having the capacity to share and receive knowledge was also important. Knowledge acquisition and transfer into the recipient organization are enacted by individuals, who develop and extend their personal knowledge, exercise judgement, link it with others, and engage in reflective practice within their own context. Deep familiarity with a particular knowledge domain (such as a service area) enables people to develop diagnostic skills, make dynamic linkages between knowledge and practice, and adapt knowledge. It helped if the visitors were curious rather than judgmental about the service in the Beacon, and interested to explore differences as well as similarities in context, political and staff cultures, and geographical and demographic challenges. Being able to engage in discussion rather than competitive attempts to show superiority helped in the exploration of strategic and operational improvements.

Recipient organizations were more effective where they had the capacity and resources to adapt learning to their own situation. Social processes of discussion, interpretation and sense making to develop new local knowledge in one council occurred in the housing benefits service, where managers consulted staff about ideas they had gathered at a Beacon event and invited them to discuss and critically to analyse the applicability of these ideas for their own council. Other local authorities ensured that a group rather than an individual visited a Beacon. This arrangement offered more scope to convey new ideas and to gather varied views about how ideas could be adapted. It also helped to sustain the motivation to continue to engage in knowledge transfer on return to the home organization.

Some local authorities established internal learning network structures that undertook processes of knowledge creation and transfer. They included regular seminars to explore learning being brought into the authority, and working groups which worked on particular service issues. The network typically comprised actors in different and complementary roles, such as elected members and officers, and across different service areas. They used dialogue to explore and generate shared meaning. Their activities began with problem identification, which informed the selection of particular learning events at specific Beacon authorities. Such internal networks helped to align knowledge requirements with goals for the service, to build internal communication processes and to build local capacity for sharing and interpreting knowledge. Internal learning networks aimed to acquire knowledge through site visits at Beacon councils, personal experience and interpretation of practical knowledge, suggesting an emphasis on tacit knowledge and person-to-person knowledge transfer.

For example, in one local authority where there was concern to improve its waste management service, local politicians and managers played complementary roles in their network. Managers valued tacit knowledge, obtained through the observation of organizational practices and talking with counterpart managers. They combined tacit with explicit knowledge of practical methods and performance measures to confirm that some aspects of their service could be rapidly improved. Local politicians focused on policy and resource issues during the visit. Their discussions on return generated shared meanings, dispelling fears that practices could not be adapted to the recipient organization. This led local politicians to mobilize support for funding pilot projects. They and local authority officers were able to test out ideas, reflect on the knowledge acquired, make linkages to practice and generate collective understanding in the informal, decision-making forum. These deliberations led to the development of a strategy and rapid implementation and then roll-out of the pilots.

Even where a practice is recognized to be potentially valuable for the recipient organization, it requires a considerable amount of work to build support for the new practice and to encourage thoughtful adaptation to local circumstances. The role of champions across the local authority and the contribution of both political and managerial leadership were reported to be critical in most services. This was especially so where more substantial changes to practices or resourcing were required. Combinations of key actors appear to be significant to enabling the knowledge transfer process between local authority organizations. Local politicians were important in prioritizing, aligning and contextualizing strategic changes. Together with senior managers, they co-created knowledge of the resource requirements to improve service performance and mobilized support for the new practices. Trust, respect and leadership were important aspects of such relationships.

Practitioners regarded local politicians as champions who actively promoted innovation, steered the improvement strategy and provided access to resources. Individual practitioners brought deep familiarity with their particular professional knowledge domain and diagnostic skills. These skills enabled dynamic linkages between new knowledge and practice, and the adaptation of knowledge transferred into the recipient organization. In this sense the champions of change are distributed through the organization and leadership was not solely a senior strategic function.

Finally, recipient organizations have the systems and the culture to evaluate (however informally) the progress and outcomes of the implementation of the knowledge transfer. Local politicians, senior and service staff encouraged a climate which enabled all to contribute to answering questions such as how is the service now performing? What is being learnt by individuals, the service and the whole organization? What is still to be learnt or developed? These are sometimes seen as the characteristics of a learning organization, but we apply these ideas here at both service and corporate levels. The emphasis is largely on formative evaluation, which is most suitable for emergent change, and the need to use evaluation of current progress to fine-tune further action. However, evaluation processes were also concerned with outcomes, exploring whether or how far changed internal practices were leading to recognizable improvements for users and citizens. In other language, this can be called an emphasis on the public value outputs and outcomes of the knowledge transfer.

Enabling processes of knowledge sharing

The third feature of the knowledge transfer framework is concerned with the enabling features of the knowledge-sharing process and the nature of the relationship between organizations. These help to create a climate of trust, collaboration and sense making and to reduce barriers to knowledge transfer, so that mistakes and dead-ends in service improvement can be shared alongside the successful actions. There is evidence that learners appreciate and learn from mistakes as well as from success in inter-organizational learning networks (Hartley and Benington 2006).

Reciprocal knowledge exchange and dialogue are enabled through first-hand person-to-person interaction between key actors. This is true even for apparently simpler lessons based on performance benchmarking, because even a comparison of factual performance data often requires knowledge of context and processes to make sense of performance. It was particularly true for more complex knowledge sharing, as with knowledge transfer which concerned more complex processes involving a range of stakeholders and with uncertain or ambiguous outcomes. One instance involved community safety: the needs of young people who lacked suitable local meeting places appeared to conflict with perceptions of youth nuisance on the streets by older residents. Finding available resources for new service provision was an initial struggle.

Complex knowledge sharing also occurred where the aim of the interaction between source and recipient managers was to explore and tease out some of the subtle organizational processes underlying substantial organizational change. An example was developing and sustaining a climate of innovation which could be transferred to supporting innovation in a different service and context. Development of trust, collaboration and the identification of common perspectives assume particular importance in public service settings. Here it is often advantageous to bring together a diversity of knowledge and actors who may come from different organizational units and from a range of partner organizations.

Face-to-face contact was also helpful where there was a need to interpret the features of a promising practice which could be transferred into an apparently dissimilar setting. Managers from one local authority visited a Beacon service for waste management. However, they felt that their own local authority could not afford such a 'Rolls-Royce' service due to resource constraints. They worked with their Beacon partners to identify and modify those features which were transferable to a more resource-constrained setting, and most likely to create impact quickly.

The transfer methods had to be customized to reflect the type of knowledge which was being transferred. Dixon (2000) has noted that different methods of transfer are needed according to whether the knowledge being transferred is routine, one-off, or complex. This was also true of knowledge transfer through Beacon visits. Some types of knowledge could be obtained in a single visit while other knowledge required 'shoulder-to-shoulder' working between the manager or staff member in the source organization and their counterpart in the recipient organization.

It could initially help if there was a high degree of similarity between the two organizations which were sharing knowledge (compatibility in Figure 9.1). People from some organizations expressed considerable interest in learning only from those organizations which were similar in key features such as political complexion, geographical circumstances (e.g. rural or urban) or demographic characteristics (e.g. with high levels of deprivation).

Similarities between organizations helped a number of visitors (and was part of the logic of having a number of Beacons in each service theme). However, the more skilled visitors were able to look beyond surface similarity to examine underlying processes of good practice which could be adapted to quite different circumstances. Often, this respect for diversity of locality and organizational practice meant that looking at another organization was a springboard for expanding horizons and being exposed to innovative ideas: a stimulus for discussion and new thinking. Where visitor organizations possessed these competencies, they were often seeking to learn not only about the good practice but also how it had been achieved, as the comparison of processes was also stimulating. In one case, the local politicians and managers were initially reluctant to learn from a local authority of a different political hue. However, through intensive discussion over a series of meetings they were able to discern some valuable lessons, which they found were worth experimenting with under a different set of policies and corporate strategies.

The framework also draws attention to the value of two-way learning, as shown by the arrows of learning between source and recipient organizations in Figure 9.1. Within 'joined-up' public service settings, members of a community of interaction are often simultaneously members of an organization and a larger, dispersed occupational group. They may also participate in cross-agency teams and formal partnerships that cut across traditional organizational boundaries, and where learning flows in all directions across the network. For instance, an organization may enter a learning network as a potential source organization and, through interaction, may acquire and apply increased understanding of the social processes and organizational characteristics to become a successful recipient organization. In many instances, an organization may enter a knowledge network with the intention of being both a source and recipient of knowledge. Knowledge creation and transfer was not limited to the 'learner' organizations in the Beacon scheme. Over two-thirds of Beacon local authority respondents in the second national survey reported that they gained knowledge and ideas from their visitors.

Policy and practice context

Features of the organizational context include its history, institutional and environmental forces, structural and disciplinary boundaries, principal accountabilities, and success criteria. It helped where knowledge-sharing partners had some sensitivity to these issues and had an awareness of how they might affect knowledge transfer from or into their own context.

The external (outer) policy context is significant too, and can shape a number of influences on inter-organizational knowledge transfer. Such influences include the varied motivations to take part in a national voluntary scheme. Institutional isomorphism and the impact of engagement on reputation could influence whether knowledge transfer is superficial compliance or skilled change management. The use of a scheme to share inter-organizational good practice among public services is undoubtedly shaped in the UK, as mentioned earlier, by a strongly centralized national government with its influence on resource allocation and even reputation. Whether such a scheme would operate as widely or as effectively in a more decentralized national context would be a profitable topic for research.

Outcomes

There is only point in developing a framework for understanding knowledge creation and transfer if there can be some degree of confidence that the knowledge transfer results in positive outcomes for the organizations which engage in it, either as source or recipient organizations, and for users of services. The literature on knowledge transfer is still relatively weak on making empirical or theoretical links between knowledge processes and outcomes (Easterby-Smith and Lyles 2005). There is reasonable evidence that the majority of local authorities aim to apply learning from the Beacon Scheme to making service improvements (Downe, Hartley and Rashman 2004) and many local authorities succeed in doing so (Rashman, Downe and Hartley 2005).

Conclusions

This chapter has focused on knowledge transfer as an element of change, innovation and improvement in public services. Our conclusions address two major themes: knowledge transfer and complex change.

First, in relation to knowledge transfer, the chapter outlines a conceptual framework, derived from a large-scale research programme, to understand knowledge transfer as a social process. It encompasses sharing both tacit and explicit knowledge to create meanings and understandings which enable ideas and practices to carry – and critically, to be adapted in the process of transfer – between one context and another. The socially constructed nature of knowledge and its transfer means that this is far from an easy task. It requires people working alongside each other to understand both surface and, in some cases, deeper aspects of change and improvement. Thus knowledge creation and transfer are intimately related to each other, as new knowledge is created or recreated with each transfer. The social processes of knowledge transfer mean that attention needs to be paid to the characteristics of both source and recipient organizations, and that the enabling processes of transfer are also critical. The organizational and policy context also shape the ways in which people are motivated and able to acquire and apply new knowledge, and influence the institutional opportunities and constraints.

The framework has been developed in the context of local government, and it is reasonable to ask whether this framework is more broadly applicable. There are particular features of the English Beacon Scheme which are context-specific, but the elucidation of knowledge-transfer processes is likely to be applicable to other public services, such as health, education and central government departments. This claim requires empirical testing, but the complexities of local government and the range of services provided are such that generalizability appears plausible.

The model of inter-organizational knowledge transfer may be applied not only to knowledge transfer between organizations but also to intra-organizational knowledge transfer between organizational sub-units. One sub-unit may be a source and another sub-unit a recipient of knowledge and good practice (and there is evidence of this in the Beacon research).

The framework is of particular interest because it is one of the very few which is based in research on the public services. As noted earlier, much of the literature on knowledge transfer is based on private-sector organizations, where two features in particular may be different. One is the competitive context of the operation of firms, compared with a stronger culture and imperative of sharing in the public sector in order to achieve a wider public value. The second feature is the nature of many public services, which are both complex and contested by different stakeholders and subject to political influences. We have argued that the context of knowledge transfer is very important but there is further research to be undertaken here about how context impacts on knowledge-transfer processes.

The second theme relates to complex and programmatic change, as outlined by Wallace and Pocklington (2002). There are more applications than can be adequately covered here but we sketch some key features. First, all complex change, by its nature, cannot be fully planned and controlled, and there are always elements of emergent change. Knowledge creation and transfer are therefore integral to complex and programmatic change. Understanding how best such knowledge transfer can be facilitated and used, and how knowledge transfer can be adapted and embedded in new contexts is critical to the success of the changes. Knowledge transfer is therefore a sub-goal to be sought in any complex change programme.

The knowledge transfer framework also has some overlap in processes with complex change. Viewing knowledge transfer not as a one-off exchange of information but as an extended set of processes of social interaction, influence, communities of practice and organizational learning means that the role of distributed leadership is significant. No single person (or group) holds all the answers, but meanings and findings from experimentation must be developed in part through discussion and debate. The knowledge transfer framework here emphasizes the contribution of members of a network with different skills and perspectives, which are used dialectically to develop and adapt knowledge. Leaders, found in a range of roles, are orchestrators of a wide array of influences on practice, and must nurture cultures to support receptivity to change and approaches to evaluation which support continuous learning and further emergent change.

ACKNOWLEDGEMENT

Jean Hartley would like to acknowledge the support of the ESRC/EPSRC Advanced Institute of Management Research for writing time, under ESRC grant number RES 331-25-008.

REFERENCES

Argote, L. McEvily, B. and Reagans, R. (2003) Introduction to the special issue on managing knowledge in organizations: creating, retaining and transferring knowledge. *Management Science*, **49**(4), v–viii.

Bapuji, H. and Crossan, M. (2004) From questions to answers: reviewing organizational learning research. *Management Learning*, **35**(4), 397–417.

Bate, S.P. and Robert, G. (2002) Knowledge management and communities of practice in the private sector: lessons for modernizing the National Health Service in England and Wales. *Public Administration*, **80**(4), 643–63.

Benington, J. (2000) The modernization and improvement of government and public services. *Public Money and Management*, **20**(2), 3–8.

Blackler, F. (1995) Knowledge, knowledge work and organizations: an overview and interpretation. *Organization Studies*, **16**, 1021–46.

Brown, J.S. and Duguid, P. (2001) Knowledge and organization: a social-practice perspective. *Organization Science*, **12**(2), 198–213.

Cohen, W. and Levinthal, D. (1990) Absorptive capacity: a new perspective on learning and innovation. *Administrative Science Quarterly*, **35**(10), 128–52.

Dixon, N. (2000) *Common Knowledge: How Companies Thrive by Sharing What They Know*. Boston: Harvard Business School Press.

Downe, J., Hartley, J. and Rashman, L. (2004) Evaluating the extent of inter-organizational learning and change through the English Beacon Council Scheme. *Public Management Review*, **6**(4), 531–53.

Easterby-Smith, M. and Lyles, M. (eds) (2005) *Handbook of Organizational Learning and Knowledge Management*: Oxford: Blackwell.

Finger, M. and Brand, S.B. (1999) The concept of the 'learning organization' applied to the transformation of the public sector: conceptual contributions for theory development. In M. Easterby-Smith, J. Burgoyne and L. Araujo (eds) (1999) *Organizational Learning and the Learning Organization*. London: Sage.

Greenhalgh, T., Robert, G., Bate, P., Kyriakidou, O., Macfarlane, F. and Peacock, R. (2004) *How to Spread Good Ideas*. London: National Co-ordinating Centre for NHS Service Delivery and Organization.

Hartley, J. (2005) Innovation in governance and public services: past and present. *Public Money and Management*, **25**(1), 27–34.

Hartley, J. and Benington, J. (2006) Copy and paste, or graft and transplant? Knowledge sharing through inter-organizational networks. *Public Money and Management*, **26**(2) 101–8.

Lave, J. (1993) The practice of learning. In S. Chaiklin and J. Lave (eds), *Understanding Practice: Perspectives on Activity and* Context. Cambridge: Cambridge University Press, pp. 3–32.

Lave, J. and Wenger, E. (1991) *Situated Learning: Peripheral Participation*. Cambridge: Cambridge University Press.

Marquand, D. (2004) *Decline of the Public*. Cambridge: Polity.

Nahapiet, J. and Ghoshal, S. (1998) Social capital, intellectual capital and the organizational advantage. *Academy of Management Review*, **23**(2), 242–66.

Newell. S., Edelman, L., Scarbrough, H., Swan, J. and Bresnen, M. (2003) 'Best practice' development and transfer in the NHS: the importance of process as well as product knowledge. *Health Services Management Research*, **16**(1), 1–12.

Newman, J. (2001) *Modernizing Governance: New Labour, Policy and Society*. London: Sage.

Newman, J., Raine, J. and Skelcher, C. (2001) Transforming local government: innovation and modernization. *Public Money and Management*, **21**(2), 61–8.

Nonaka, I. (1994) A dynamic theory of organizational knowledge creation. *Organization Science*, **5**(1), 14–37.

Nonaka, I. and Takeuchi, H. (1995) *The Knowledge-Creating Company*. Oxford: Oxford University Press.

Polanyi, M. (1966) *The Tacit Dimension*. New York: Doubleday.

Rashman, L., Downe, J. and Hartley, J. (2005) Knowledge creation and transfer in the Beacon Scheme: improving services through sharing good practice. *Local Government Studies*, **31**(5), 683–700.

Rashman, L. and Hartley, J. (2002) Leading and learning? Knowledge transfer in the Beacon Council Scheme. *Public Administration*, **80**, 523–42.

Rashman, L. and Radnor, Z. (2005) Learning to improve: approaches to improving local government services. *Public Money and Management*, **25**(1), 19–26.

Szulanski, G. (2003) *Sticky Knowledge*. London: Sage.

Szulanski, G. and Winter, S. (2002) Getting it right the second time. *Harvard Business Review*, January, 62–9.

Tsoukas, H. and Vladimirou, E. (2001) What is organizational knowledge? *Journal of Management Studies*, **38**(7), 973–93.

Wallace, M. and Pocklington, K. (2002) *Managing Complex Educational Change: Large-Scale Reorganisation of Schools*. London: RoutledgeFalmer.

CHAPTER 10

LEARNING TO NAVIGATE THE NOISE OF CHANGE: LESSONS FROM COMPLEX HEALTH SYSTEM CONTEXTS

Ann Casebeer

The argument is developed that central policy making can have, at most, a condition-setting and nurturing role in seeking to bring about deep and sustainable change capable of genuinely improving public services in complex service systems. Ann Casebeer suggests that deep change in practice which gets to the heart of service provision cannot be so much orchestrated in any coherent and directive way from the centre as incrementally improvised within and between organizations at the local level. A key to success is encouragement and support for collective learning among the network of professionals and other stakeholders concerned with improving practice. Such group-ings are conceived as local 'communities of learning', whose potential for collective improvement efforts should be maximized through interventions to provide ongoing learning support. This position resonates with Hartley and Rashman's (Chapter 9) view that where a central initiative is undertaken to disseminate good practice, it should actively promote adaptation to local settings rather than 'one-size-fits-all' adoption.

Academics from higher education institutions can play a very positive part, becom-ing in effect leading members of communities of learning with specialist expertise to offer. Casebeer draws on her extensive experience of supporting local innovation in the context of the regionalization (and re-regionalization) of health care in the Canadian province of Alberta. This work is driven by the pursuit of knowledge-for-action, seek-ing both to inform and, through collaborative activity, directly to engage in helping healthcare professionals and those involved in local governance to improve practice. She makes the normative case for policy-makers to facilitate innovation and har-ness it, as far as possible, towards the achievement of broad policy goals. The role Casebeer conceives as appropriate for central policy-makers in creating conditions for flexible and incremental local innovation echoes the normative idea of 'temperate' policy making advocated by Wallace and Hoyle (Chapter 4).

Introduction

This chapter draws from a broad range of research and practice-based experience focused on understanding the structure, process and outcome of complex change in the context of health system innovation and health improvement. While the mechanisms for attempting to manage complex and programmatic change are often composed of targeted government planning efforts and usually rely heavily on structural interventions, the results of such efforts remain disappointing at best (Buchanan, Claydon and Doyle 1999; Van de Ven *et al.* 1999; Quinn 2000; Plsek and Greenhalgh 2001; Ferlie *et al.* 2005). This chapter suggests that traditional notions of capacity to programme and control complex change are getting in the way of understanding and subsequently enabling such change to occur. Rather, only through careful but loose nurturing of change and opportunities for learning can innovation hope to emerge which, in turn, may create opportunities to diffuse and communicate sustained change within the messy, noisy, complex contexts of large and dynamic systems. This recognition poses a significant shift of mindset for governments whose ministers are serious about enabling improvements in public sector services.

Several case examples and developing constructs are presented, providing contributions to how we might begin to think differently about supporting change capacity. Most of the insights are drawn from within Canadian health-care jurisdictions, particularly Western Canada. They are augmented by a reasonable understanding of the English NHS, a more meagre understanding of the Scottish and Welsh systems, a smattering of knowledge of the New Zealand and Australian contexts, and some probably quite biased knowledge about impacts of the lack of a public sector system of care in the United States.

Insights and ideas from research and practice experience concerning the enabling of change are loosely framed around five areas:

- Empirical lessons – highlighting 'positively deviant cases' of innovation under circumstances of complex change and uncertainty within supposedly programmatic health policy shifts.
- Methodological challenges – identifying opportunities to expand and adjust approaches to researching complex and programmatic change.
- Theoretical insights – considering the implications for current theoretical constructs of new and emergent research findings and practice experience.
- New directions – discussing opportunities for exchanging, creating and using evidence to enable, or at least more successfully navigate, complex change.
- An emergent frame for learning to change – making the case for investing in communities of learning as an integral part of framing and understanding the potential for complex change and in turn enhancing change capacity.

The ideas developed here are meant to generate questions and reactions, some of which link to ideas that other authors within this text have helped to shape.

Specifically, experience shared collaboratively from cross-sectoral and international perspectives of complex change within public sector settings has allowed collective ideas and comparative frames for understanding the nature of change to emerge. For example, the questions and issues raised warrant consideration within and alongside Wallace and Pocklington's (2002) conceptualization of the potential for 'orchestrated' change within the UK education sector. Experience with the dynamics of change at play within regionalized systems of health care in the Canadian context suggests that these dynamics may well be too diffuse, diverse and too uncoupled to be 'orchestrated' except in the most 'unobtrusive' sense of the word. There is simply too much 'cacophony' – discordant sound or noise – within healthcare system environments for large-scale programmatic change to succeed.

This observed noise of change may well be due in part to the 'inevitable tensions' that Levin describes as inherent to managing large-scale public reform (Chapter 7) and better understood when remembering Louis's call to bring back the 'meso-politics' of change when considering how to manage it (Chapter 5). Clearly, there is a broad range of perspectives and experience with complex change theory and practice contained within this book suggesting the possibility of an equally broad range of approaches and potential for facilitating change. Mindful of these possibilities, empirical findings to date in health care in Canada suggest that loosely supporting experimentation, differentiation and a multiplicity of opportunities for learning have had more success in building change capacity and leading to sustained innovation, than more usual, highly planned and structured approaches to managing change.

The joint testing of some possibilities has helped to deepen understanding of change processes and outcomes. It has also helped to elucidate ways of using that knowledge to support, encourage and maybe even engender complex change that fosters both desired innovation and takes advantage of positive unintended learning. So, although the lessons for change here are grounded within health and healthcare settings, they may have some resonance for other public sector jurisdictions. They all draw from public sector cases, although some of the research questions and approaches have been informed by learning from the business and voluntary sectors. Given the increasingly mixed organizational forms that many of our health and education systems seem to be trying on, this transference and testing across multiple sector experiences could be a crucial future direction for both research and practice.

I am increasingly of the belief that the best hope for future innovation through complex change (and especially in complex system environments) will come not from either the most brilliant single practice pilots or research studies, or from sustained programmes of orchestrated change or collaborative research. Rather it will come from building what many refer to as communities of practice, but what might be better framed as multidisciplinary 'communities of learning'. It is within and through opportunities for *learning* that complex change may hope to emerge and be sustained. Nurtured spaces of learning – whether our main sector focus is health or education – might arguably represent the best we can do. If this is the case, then more of our concerted and resourced efforts must support public sector jurisdictions to foster these spaces of learning with the goal of enabling rather than managing change.

Empirical Lessons

Looking to empirical lessons remains critical, especially given the relative dearth of positive examples of sustained change in complicated circumstances that significantly advance performance improvement within complex healthcare settings (e.g. Buchanan, Claydon and Doyle 1999; Adair *et al.* 2003; Greenhalgh *et al.* 2004). Active study and observation of a number of health system change processes associated with significant policy shifts has provided insights into how change occurs (see Pettigrew 1986; Shortell *et al.* 1996; Denis *et al.* 1996, 2002; Ferlie *et al.* 1996, 2005).

The focused long-term and in-depth studies that I have been directly involved in over the past decade have been in relation to the experience of regionalization in Alberta and elsewhere in Canada. The experience has been marked, on the one hand, by the natural progression of what Hinings describes as loosely coupled processes of change in health and health care that would have occurred regardless of new change policy mechanisms (such as regionalization). On the other hand, we also have been seeing change that is more embedded in the context of regionalization (and more recently, re-regionalization). It has sometimes enhanced patterns of learning and subsequent innovation (Hinings *et al.* 2003; Thurston *et al.* 2004). Some programmes of organizational change research are generating valuable lessons concerning where and how actual innovative change happens. For example, several members of a team of organizational and health researchers based in Western Canada have been watching and analysing change experiences embedded within regionalization for over a decade. Our separate and combined efforts are reported for lessons concerning the nature of change and innovation within large health system contexts.

An early study of the Alberta healthcare system's actual and initial transition to a regionalized form of system between 1994 and 1995 (Casebeer and Hannah 1998) baselined experiences of this policy shift (government-mandated change). The research focused on the perspectives of newly appointed chief executive officers and chairs of the new regional health authorities, and the lead government bureaucrats responsible for managing the change process. The findings suggest that when advancing such a complex, albeit primarily structural, change at a system level, several prerequisite change processes are required for positive shift to occur. Several additional processes are inherent to continued or sustained ability to make progress within such a change experience. Figure 10.1 identifies ten processes that leaders indicated were far more important to successful implementation than either the specific initiating policy or the structural change adopted. These categories of change process emerged as critical to enabling and sustaining the health policy shift.

Prerequisite continua:		
Absent	**Sustaining political will**	Present
Inappropriate	**Pacing**	Appropriate
Inadequate	**Resourcing**	Adequate
Resistance	**Committing to change**	Acceptance
Additional continua:		
Ineffective	**Leading**	Effective
Closed, unclear	**Communicating**	Open, clear
Unavailable	**Informing**	Available
Avoided	**Learning***	Supported
Discrete	**Planning**	Continuous
Thinking	**Adjusting**	Acting

Figure 10.1   Critical change processes within a health policy shift
Note: *Given the lessons of subsequent work, at least the 'capacity to learn' is likely to be an implicit and/or unrecognized prerequisite to enabling the additional change processes to thrive.

The anchors of the process continua delineate the potential nature and range of activity connected with each process category. They can also provide a vehicle for reviewing dynamic tensions among process categories. Used across time, they provide important temporal data concerning the change trajectory. Given the array of interrelated processes that need to be in play, the opportunity for failure is high.

Revisiting the robustness of this earlier work is timely given the fact that many healthcare jurisdictions are now in the process of essentially re-regionalizing (Healthcare Papers 2004; Casebeer *et al.* 2006). Connected research efforts are particularly important when attempting to validate the extent of real sustained change, especially beyond the level of restructuring. Anchored scales related to pivotal change processes could enhance our understanding of how much actual change has occurred over a decade of planned structural governmental intervention, and how much we might capture in the future. The 'bottom-line' lesson is that structure can be enabling, but it is the complex interplay of multiple processes that actually secures change.

Later empirical examples of case studies of complex health system change in Canada (Casebeer, Scott and Hannah 2000; Hinings *et al.* 2003; Denis *et al.* 1996, 2002) and elsewhere (Ferlie 2001; Ferlie *et al.* 1996, 2005) derive from multiple spaces and places. While these separate efforts do not share specific theoretical frames or replicate specific findings, the cases all present change efforts within health-care settings which are complex and chaotic, and not easily orchestrated or controlled. Their messages about the inherent messiness of health system change are consistent: 'A key challenge for research in health service delivery and organization is that the phenomena under study (for example, a change to the way a service is delivered or organized) are complex and difficult to define' (Fulop *et al.* 2001: 9).

Observation of a primary healthcare innovation across time in a regional health authority context is beginning to fill the knowledge gap between the notion of strategy as craft (Mintzberg 1987, 1994) rather than plan or prescription, and the attainment of positive change outcomes. This case study of primary healthcare reform provides important lessons for what strategic action and leadership as vehicles for organizational policy guidance can and cannot achieve (Casebeer and Reay 2004). In this case, the key events occurred at the middle and front-line levels in the organization. If these findings replicate elsewhere, and the work of Ferlie *et al.* (2005) and Denis *et al.* (2002) is instructive here, they suggest that the effort to establish large-scale programmes of change controlled centrally may simply miss the point of how and where change efforts need to be encouraged and supported (Reay, Golden-Biddle and GermAnn 2006). Therefore, the implications arising from this case are potentially fundamental to how we describe, use and diffuse such mechanisms for best purpose in future situations attempting policy change supporting health reform.

Findings across several strands of large-scale change have focused in on uncovering and analysing 'positively deviant' change efforts: experiments and pilots demonstrating the capacity to generate innovation and learning. They have sometimes led to sustainable organizational or system level adoption (Casebeer 2004). I increasingly believe that there is more to learn from these positively deviant cases than from continuing to amass evidence of the potential for large-scale complex change strategy to fail (Staudenmayer, Tyre and Perlow 2002; Berwick 2003).

Moreover, some recurring patterns are emerging across these cases. Middle managers are critical actors when changes move beyond the specific pilot or programme level. Activity and leadership in the middle as well as the degree of commitment to learning at the frontline would appear to be more critical than the degree of specific or targeted planning at the system level. Through longitudinal, in-depth studies that follow the actions of managers in the middle of the organization and lower down, insights are being gained about the actual process of change within large and complex health system contexts. Watching long enough and deeply enough allows the underpinnings of innovation to be exposed and the large-scale changes that do sometimes emerge to be understood and potentially replicated. Staying the distance with the researching and the implementing of large-scale changes also illuminates these changes: not just as central planning or strategic policy successes or failures, but as a creative and complicated combination of flexible frames and processes that connect with difficulty across sectors and turfs, and sometimes make a real difference.

Methodological Challenges

Research challenges associated with understanding the process and impact of large-scale complex change are multiple and multidimensional. Effective research processes are therefore themselves complex, requiring combined methods and multidisciplinary expertise.

Current literature is sparse in relation to identifying models or frameworks for approaching this type of research in a collaborative way, and experience of the research process from both the researcher and the decision-maker perspective has not usually targeted cooperative partnership. Instead it has more often emphasized controlled observation and at least quasi-experimental designs. These designs have not led to the knowledge transfers hoped for (Casebeer *et al.* 2003b: 351).

For some researchers, deepening the understanding of change has become increasingly and necessarily some form of negotiated collaborative partnership. This implies a collective activity involving a diverse group of researchers and practice partners. Together they share an interest in improvement through better understanding of how to seek and support innovation within evolving policy environments, marked by constant restructuring and uncertainty (Brazil, MacLeod and Guest 2002). For other researchers, this collective approach raises serious issues concerning objectivity and bias in the research process. It also challenges researchers trained to work within specific scientific paradigms. Clearly, the research approach must fit the question of interest and the underlying problem that is being addressed (Sackett and Wennberg 1997). If the co-production of knowledge is not an appropriate fit to the research or practice intent, then a separate and parallel research design may be more relevant. Complementary research by 'outsiders' may be called for. Or a mixing of approaches may yield more insightful findings than either on their own (Verhoef, Casebeer and Hilsden 2002). However, when trying to shift policy in complex real-world settings such as public sector systems, working together seems most likely to succeed.

When collective approaches are warranted, what do cooperative researcher and decision-maker partnerships look like in practice? How can a partnership be implemented in a way that works in both the academic and healthcare practice worlds? One large national project (Abelson *et al.* 2004) focused on understanding and then testing effective involvement of public participation in healthcare decision making. The benefits of an academia–practice partnership for advancing knowledge in this area were articulated as follows.

- The quiet observer presence of the researchers on the consultation days seemed to strike the appropriate stance, focusing on the community participants as the experts and the researchers as learners.
- A collaborative approach to team process allowed research and practice issues and goals to merge, ensuring that both sets of needs were met.
- The combined financial and intellectual resources of practitioners and researchers enabled improved efforts at public consultation to be advanced in support of improved health services' contribution to the health of children and families in the communities involved.

There are messages here suggesting a fundamental shift that may transfer to policy-makers' roles as well. Just as collaborative research secures improved practice uptake, the potential for system change seems likely to be enhanced where policy making is collaborative and flexible, supportive rather than controlling, and conducive to shared learning and growth in line with broad goals. Such an approach accords with Wallace and Hoyle's (Chapter 4) advocacy of 'temperance' in policy making.

Within our partnership following organizational change in the health sector, we have formed a group of multi-site, multidisciplinary researchers and decision-makers. Together we are undertaking a longitudinal programme of work. It has been a collaborative journey of give and take among all partners and one of learning for all of us (Golden-Biddle *et al.* 2003). Because the research is designed to assist providers, managers and policy-makers in their future efforts to develop and implement appropriate change strategies, collaborative, action-oriented partnering is congruent with our efforts.

We believe that both researchers and decision-makers gain from this style of research. In all facets of the research to date there has been an emphasis on 'learning along the way'. It has sustained the efforts of all partners to maintain a 'strength-based approach' to collaborative working. An unintended but positive consequence of this way of doing things has been a mutual orientation to understanding innovation and learning: how they occur within our various partner organizations, and how we extend our research competencies and enhance our own learning. Framing the research partnership at least in part as a joint learning opportunity creates an overlap between research and practice interests that encourages shared ownership and trust. This, in turn, leads to a greater willingness to allow longer and more in-depth observation. Conversely, and as importantly, clarity of divergent or separate research and practice objectives at the onset of the partnership enhances the rigour of the research and the value of findings for practice.

Our research efforts allow sustained connection and progress. They are at once almost constantly formative and informative and simultaneously systematic and rigorous. They allow us to observe close enough and long enough to unpick what is occurring within large, complex change initiatives. Policy-makers are joining us as partners in these efforts and accepting new roles in the process that fundamentally alter traditional policy-making pathways.

Theoretical Insights

This section is framed by the premise that complex changes in public sector practices require equally complex theoretical constructs (Fulop *et al.* 2001). Further, consideration of the experience of change gains and failures within public sector contexts suggests that there remains some lack of fit between many theoretical constructs of how change occurs and how to plan or implement change. This may in part be due to the relative dearth of long-term change studies in public sector contexts. It also may be in part due to the limited transferability of theory based on private sector contexts that are not as complex as public sector systems.

It is not that many theories of change make little sense, that they have yet to mature across time, or that they do not attempt to encompass the ambiguity and uncertainty of change processes. Rather, it is that 'the devil is still in the detail'. These theories seem to hold up pretty well and make sense in the real world when our lens is broad and when we are identifying what does not work (Mitroff 1998). However, it is this level of abstraction or focus on failure that gets us into trouble. Difficulties arise when theories do not embrace the detail of what actually happens and what works in complex settings. They also arise where we try to 'detail the theory', and fall back into old traps about inappropriate assumptions. Such assumptions overestimate the significance of issues such as the locus of control, the degree of 'wickedness' (uncertainty, complexity, variability) of change processes, and the extent of non-rational, non-linear relationships within successful change.

We begin to make progress when we let go of notions of strategy as the rational framing for a logical linear process that leads to planned change outcomes in however incremental a manner. While this is a proposition that most researchers of change and some practitioners will embrace, it is much less apparent that many governments and their policy-makers would agree. Hence we are still left with a practical problem and a theoretical gap concerning the role of policy making within large-scale complex change. The range of ideas and insights from contributions in this book brings together issues and potential solutions that may well be filling this theory–practice gap. Some of the empirical work and in-depth practice experience offer insights that are critical to consider alongside theory-informed research efforts. Both strands of knowledge development will be a part of the answers to questions we are still grappling with:

- How do we understand the messiness of change?
- Can we harness the mess in useful ways for progress, for learning, and for improvements to health care and health?
- Is an understanding of how 'good messy change processes' lead to fruitful innovation in one setting transferable to practice in other settings?

Perhaps we need a 'theory of watching' that informs our observation of how the mess is tackled across organizations and systems. Such a theory would not only be useful but may be imperative for breakthroughs in theoretical constructs that are of practical use.

It is disconcerting how wide the gap between research and practice remains (Mason, Wood and Freemantle 1999; Lehman, Greener and Simpson 2002; Simpson 2002). If we cannot fill this gap, our chances are slim of moving beyond situations where complex change unfolds successfully by good luck and happenstance, rather than through concerted effort. We seem all too often not to invite each other to the same conferences or seek a shared language for the common needs and goals we have. This gap requires addressing through making time for joint interaction among decision-makers and researchers. Better substantive theories conceptualizing collaborative research processes would also help create both greater awareness and greater acceptance of their value. This is particularly important but particularly difficult in the healthcare sector, where notions of good science and strong evidence remain heavily weighted towards the biomedical and positivist paradigms. That said, there are signs of hope.

> Research, for all its claims to objectivity, cannot sit outside the influence of broader systems of norms and rules . . . we argue that the current popularity of collaborative research is a convergence between emerging forces and traditions within academia and changing rules and norms within policy and management, particularly the public management of health and social policy (Denis and Lomas 2003).

Yet such forces are converging unevenly within varying traditions and paradigms in academia. The convergence is more obvious and more acceptable outside of faculties of medicine. There, notions of combined methods research – let alone collaborative research – still require a major shift away from prevailing views of what counts as the 'gold standard' for research and evidence (Miller and Crabtree 2000).

New Directions

Of the many promising new directions that warrant consideration, one stands in bold relief: a stronger emphasis on *learning*. Within the health sector, learning is often referred to as knowledge development, transfer, brokering, exchange, or supporting the capacity for evidence-based decision making. This direction should be on everyone's agenda for the future. The potential for successful complex change and sustained innovation within complex organization, system or sector environments will depend in large part on our ability to think differently about learning (Crossan, Lane and White 1999; Bohmer and Edmondson 2001). There are extensive opportunities for the public services, especially the health and education sectors, to lead the way in establishing support for learning to and for change. These sectors are particularly well suited to learning as a vehicle for enabling desired change: they embody shared collective goals such as societal literacy and population health that are broadly acceptable to a wide range of stakeholders. So, even in turf- and status-ridden healthcare settings, a common focus on learning to improve the quality of patient care can form powerful bridges across sectors and between professional divides.

I will present a brief account of one community of learning that develops enhanced evidence-based healthcare decision-making capacity in supporting community health. It offers a case example of what is possible now as a point of reference for discussion of what might be possible in the future. An indication of the theoretical underpinnings of this learning community is provided in order to encourage future discussion on the relationships between the theories and the practices of learning. 'Learning in practice' and 'learning as practice' are seen as constructs that are key enablers of change, particularly within complex and dynamic settings (Spencer and Jordan 1999).

SEARCH Canada is a public service organization supporting a network of health practitioners and health researchers. This network is dedicated to enhancing health research knowledge and capacity for quality health and healthcare decision making. SEARCH Canada engages diverse groups of practising health professionals in training and mentoring, and establishes linkage and exchange of research activity across diverse sectors. The SEARCH Classic Program (Swift, Efficient Application of Research in Community Health) is an innovative multidisciplinary learning community. It was established to accelerate the use of research findings and facilitate the uptake of knowledge across Alberta. Guided by a steering committee of stakeholders, and committed to continuous improvement, the learning community has evolved over the course of ten years and five cohorts of practitioner learners. Learning and communication occur through a combination of face-to-face training modules and a web-based, distance-learning network, supported by mentoring of practitioners back in their workplaces (Casebeer *et al.* 2003a).

SEARCH Canada supports a virtual learning network that survives outside the scheduled periods of learning and beyond the boundaries of the formal programme. As such, it has attracted international interest for its innovative approaches (International Board of Review 2004). The learning programme's focus on capacity building through multifaceted learning is making a difference. People in practice and management settings are supported in developing and using research skills and research results within their own organizational decision-making contexts. Various evaluation efforts have consistently identified the following characteristics of SEARCH that account for its success: it is sustainable, multidisciplinary, intensive, development-focused, virtual, community-oriented, project-based and organizationally embedded (Birdsell and O'Connell 2003; McCaffrey Consulting 2004).

The theoretical grounding of SEARCH Canada's programmes and services is adapted from a combination of existing frames for effective organizational learning (Argyris 1999). It is informed by the literature examining effective partnerships and networks (Huxham 1996; Roussos and Fawcett 2000); the role of information tools and technologies in learning (Lau and Hayward 2000) and behaviour change (Rosenstock, Strecher and Becker 1988); principles of adult and appreciative learning (Cooperrider 1997); and successful research transfer and exchange in and for health (Gray 2001). The conceptual frame of education as a means for change and growth is paramount within SEARCH as a learning and communications network. The works of Friere (1990) and later Church (2002) provide strong theoretical underpinning for the experience as a whole. At their best, SEARCH and other multidisciplinary learning communities develop beyond time-limited learning experiences or experiments into long-term learning networks. As such, they become inherently collaborative and dynamic in nature and depend on creating relationships that are reciprocal across boundaries and sustainable across time. If nurtured and resourced, they become an intrinsic and powerful resource of an organization or system.

This case example of an existing community of learning offers a reference point for discussing the contribution that innovative and multidisciplinary communities of practice and learning can make towards enhancing our capacity to advance complex change initiatives: in education for improved learning capacity, and in health for enabling change for health gain. Its relevance ties back to the ways in which innovation actually occurs in complex healthcare systems. Innovation is inherently derived from creating the capacity for learning that can in part be supported loosely via system-level policy frames and encouraged via broad organizational vision. Arguably, the pivotal roles of policy making become nurturing and harnessing opportunities for individuals to learn, to experiment and to innovate within and across organizational spaces (Martin 2003). Only then can the potential for system-level learning emerge and possible diffusion of sustainable change be enabled. Far more concerted attention to learning in and across organizational contexts (and in studying and evaluating impacts) is warranted in support of innovation and change capacity within public service sector environments.

An Emergent Frame for Learning to Change

Given experiences of change within complex healthcare jurisdictions, and with growing theoretical insights into the complexity of large-scale change more generally, learning as an explicit component of change capacity warrants enhanced support. Some early thinking is presented as working towards a framework for nurturing complex change efforts in the context of healthcare system environments, and perhaps in public sector systems more widely. It represents learning in progress.

We know that the potential for diffusion of both learning and subsequent innovation is high when the capacity to champion change is high (Rogers 1995; Pearce and Ensley 2004). In complex health system environments, we are seeing that where the capacity for learning is well supported, the ability to innovate is enhanced and the potential for complex changes to be adopted and sustained are greater. Figure 10.2 frames a range of potential relationships between learning and innovation in relation to change capacity. This capacity is rarely the result of highly centralized or planned change even in the presence of strong leadership. Rather, it is more likely to occur when learning is supported throughout the system and innovation is left to emerge dynamically where the learning is happening. Herein lies a repeated dilemma.

Instead of developing strong and sustained infrastructure and capacity for shared development and learning in order to enhance innovation potential, approaches to large-scale complex change within healthcare jurisdictions tend to remain time limited and structural. Therefore, at most they foster other processes of change that in turn require multiple and largely chaotic responses in order for something noticeable to happen. Otherwise, change comes from largely unplanned and

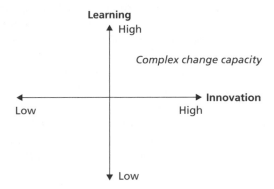

Figure 10.2   Learning and innovation capacity in complex change for health gain

unpredictable breakthroughs in technologies and treatments. However, diffusion of this kind of change also often occurs through a series of loosely connected actions from some 'early adopters' and is sometimes followed eventually by some or many 'laggards' (Rogers 1995), but not necessarily with any evaluative learning component, and rarely with any early policy attention.

Figure 10.3 frames the relationship between planned and unplanned change, and the degree of reliance on structural or more process-oriented mechanisms. If the construct is correct that complex change is more likely when there is high learning (consequent on strong learning support) and high innovation capacity, then resources and incentives enhancing these characteristics will enlarge the scope of planned and process-oriented change activities. They also will allow better capture of unplanned and process-oriented change possibilities as and when they occur. Using the typology of Greenhalgh *et al.* (2004), you might be able to better 'make it happen' by creating capacities that support 'letting it happen'.

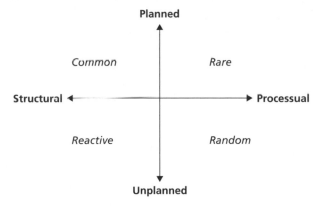

Figure 10.3   Approaches to large-scale complex change

Conceived in this way, the role of government policy is not negated or reduced, rather it is radically altered. The agency role for central action or decision making becomes much less about implementing structures, plans and controls and more about creating flexible and varied opportunities for learning and the harnessing of emergent innovation in line with broad system vision and shared policy goals.

Multidisciplinary practice-based learning networks can help create sufficient overlap of understanding and commitment to innovate in relatively uncharted territory towards loosely shared goals such as 'health gain' or 'social capital'. The real promise for creating capacity for complex change within complex public service environments may well lay primarily in our ability to develop and support what Wenger (1998) frames as ongoing communities of practice (in this instance for learning). If so, rethinking how or even if we can actively manage change is a requirement that needs tackling as soon as possible.

Final Thoughts for Further Reflection and Action

Insights concerning how to encourage innovative change in complex public sector settings (outlined in this chapter) include a combination of empirical lessons from observing change within several health system jurisdictions; the identification of methodological challenges in our as yet insufficient research efforts; some theoretical ideas on possible emergent solutions; and suggestions concerning emergent gains and alternative frames. A few final reflections in light of these ideas are offered for further debate and development.

First, capturing positively deviant cases of successful change and innovation will advance our understanding of how far we can enable and harness complex change in the public sector, more than cataloguing additional failures and barriers will. There is a vast and growing literature cataloguing our failures to manage complex change that actually enhances performance in health system environments. It is time to increase our efforts to identify when and where and how complex change processes actually make a difference in sustainable and meaningful ways.

Second, the gaps between research and practice and researchers and practitioners need to be narrowed. If we cannot communicate, we cannot deal with the noise – the cacophony – in both our change theories and our change practices. When researchers, policy-makers and practitioners share even a vague common interest in improving health care or other public 'goods' such as basic education, they should endeavour to work on the solutions collectively and collaboratively. The efforts may appear more problematic, more arduous and more 'messy', but the longer term, sustainable outcomes usually warrant the harder work. Enabling complex change within complex public sector environments is a contact sport that requires a team effort.

Third, complex change in complex public sector environments requires equally complex theoretical constructs and practical approaches. Just as Colebatch (2004) reminds us that policy making is 'messy' but critical for us to 'make sense of the real world', our research training and paradigms and approaches need to be equally messy and mixed. If we are going to be able to comprehend the complexity of large-scale public sector change, and more importantly, if we are going to be able to extend our theoretical insights in ways that actually allow learning and progress, then we need to move beyond the veneer of structural or surface level change to encompass dynamic, emergent, deeper level cognition and action.

Fourth, creating and sustaining multidisciplinary communities of learning in practice will help secure the potential to change and innovate in complex ways in complex settings. Uniprofessional communities of practice are a reality within highly professionalized organizations such as health care (Ferlie *et al.* 2005). Wenger and Snyder (2000) speak of communities of practice as 'the organizational frontier'. If we can support and encourage multidisciplinary communities, the potential to harness learning and innovation for the system is intensified. Perhaps multidisciplinary communities of learning should become 'the organizational standard' of the future if we want to nurture change and harness innovation within complex large-scale systems.

Fifth, reframing the fundamental role of policy making within and for change will strengthen the potential for sustained innovation. Policy- and decision-makers are key stakeholders when it comes to learning to better support change. Akin to Wallace and Hoyle's 'temperate policy making' (Chapter 4), large-scale policy efforts should target creating favourable conditions for local solutions mindful of parameters such as legislation, resourcing, safety and accountability concerns. Less effort on elaborate detailed plans, and more effort on flexible responsive incentives, will enhance chances for success.

To sum up, maybe change can't be managed. Perhaps it can only be nurtured. Simply put, we make a mistake when we believe we can programme or control complex change within complex public service system environments. However, we can provide opportunity and encouragement to accept higher levels of risk within experimentation, letting innovation emerge wherever and however it can. If this is so, a fundamental policy objective becomes capturing innovation aligned to desired progress. In turn, the key leadership and management responsibilities would need to focus more on enabling change where and when it happens, rather than trying to manage it or make it happen. The real challenge then becomes understanding and supporting learning at multiple levels and capturing innovations in line with organizational mission and goals. 'Improvising' positive pathways for change is likely to be more critical to nurturing sustainable innovation than initially 'orchestrating' the way.

ACKNOWLEDGEMENTS

It is important to acknowledge several valuable sources of contribution to this chapter. The following groups of investigators, funders and publishers are thanked for their leadership, insights, support and help in developing and sharing knowledge related to better understanding complex change.

- The team of organizational and health researchers following innovative change processes in Canadian health system contexts includes: Karen Golden-Biddle, Bob Hinings and Trish Reay at the School of Business at the University of Alberta, and Amy Pablo at the Haskayne School of Business, and myself from the Department of Community Health Sciences, both at the University of Calgary. This five-year Programme of Research into Organizational Change in the Healthcare Sector was jointly funded by the Canadian Health Services Research Foundation (CHSRF) and the Alberta Heritage Foundation for Medical Research (AHFMR).
- The national project team researching public participation comprised investigators from five Canadian provinces – led by Julia Abelson at McMaster University and Pierre-Gelier Forest at Laval University, and also was funded by CHSRF and AHFMR.
- Segments of the researcher – decision-maker partnership described within the section on methodological challenges were first published as Appendix A of *Collaboration in Context* (Scott and Thurston 2003).
- Segments of the description of SEARCH as a learning community first appeared in Casebeer *et al.* (2003a), Chapter 16 in *Collaboration in Context* (Scott and Thurston 2003).

Finally, all of the practitioners, managers and policy-makers who have participated in the empirical work cited are thanked for their willingness to collaborate and for their critical insights concerning complex change on the ground.

REFERENCES

Abelson, J., Forest, P.G., Eyles, J., Casebeer, A. and MacKean, G. (2004) Will it make a difference if I show up and share? Citizen perspectives on improving public involvement in health system decision making. *Journal of Health Service Research and Policy*, **9**(4), 205–12.

Adair, C.E., Simpson, L., Birdsell, J.M., Omelchuk, K., Casebeer, A., Gardiner, H.P., Newman, S., Beckie, A., Clelland, S., Hayden, K.A. and Beausejour, P. (2003) *Performance Measurement Systems in Health and Mental Health Services: Models, Practices and Effectiveness – a State of the Science Review*. Edmonton, Alberta: Alberta Heritage Foundation for Medical Research.

Argyris, C. (1999) *On Organizational Learning*. Oxford: Blackwell.

Berwick, D.M. (2003) Improvement, trust, and the healthcare workforce. *Quality and Safety in Health Care*, **12**, 448–52.

Birdsell, J.M. and O'Connell, P. (2003) *The Impact of SEARCH on Participating Organizations: Evaluation Report. Developed for the Applied Health Research Programs*. Edmonton, Alberta: Alberta Heritage Foundation for Medical Research.

Bohmer, R.M.J. and Edmondson, A. (2001) Organizational: health care leaders need to design structures and processes that enhance collective learning. *Health Forum Journal*, **44**(2), 32–5.

Brazil, K., MacLeod, S. and Guest, B. (2002) Collaborative practice: a strategy to improve the relevance of health services research. *Healthcare Management Forum*, **15**(3), 18–24.

Buchanan, D., Claydon, T. and Doyle, M. (1999) Organization development and change: the legacy of the nineties. *Human Resource Management Journal*, **9**(2), 20–37.

Casebeer, A. (2004) Regionalizing Canadian health care: the good – the bad – the ugly. *Health Care Papers*, **5**(1), 88–93.

Casebeer, A. and Hannah, K.J. (1998) The process of change related to health policy shift: reforming a health care system. *International Journal of Public Sector Management*, **11**(7), 566–82.

Casebeer, A. and Reay, T. (2004) Reinventing primary health care: physicians have a pivotal part to play. *Canadian Family Physician*, **50**, 1345–7.

Casebeer, A., Scott, C. and Hannah, K. (2000) Transforming a health care system: managing change for community gain. *Canadian Journal of Public Health*, **91**(2), 89–93.

Casebeer, A., Hayward, S., Hayward, R. and Matthias, S. (2003a) SEARCH – a learning and communication network. In C.M. Scott and W.E. Thurston (eds), *Collaboration in Context*. Calgary: University of Calgary, pp. 183–93.

Casebeer, A., Besner, J., Golden-Biddle, K. and Reay, T. (2003b) The researcher–decision maker partnership: a collaborative journey. In C.M. Scott and W.E. Thurston (eds), *Collaboration in Context*. Calgary: University of Calgary, pp. 351–4.

Casebeer, A., Reay, T., Golden-Biddle, K., Pablo, A., Wiebe, E. and Hinings, C.R. (2006) Experiences of regionalization: assessing multiple stakeholder perspectives across time. *Healthcare Quarterly*, **9**(2), 32–43.

Church, E. (2002) *Tempered Radicals: How People Use Difference to Inspire Change at Work*. Boston: Harvard Business School Press.

Colebatch, H.K. (2002) *Policy*, 2nd edn. Milton Keynes: Open University Press.

Cooperrider, D. (1997) *Appreciative Inquiry: a Constructive Approach to Organizational Change and Development*. Cleveland, OH: Case Western Reserve University.

Crossan, M.M., Lane, H.W. and White, R.E. (1999) An organizational learning framework: from intuition to institution. *Academy of Management Review*, **24**, 522–37.

Denis, J.-L. and Lomas, J. (2003) Editorial – convergent evolution: the academic and policy roots of collaborative research. *Journal of Health Services Research and Policy*, **8**(4), Supplement 2, S2-1–S2-6.

Denis, J.-L., Langley, A. and Cazale, L. (1996) Leadership and strategic change under ambiguity. *Organization Studies*, **17**, 673–99.

Denis, J.-L., Herbert, Y., Langley, A., Lozeau, D. and Trotier, L. (2002) Explaining different patterns for complex health care innovations. *Health Care Management Review*, **27**(3), 60–73.

Ferlie, E. (2001) Organizational studies. In N. Fulop, P. Allen, A. Clarke and N. Black (eds), *Studying the Organization and Delivery of Health Services: Research Methods*. London: Routledge, pp. 24–39.

Ferlie, E., Ashburner, L., Fitzgerald, L. and Pettigrew, A. (1996) *The New Public Management in Action*. Oxford: Oxford University Press.

Ferlie, E., Fitzgerald, L., Wood, M. and Hawkins, C. (2005) The nonspread of innovations: the mediating role of professionals. *Academy of Management Journal*, **48**(1), 117–34.

Friere, P. (1990) *Education for the Critical Consciousness*. New York: Continuum.

Fulop, N., Allen, P., Clarke, A. and Black, N. (2001) *Studying the Organization and Delivery of Health Services: Research Methods*. London: Routledge.

Golden-Biddle, K., Reay, T., Petz, S., Witt, C., Pablo, A., Casebeer, A., Greenwood, R. and Hinings, C.R. (2003) Toward a communicative perspective of research collaboration as communicative endeavor: the case of the researcher-decision maker partnership. *Journal of Health Services Research and Policy*, **8**(4), Supplement 2, 20–5.

Gray, J.A.M. (2001) *Evidence-Based Healthcare: How to Make Policy and Management Decisions*, 2nd edn. Edinburgh: Churchill Livingstone.

Greenhalgh, T., Robert, G., MacFarlane, F., Bate, P. and Kyriakidou, O. (2004) Diffusion of innovations in service organizations: systematic review and recommendations. *The Milbank Quarterly*, **82**(4), 581–629.

Healthcare Papers (2004) Regionalization of health systems. *Healthcare Papers*, **5**(1).

Hinings, C.R., Casebeer, A., Reay, T., Golden-Biddle, K., Pablo, A. and Greenwood, R. (2003) Regionalizing health care in Alberta: legislated change, uncertainty and loose coupling. *British Journal of Management*, **14**(1), S15–S30.

Huxham, C. (ed.) (1996) *Creating Collaborative Advantage*. London: Sage.

International Board of Review (2004) *A Review of the Operation of the Alberta Heritage Foundation for Medical Research: 1998–2004*. Edmonton, Alberta: International Board of Review.

Lau, F. and Hayward, R. (2000) Building a virtual network in a community health research training program. *Journal of the American Medical Informatics Association*, **7**(4), 361–77.

Lehman, W.E., Greener, J.M. and Simpson, D.D. (2002) Assessing organizational readiness for change. *Journal of Substance Abuse Treatment*, **22**, 197–209.

Martin, V. (2003) *Leading Change in Health and Social Care*. RoutledgeFalmer: London.

Mason, J., Wood, J. and Freemantle, N. (1999) Designing evaluations of interventions to change professional practice. *Journal of Health Service Research and Policy*, **4**(2), 106–11.

McCaffrey Consulting (2004) *The Swift Efficient Application of Research in Community Health (SEARCH): Project Tracking Report Developed for the Applied Health Research Programs*. Edmonton, Alberta: Alberta Heritage Foundation for Medical Research.

Miller, W.L. and Crabtree, B.F. (2000) Conversing at the wall. In N.K. Denzin and Y.S. Lincoln (eds), *Handbook of Qualitative Research*, 2nd edn. Newbury Park, CA: Sage, pp. 607–31.

Mintzberg, H. (1987) Crafting strategy. *Harvard Business Review*, July–August, 66–75.

Mintzberg, H. (1994) *The Rise and Fall of Strategic Planning*. New York: Free Press.

Mitroff, I. (1998) *Smart Thinking for Crazy Times*. San Francisco: Berrett-Koehler.

Pearce, C.L. and Ensley, M.D. (2004) A reciprocal and longitudinal investigation of the innovation process: the central role of shared vision in product and process innovation teams (PPITs). *Journal of Organizational Behavior*, **25**(2), 259–78.

Pettigrew, A.M. (1986) Health service managers reflecting on practice. In G. Parston (ed.), *Managers as Strategists*. London: Hollen Street Press.

Plsek, P.E. and Greenhalgh, T. (2001) Complexity science: the challenge of complexity in health care. *British Medical Journal*, **323**, 625–8.

Quinn, R.E. (2000) *Change the World: How Ordinary People Can Accomplish Extraordinary Results*. San Francisco: Jossey-Bass.

Reay, T., Golden-Biddle, K. and GermAnn, K. (2006) Legitimizing a new role: small wins and micro-processes of change. *Academy of Management Journal* (in press).

Rogers, E.M. (1995) *Diffusion of Innovations*, 3rd edn. New York: Sage.

Rosenstock, I.M., Strecher, V.J. and Becker, M.H. (1988) Social learning theory and the health belief model. *Health Education Quarterly*, **15**(2), 175–83.

Roussos, S.T. and Fawcett, S.B. (2000) A review of collaborative partnerships as a strategy for improving community health. *Annual Review of Public Health*, **21**, 369–402.

Sackett, D.L. and Wennberg, J.E. (1997) Choosing the best research design for each question. *British Medical Journal*, **315**, 20–7.

Scott, C.M. and Thurston, W.E. (eds) (2003) *Collaboration in Context*. University of Calgary: The Institute for Gender Research and Health Promotion Research Group.

Shortell, M.S., Gillies, R.R., Anderson, D.A., Erickson, K.M. and Mitchell, J.B. (1996) *Remaking Health Care in America: Building Organized Delivery Systems*. San Francisco: Jossey-Bass.

Simpson, D.D. (2002) A conceptual framework for transferring research to practice. *Journal of Substance Abuse Treatment*, **22**(4), 171–82.

Spencer, J.A. and Jordan, R.K. (1999) Learner-centred approaches in medical education. *British Medical Journal*, **318**, 1280–3.

Staudenmayer, N., Tyre, M. and Perlow, L. (2002) Time to change: temporal shifts as enablers of organizational change. *Organization Science*, **13**(5), 583–97.

Thurston, W.E., MacKean, G., Vollman, A., Casebeer, A., Weber, M., Maloff, B. and Bader, J. (2004) Public participation in regional health policy: a theoretical framework. *Health Policy*, **73**(3), 237–52.

Van de Ven, A., Polley, D., Garud, R. and Venkataraman, S. (1999) *The Innovation Journey*. Oxford: Oxford University Press.

Verhoef, M.J., Casebeer, A.L. and Hilsden, R.J. (2002) Assessing efficacy of complementary medicine: adding qualitative research methods to the 'gold standard'. *Journal of Alternative and Complimentary Medicine*, **8**(3), 275–81.

Wallace, M. and Pocklington, K. (2002) *Managing Complex Educational Change: Large-Scale Reorganization of Schools*. London: RoutledgeFalmer.

Wenger, E. (1998) *Communities of Practice: Learning, Meaning, and Identity*. Cambridge: Cambridge University Press.

Wenger, E.C. and Snyder, W.M. (2000) Communities of practice: the organizational frontier. *Harvard Business Review*, **78**(1), 139–45.

CHAPTER 11

ORCHESTRATION, COHERENCE AND THE PROBLEM OF CONFLICTING ACCOUNTABILITIES

William Firestone and Dorothy Shipps

This chapter focuses squarely on the service organizations that are both the target sites of implementation of many complex and programmatic changes connected with government-driven reforms, and the source of local innovation which may, in time, spread to become more complex. William Firestone and Dorothy Shipps develop the notion of trying to maximize 'coherence' in seeking to sustain and incrementally to improve practice in public service organizations as complementary (and logically prior) to a focus on orchestrating the process of complex and programmatic change at this service organization level. Their intellectual project is to develop knowledge-for-action which will assist organization leaders with working to improve practice in the face of inconsistent external pressures for change. Their normative concern lies with the mediation of external demands for change in settings where government intervention is on the increase, as with US education.

Firestone and Shipps put forward the ideal of attaining a coherent direction for change at the service organizational level in order to maximize the potential for improvement. They discuss how difficult it can be for organization leaders to achieve this ideal in the face of multiple and sometimes contradictory external pressures for reform and other kinds of change, coupled with interacting but not wholly compatible accountability requirements (part of many reform efforts, as Chapter 6 depicts for Canadian health care). A way forward may be to develop a clear and consistent idea of 'internal accountability' as a basis for making sense of, and considering how far to mediate, external demands. A sense of internal accountability may act as a filter, which guides a selective response to such pressures, legitimating their adaptation where possible to promote coherence in line with shared organization-level educational values. (The response advocated here is consistent with the idea of mediation through 'principled infidelity' discussed in Chapter 4.)

Introduction

In an effort to bring greater clarity to the challenges of leading complex change, Mike Wallace (Chapter 1) has focused on the metatask of 'orchestration' (Wallace and Pocklington 2002). He defines orchestration as 'coordinated activity within set parameters expressed by a network of senior leaders at different administrative levels to instigate, organize, oversee and consolidate complex change across part or all of a multi-organisational system'. Orchestration is explicitly contrasted with transformational and transactional leadership as having some elements of both, but identifying additional special tasks that must be accomplished if complex changes are to be brought about.

Orchestration emphasizes the process of change leadership over time, but it tends to focus on the enactment of a particular change or programme of change, however complex it may be. Coherence is a complementary concept that refers to the extent of fit or compatibility among changes, reforms and/or policies in place at any given time, usually – unlike orchestration – at one level of the educational system. The frequently noted absence of coherence at each level of the system highlights the difficulties of orchestrating any particular change.

There is a rather extensive tradition of writing about (and a smaller tradition of studying) coherence in the American educational policy literature (Smith and O'Day 1991) and to a lesser extent in research on local educational change (Hatch 2001). Much of this literature portrays coherence not as a process but as a state, one in which practitioners receive consistent messages about what intended outcomes and modes of achieving them are valued (Fuhrman 1993a). While coherence is desirable, it is almost unachievable for local organizations because the growing role of central government exacerbates conflicting external accountabilities to which local leaders and administrators must respond. To illustrate the difficulty of achieving coherence, we provide a typology of such accountabilities and illustrate their conflicts after we elaborate on the idea of coherence.

Yet the meanings of external accountabilities are not straightforward. In fact, the messages communicating accountability demands are always interpreted locally through processes that differ from location to location. In the following section, we suggest that the way accountability demands are interpreted makes a difference. One new idea is that leaders and practitioners on the scene can interpret the signals they receive and their own values to create their own sense of 'internal accountability', and that such internal accountability may be more powerful than external accountability demands. After exploring the dynamics of external accountability interpretation, we argue that the idea of internal accountability provides a potential basis for making sense of conflicting external demands.

Coherence

Wallace's definition of orchestration focuses on the process of change. The idea of coherence refers more to an ideal state of school organization. Yet it seems important to focus on the target – the state to be attained – while considering the process.

American discussions of coherence were a response to the blizzard of changing and contradictory directions that federal and state governments give to schools. Coherence is achieved when polices avoid contradictions, send similar messages and give direction to the educational system as a whole. Advocates for coherence argue that the message to be sent should be that intellectually challenging goals must be set for all children, and policies should provide a coherent framework for achieving those goals (Fuhrman 1993b).

Advocates of coherence quickly began to focus on what some called instructional guidance systems (Cohen and Spillane 1993). They argued that policy making in the early 1990s focused too much on finance, groups with special needs and ancillary services. Improving education, they argued, meant improving instruction. That was best achieved by focusing on policy levers most directly affecting teachers: standards, student assessments, instructional materials, the oversight of instruction and requirements for teacher education and licensure. This analysis contributed to the vast spread of standards and national curricula and assessments during the 1990s (Ball 1990; Editorial Projects in Education 2001). The latest chapter in that development in the US is the 'No Child Left Behind' legislation. It mandated the subjects and grades at which states should test, and identified sanctions for schools if students failed to meet annual performance targets for several years in a row.

Coherence is an issue for schools and districts too. The introduction of multiple major reforms simultaneously is a recipe for chaos (Hatch 2001). Although coherence is difficult to achieve at both the school and district level, it is an important prescription for increased student achievement at both levels (Reynolds and Teddlie 2000; Hightower *et al.* 2002). Thus, one would hope that changes could be managed in ways that would build internal coherence.

Conflicting External Accountabilities

Coherence is an elusive ideal if only because the external policy environment is so fragmented. As that environment becomes more active, local educators find themselves held accountable for more and more things. Those things are rarely well aligned. To illustrate the breadth of external accountabilities that local leaders face, we identify and describe four accountabilities and point out some conflicts among them.

When we say that an educational leader (or anyone else) is held accountable, it means that the leader has made a commitment to provide an account of her or his actions to some constituent, customer or formal superior. This makes the person giving that account the agent of some other authority. Policies that increase accountability generally assume that the leader is extrinsically motivated, or at least that external motivation is required to make the agent accountable to the authority in question. If providing an account is not sufficient in and of itself, the agent may be subject to rewards or sanctions depending on how well the agent's actions – as described in that account – meet criteria set by the authority (Adams and Kirst 1999).

Most analyses of accountability focus on the relationship between the agent and one authority at a time. We highlight the variety of authorities to which educational leaders are held accountable and explore the problems that come from these multiple accountabilities.

Political accountability

The core of political accountability is responsiveness to the electorate. As the American educational system was formalized in the nineteenth and twentieth centuries, the first authority to whom local educational leaders were accountable was the locally elected school board. The constituents to whom educators are held accountable politically has expanded over time to include parents, teachers' unions and local civic and business groups who are represented through advisory councils and Parent Teachers Associations (Tyack 1974). Hence, educational leaders have a variety of local constituents vying for their attention and for special consideration (Adams and Kirst 1999). Often they are more concerned about reducing taxes or keeping their jobs than about educational outcomes (Shipps 2003).

Political accountability is not as strong in several former Commonwealth countries (Farrell and Law 1999; Earley 2003; Robinson, Ward and Timperley 2003). England and Wales and New Zealand both introduced boards of governors for individual schools during governance reforms in the late 1980s. These boards include at least elected parent representatives, teacher representatives, and representatives that the boards themselves co-opt. The intent is for the boards to have a majority who are not school employees.

Several factors work against strong political accountability in commonwealth countries. First, while one intent of the legislation establishing these bodies is to promote political accountability, that is only one of their functions. Second, the impact of locally elected governors is blunted by the presence of others on the boards. Finally, evidence suggests that local governors lack the capacity to understand many of the issues they face, especially when the schools serve poor and minority communities, creating a strong dependence on the school headteacher (Earley 2003; Robinson, Ward and Timperley 2003).

The multitude of political pressures that American educators face encourages the satisfaction of specific demands, rather than thinking more globally and strategically about how to engage the public or build a general base of support. The implications of such pressures are for local leaders to become negotiators who can build coalitions by bringing together individuals and groups with divergent interests around relatively common goals.

School leaders handle these political pressures poorly. Relatively few urban superintendents learned to negotiate such pressure at mid-century (Cuban 1976). While we know little about their decision making since then, writings that seek to capture superintendents' views of their work often portray them as highly reactive and at the mercy of larger political forces they can neither control nor accommodate effectively (Brunner and Bjork 2001). Working with the community appears to be a major challenge for which many principals are not well prepared. Their capacity to address community interests effectively while addressing internal concerns appears limited. The circumstances in which they cope with external constituencies while promoting improved teaching and learning appear highly conditional (Bizar and Barr 2001). Recent surveys suggest that political accountability continues to bedevil coping with both external and internal concerns. School leaders report being driven out of the field by the combination of political and bureaucratic demands (Public Agenda 2001).

Bureaucratic accountability

Bureaucratic accountability is supposed to ensure that the decisions and orders of formal superiors are carried out. It is usually embodied in formal rules, regulations and standard operating procedures (SOPs) that specify what subordinates are expected to do. Such accountability usually encompasses controls over subordinates' work, and rewards and sanctions linked to the performance (Adams and Kirst 1999).

Bureaucratic and political accountability become enmeshed when politics generates rules and regulations. Thus federal legislation specifying what services are available for categories of children results from a political process. Yet, from the school or district perspective, it is a bureaucratic accountability; the school faces regulations that must be followed. Such regulations are usually non-negotiable for a specific school or its leader.

Bureaucratic accountability has changed radically in the last decade or two. Initially, regulations coming from the state or federal government specified the processes to be used: what textbooks would be employed, how many hours constitute a school day, what courses a student must take to graduate, how teachers are certified. The rise of the 'standards movement' and interest in instructional guidance has spread the use of outcome accountability. Increasingly, American states adopt standards specifying what children are expected to learn, backing them up with tests and assessments that are supposed to measure the extent to which children achieve those standards. In many instances, rewards and sanctions are linked to their performance. This has led to various forms of 'teaching to the test' where high scores become an end in themselves rather than an indicator of student learning. Researchers disagree about how much displacement outcome accountability creates. Some see uniformly negative results (McNeil 2000) and others seeing more of a mixed picture (Firestone, Schorr and Monfils 2004). While the instructional effects of outcome accountability are debated, it is becoming increasingly clear that tested subjects receive more attention than those not tested.

A similar development happened in the UK with the introduction of the National Curriculum and its assessment in the 1988 Education Reform Act. The English–Welsh approach goes beyond standards to specifying the curriculum students should be taught, and testing them on their mastery of that curriculum. Nevertheless, as a form of accountability, there are substantial similarities between the English and American approaches to testing (Firestone, Broadfoot and Fitz 1999). This kind of outcome standardization is well within the bureaucratic approach to accountability (Mintzberg 1983).

Yet process accountability continues to be a major focus of attention in England and Wales. It is most prominently reflected in the current Office for Standards in Education (OFSTED) inspection system. Through OFSTED visitations, the government generates a report that assesses a variety of dimensions of instruction and school leadership (Office for Standards in Education 2003). Some of these reflect the practices that are likely to contribute to increased test scores; others reflect different criteria for a good school experience. Whatever the value of these dimensions, OFSTED inspections are experienced as a strong form of accountability for schools (Case, Case and Catling 2000; Ouston, Fidler and Earley 1997).

In the face of bureaucratic accountability, school leaders are expected to serve as functionaries who comply with external regulations. This is easier with process regulations that specify specific actions to be taken or procedures to follow. It is more challenging when authorities specify outcomes. Especially so when there is substantial doubt about how to achieve those outcomes, for instance when schools are accountable for raising the achievement of groups of students that historically have scored poorly. Then, leaders must become problem solvers who mobilize available resources and align them to achieve externally specified goals.

Market accountability

Market accountability aims to improve schooling through increased competition: between educators for jobs, educators and external service providers for contracts, and schools for students. Competition with alternative providers is supposed to increase teaching and learning efficiency, and competition between schools for students and staff is expected to encourage innovation. Leaders are expected to become better managers or learn to function as entrepreneurs. With market accountability, district leaders are expected to treat parents and students as customers, and to adopt corporate 'restructuring' to get more effort from school employees for the same (or fewer) tax dollars. Market logic dictates that leaders who show improvements in student performance should receive material incentives, while failure to improve leads to removal. Similar material incentive systems for teachers have not proven especially effective except when they are provided collectively (O'Day 2002), although the use of bonuses has not been systematically researched for their effects on educational leaders.

Market accountability that has been attempted by outsourcing special education, school support and school management services comes from similar arguments about market efficiencies that leaders can capture when serving special populations. Such contracting aims to take advantage of private sector expertise, while encouraging leaders to become more efficient and creative managers. Research has noted a lack of real savings (Hannaway 1999), but has not yet explained whether the core assumption about promoting efficiency really spurs performance as intended.

More attention has focused on accountability mechanisms that use school choice – charters, vouchers and open attendance zones where parents choose as opposed to going to an assigned school – to create market-like situations in education (Clotfelter and Ladd 1996). The idea has been justified as a way to provide children with access to the schooling their parents want, rather than that which local civic elites and governments provide. The concept suggests a bargain. Individual schools are substantially deregulated. In exchange, their leaders become flexible, risk-taking entrepreneurs who invent new ways to close performance gaps.

With market accountability, school leaders are expected to act as corporate managers and entrepreneurs. The hope is that market incentives will promote creativity and efficiency. The fear is that increased attention to marketing will distract attention and siphon resources from efforts to improve core instructional processes.

Professional accountability

Professional models place great discretion with the agents rather than some outside authority. They assume that the services required are typically non-routine. These services can be provided only with a great deal of expertise, and the discretion to use that expertise in order to tailor the work to the needs of the client or student (Adams and Kirst 1999). In principle, however, professional accountability implies collective responsibility rather than individual responsibility. That is, the profession defines best practice for specific problems, recognizing that such practice must be tailored to specific circumstances. Then individual practitioners can be held accountable for following standards of good practice.

The last decade has seen an effort to increase professional accountability by specifying professional standards. Perhaps the best example is the *Principles and Standards for School Mathematics* of the National Council of Teachers of Mathematics (NCTM 2000). Unlike state standards, these provide as much attention to the process of teaching as to what students should learn, although the two are interwoven. A related effort is that by the Interstate School Leaders Licensure Consortium (1996) to develop training and performance standards for principals. Such standards have been widely disseminated and often serve as a point of reference for determining good practice. Nevertheless, there is too little consensus around these standards for them to serve as broadly accepted yardsticks of good practice, much less for enforcement panels (such as professional review boards) to develop around them. Instead, where professional consensus develops, it appears to be more of a school-by-school phenomenon, and even that is unusual (Carnoy, Elmore and Siskin 2003).

Nevertheless, the ideal of professional accountability creates new demands upon leaders. They are expected to become expert educators who can guide teachers to good practice, either by providing such knowledge themselves or by directing teachers to sources of such information (Stein and Nelson 2003).

Conflicting accountabilities

The point of this analysis is to indicate that school and district leaders are likely to experience many accountability claims simultaneously, making the task of creating coherence out of mixed signals vastly more complex than it appears to most policy-makers, advocates or researchers. In practice, these obligations often conflict, pinning leaders between constituents and superiors, professional standards and public expectations, market forces and regulators. Three examples illustrate such conflicts.

The major conflict in England and some other commonwealth countries is between *market* demands and *bureaucratic* accountability stemming from national assessment. School leaders and boards of governors become driven by marketing concerns. One would think that market and outcome decisions would push leaders and governors in the same direction, given the prevalence of league tables and the theory that parents will select schools where children consistently do well on national assessments. Yet, other, often more cosmetic, issues arise like the quality and aesthetics of buildings, uniforms and marketing materials. School governors may fear discussing embarrassing issues in open meetings because of negative consequences for recruitment. Investment decisions are made with an eye to recruitment, sometimes regardless of educational consequences. Moreover, the major competition is often for middle to upper middle class children who are likely to score well on state tests. Other groups become less valued (Deem and Brehony 1994; Fiske and Ladd 2000).

In the US, superintendents often cite accountability conflicts between the *political* demands of their local communities and *bureaucratic* accountability required by state and federal bureaucratic mandates. Most state departments of education have asked superintendents to show regular increases in student achievement, anticipating that they will comply by redirecting fiscal resources and staff efforts to that goal. But this ignores the political accountability that a superintendent inherits as the head of a large, local government agency that depends on local tax revenues and is both a major employer and a significant purchaser of goods and services. Frequently, raising test scores requires new instructional materials, additional training and, some would argue, a longer school day and year. Yet all of these things cost money. Moreover, state-funded schools open a pathway to social mobility for adults, especially from immigrants and minorities. Local constituents may care more about hiring local people than those with the strongest technical credentials. Superintendents may feel forced between choosing those who could contribute most to state mandates and those with local support (Fuller *et al.* 2003).

Professional and *political* accountability also clash. In 1993, in Littleton, Colorado, the district began to introduce performance-based assessments. In this high achieving district, the local professional consensus was that more open-ended assessments would challenge students not only to provide 'right answers' but also better justify their conclusions and use the language and representation systems of the disciplines in which they were assessed. Within a few years, Littleton parents were deeply divided about the new assessments. After one of the bitterest elections in the district's history, three critics of the system won seats on the school board by two-to-one margins, the superintendent was fired, and – at least at the high school – the assessment system was dismantled (Rothman 1995).

Sense Making and Orchestration

Conflicting accountabilities add a level of complexity to change management that is qualitatively different from responding to one source of accountability or making one change. A complex and conflicted environment raises numerous questions about what should be done that precede the challenge of orchestrating any one change. Leaders undoubtedly grapple with what to do while simultaneously orchestrating changes begun earlier.

To complement Wallace's work on orchestration, we explore the complexities of figuring out a course of action. In doing so, we are aware that such decisions are made in systems where different people have access to different information and authority over different internal decisions. To make sense of this challenge we employ an information-processing model that focuses on knowledge acquisition, distribution and interpretation (Huber 1996) and then consider internal accountability as a way to bring coherence to the decision process. (The conceptual focus on knowledge as a basis for internal decision making has affinities with the exploration in Chapter 9 of the way good practice knowledge becomes reconfigured as it is deliberatively transferred between organizations.)

Knowledge acquisition

Knowledge initially comes into a school or district through some mix of scanning, focused search or having it thrust upon one. Most search and retrieval is done by formal gatekeepers with ties to specific elements in the environment (Huber

1996). Different people get information from different sources. Superintendents are sensitive to demands from the school board and the general community. Principals get the most information about parents at their schools. Central office curriculum and content specialists learn first, and perhaps the most, about state standards and assessments. Student specialists (in other words, Title I or special education directors) know about policies related to those groups. Central office staff may also have access to the most information about professional accountability expectations in their areas. It is not clear who has the greatest information about relevant market conditions, but superintendents, financial officers and board members are candidates.

It is difficult to assess the impact of gross factors, such as size, on access. For instance, when controlling for socioeconomic status (SES), larger districts have more boundary-spanning personnel with great entrée to many sources of information (Hannaway and Kimball 2001). Regardless of district size, certain kinds of information are also more broadly available than others. New professional expectations about good practice are probably less readily accessed than information coming from the public media. Once accountability demands become known to someone in a school or district, that information has to be distributed and interpreted.

Knowledge distribution

Knowledge may exist in the district and still be inaccessible. Knowledge travels through some internal pathways better than others. Bureaucratic information and some political information travel down the hierarchy easily when leaders near the top want it to (Huber 1996). Superintendents can broadcast formal announcements, but they may not widely share some board demands or the competitive pressures coming from private or parochial schools. Knowledge at the bottom of the hierarchy may also remain hidden. An elementary teacher's deep understanding about the National Council of Teachers of Mathematics standards and their implications for the curriculum and instruction may not be known to district decision-makers or even fellow teachers.

At least three characteristics affect the distribution of knowledge. One is its complexity. Information about the percentage of children who must score at a 'proficient' level on a state test to avoid a takeover is easier to communicate than understandings about how to help children achieve 'proficiency'. The urgency attached to information is a second characteristic. Urgency can be increased by the threat of credible bureaucratic sanctions – including high stakes directly linked to assessments – but also by more diffuse means, including fear of political repercussions from the community like declining to pass a school budget. A mix of potential punishments, the strength of ties between state and district and political culture all affect the attention that districts give to different external accountability demands. The quality of internal networks is the third factor. In schools, principals who are central to networks facilitate sharing information (Friedkin and Slater 1994).

Interpretation

Interpretation gives information shared meaning (Huber 1996). At issue here is how to weigh demands, relate them to each other, and strengthen or weaken links between those demands and leaders' views of purpose and means for achieving purposes. Interpretations influence ways of relating among adults and between adults and students. It is much more complex and much less rational than demand–response accountability theories would lead one to believe. Conflicting accountabilities and pre-existing beliefs combine in an intricate calculus.

As an example of an interpretation of several accountability demands, one super-intendent doubted that his district would be sanctioned by his state for low test scores. He did worry that low scores would undermine public confidence and impede budget passage. His understanding of the state standards and professional definitions of effective teaching in some areas was rather limited. To the extent that he understood state standards, he did not support them. Thus he com-municated to his staff the political importance of raising test scores, but without support for some of the practice innovations that standards advocates wanted to accompany the state's assessments. The central office staff communicated that inter-pretation to others throughout the district (Fairman and Firestone 2001).

This instance illustrates how the joint interpretation of conflicting professional, bureaucratic and political accountability demands, when filtered through personal beliefs, can lead to interpretations that the designers of accountability systems may not support. The ideal is to wind up with broadly shared interpretations. The research on school effectiveness argues that uniformity of beliefs promotes student learning (Reynolds and Teddlie 2000). Sometimes it is important to have a shared sense of purpose, but a wide variety of knowledge and beliefs may help implement that vision. Some districts appear to have raised student achievement by developing a culture that focuses on instructional improvement. This shared culture facilitates the use of the staff's diverse knowledge to figure out how to improve (Elmore 1997).

Several factors affect the likelihood of generating shared interpretations. Some are cultural. Norms about sharing and privacy affect the spread of information. So do interpretations that suggest which accountability demands are important. Transformational leaders use a variety of more or less symbolic means to generate strong, shared norms and a sense of purpose. But how they do it is unclear (Leithwood, Jantzi and Steinbach 1999). District leaders who create a culture focus-ing on the continuous improvement of instruction appear to create a demand for information from several sources, including test data and knowledge about teaching that comes from local enquiry. These leaders encourage interpretation of external accountabilities to fit the culturally dominant view (Hightower *et al.* 2002). Where leaders focus more narrowly on raising scores in direct response to bureaucratic accountability pressures, enquiry about instruction may be less common and test data may be used differently.

Power is also important (Blase 1993). Formal authority confers on its incum-bents considerable control over what information is shared and what is suppressed, as well as the right to determine official interpretations. Yet teachers and others have considerable resources coming from diverse sources, such as the power of unions or the previously mentioned capacity to close the door on one's classroom and proceed in many areas as one prefers. They can successfully resist the interpretations of top leadership. Moreover, different district offices have divergent interpretations and compete to set the dominant interpretation (Spillane 1998).

Local interpretations determine the extent to which people acquiesce to specific accountability demands, but acquiescence is only one possible response. Others include compromise, avoidance, defiance and manipulation (Oliver 1991). The partial response to state standards where teachers adopt specific instructional procedures but accommodate them to their old modes of teaching is a common compromise in the face of new testing regimes (Firestone, Schorr and Monfils 2004). The ways in which superintendents have sought to manipulate school boards through representing local accountability demands have been extensively documented (Burlingame 1988). The symbolic adoption of policies without following through on implementation is a form of avoidance.

Internal Accountability, Interpretation and Coherence

While interpretation is subject to historical, social and political forces, there is also a substantial moral component. This is sometimes referred to as internal accountability – in explicit contrast to external accountability and defined as a situation:

> where essential components of accountability [a]re generated largely within a school staff. Staff identify clear standards for student performance, collect ... information to inform themselves about their levels of success, and exert ... strong peer pressure within the faculty to meet the goals (Newmann, King and Rigdon 1997).

Although it depends on a few case studies, the idea of internal accountability makes professional and moral leadership explicit and defensible. Extant definitions emphasize a shared culture with strong professional norms governing expectations for students. They also suggest a well-developed capacity for teachers to collaborate around shared values. Thus, this concept supports research linking strong school professional communities with improved student performance (Newmann and Associates 1996). It also fits with the research on transformational leadership, which suggests that leaders could promote this sense of internal accountability. Thus, a strongly developed sense of internal accountability may provide a filter for interpreting external accountabilities in ways that promote ends to which a school or district is deeply committed. These pre-existing commitments, more than external accountability, may prove to be the key to collective action that actually promotes student learning.

Research Agenda

Nevertheless, writing about internal accountability raises several important questions that deserve more extensive enquiry and provide the starting point for a research agenda. The first question is: what do educators in schools or districts hold each other accountable for? Is it student achievement? Equal educational outcomes? Educational achievement but only for those that 'everyone' already knows will do well in school? 'Good behaviour?' There is modest evidence that in some schools, the content of the internal accountability system works against high achievement for all students, but works for positive, equal outcomes (Carnoy, Elmore and Siskin 2003).

A related question is: what factors contribute to and shape internal accountability? There are some indications that internal accountability is easier to develop in schools serving a higher socioeconomic student body. If that is the case, using internal accountability to promote equity may be an uphill battle. It is also critical to understand how leaders in different positions contribute to internal accountability for high standards for all students, especially in the most challenging contexts.

Finally: does internal accountability contribute to deeper and more equitable student learning? Few, if any, studies have attempted to operationalize the concept in ways that would link it to student outcomes. Such studies would have to take the content of the internal accountability system into account because, as the previous question suggests, it may be that not all strong internal accountability systems have the same effect.

These questions put into perspective a more frequently asked question: how do external accountabilities promote or undermine internal accountability for student learning for all students? This question seems especially important to ask about external accountabilities that are intended to promote student achievement by contributing to internal capacity. The evidence to date is that the theory behind external accountability systems is wrong. This theory was that external accountability, in the form of standards, national curricula, assessments and sanctions, was necessary to build internal accountability. It now appears that schools do not respond effectively to external accountability unless they have the requisite capacity and sense of internal accountability. Moreover, sanctions that are too strong may undermine the development of strong internal accountability that supports learning for all students (Newmann, King and Rigdon; Carnoy, Elmore and Siskin 2003). However, the basis for this conclusion is thin. It rests on a few case studies.

Nevertheless, the work to date is promising enough to suggest two hypotheses to be explored in education and other sectors as well. The first is that internal accountability will strongly influence how external accountability is enacted. This is a variation on the old idea that street-level bureaucrats interpret central policy (Lipsky 1980), but it points to specific mechanisms and roles that are critical to the interpretation process. The second is that the intent behind higher level policy will most likely be met when external and internal accountabilities are aligned.

The implication of this hypothesis – if it proves true – is that conventional accountability enforcement policies will not be enough to ensure that central policies are carried out. Other actions will be needed to help develop a local sense of internal accountability, one that is congruent with the policy in question. These hypotheses suggest that we need to know a lot more about the interplay of external and internal accountability and the whole process by which different external accountabilities interact and how they are interpreted and enacted locally.

Conclusion

In sum, we have argued that it is useful to think of building coherence as an important part of orchestration. One challenge to building coherence is the constant problem of interpreting conflicting accountability demands (and other pressures). This chapter has identified key sources of conflicting accountabilities and some elements in the process of interpreting them. It also suggests that internal accountability provides a critical filter for interpreting external accountabilities. It also suggests that internal accountability may influence whether external accountabilities have their desired effects. By pointing to the importance of internal accountability, it has clarified a central challenge for orchestration and suggested one condition that should promote its success.

REFERENCES

Adams, J.E. and Kirst, M.W. (1999) New demands and concepts for educational accountability: striving for results in an era of excellence. In J. Murphy and K.S. Louis (eds), *Handbook of Research on Educational Administration*, 2nd edn. San Francisco: Jossey-Bass, pp. 463–90.

Ball, S.J. (1990) *Politics and Policy-Making in Education*. London: Routledge.

Bizar, M. and Barr, R. (2001) *School Leadership in Times of Urban Reform*. Mahwah, NJ: Lawrence Erlbaum Associates.

Blase, J. (1993) The micropolitics of effective school-based leadership: teachers' perspectives. *Educational Administration Quarterly*, **29**(2), 142–63.

Brunner, C.C. and Bjork, L.G. (2001) *The New Superintendency*. Amsterdam: JAI Press.

Burlingame, M. (1988) The politics of education and educational policy: the local level. In N.J. Boyan (ed.), *Handbook of Research on Educational Administration*. New York: Longman, pp. 439–52.

Carnoy, M., Elmore, R.F. and Siskin, L.S. (2003) *The New Accountability: High Schools and High Stakes Testing*. New York: RoutledgeFalmer.

Case, P., Case, S. and Catling, S. (2000) Please show you're working: a critical assessment of the impact of OFSTED inspection on primary teachers. *British Journal of Sociology of Education*, **21**(4), 605–21.

Clotfelter, C.T. and Ladd, H.F. (1996) Recognizing and rewarding success in public schools. In H.F. Ladd (ed.), *Holding Schools Accountable: Perfomance-based Reform in Education*. Washington, DC: Brookings Institution, pp. 23–63.

Cohen, D.K. and Spillane, J.P. (1993) Policy and practice: the relations between govern-ance and instruction. In S.H. Fuhrman (ed.), *Designing Coherent Education Policy*. San Francisco: Jossey Bass, pp. 35–95.

Cuban, L. (1976) *Urban School Chiefs under Fire*. Chicago: University of Chicago Press.

Deem, R. and Brehony, K. (1994) Governors, schools and miasma of the market. *British Educational Research Journal*, **20**(5), 535–50.

Earley, P. (2003) Leaders or followers: governing bodies and their role in school leader-ship. *Educational Management and Administration*, **31**(4), 353–67.

Editorial Projects in Education (2001) *A Better Balance: Standards, Tests, and the Tools to Succeed: Quality Counts 2001*. Bethesda, MD: Editorial Projects in Education.

Elmore, R.F. (1997) *Investing in Teacher Learning: Staff Development and Instructional Improvement in Community School District #2*. New York: National Commission on Teaching and America's Future.

Fairman, J. and Firestone, W.A. (2001) The district role in state assessment policy: An exploratory study. In S.H. Fuhrman (ed.), *From the Capitol to the Classroom: Standards-Based Reform in the States*. Chicago: University of Chicago Press, pp. 124–47.

Farrell, C. and Law, J. (1999) The accountability of school governing bodies. *Educational Management and Administration*, **27**(1), 5–15.

Firestone, W.A., Broadfoot, P. and Fitz, J. (1999) Power, learning, and legitimation: assess-ment implementation across levels in the US and the UK. *American Educational Research Journal*, **36**(4), 759–96.

Firestone, W.A., Schorr, R.Y. and Monfils, L. (2004) *The Ambiguity of Teaching to the Test*. Mahwah, NJ: Lawrence Erlbaum Associates.

Fiske, E.B. and Ladd, H.F. (2000) *When Schools Compete: a Cautionary Tale*. Washington, DC: Brookings Institution.

Friedkin, N.E. and Slater, M.R. (1994) School leadership and performance: a social network approach. *Sociology of Education*, **67**(2), 139–57.

Fuhrman, S.H. (ed.) (1993a) *Designing Coherent Education Policy: Improving the System*. San Francisco: Jossey-Bass.

Fuhrman, S.H. (1993b) Preface. In S.H. Fuhrman (ed.), *Designing Coherent Educational Policy*. San Francisco: Jossey-Bass, pp. xi–xx.

Fuller, H.L., Campbell, C., Celio, M.B., Harvey, J., Immerwahr, J. and Winger, A. (2003) *An Impossible Job? The View from the Urban Superintendent's Chair*. Seattle, WA: University of Washington, Daniel J. Evans School of Public Affairs, Center on Reinventing Public Education.

Hannaway, J. (1999) *Contracting as a Mechanism for Managing Public Services*. Philadelphia, PA: University of Pennsylvania, Consortium for Policy Research in Education.

Hannaway, J. and Kimball, K. (2001) Big isn't always bad: school district size, poverty, and standards-based reform. In S.H. Fuhrman (ed.), *From the Capitol to the Classroom: Standards-Based Reform in the States*. Chicago: University of Chicago Press, pp. 99–123.

Hatch, T. (2001) Incoherence in the system: three perspectives on the implementation of multiple initiatives in one district. *American Journal of Education*, **109**(4), 407–37.

Hightower, A., Knapp, M.S., Marsh, J.A. and McLaughlin, M.W. (2002) *School Districts and Institutional Renewal*. New York: Teachers College Press.

Huber, G.P. (1996) Organizational learning: the contributing processes and the literature. In M.D. Cohen, and L.S. Sproull (eds), *Organizational Learning*. Thousand Oaks, CA: Sage, pp. 124–62.

Interstate School Leaders Licensure Consortium (1996) *Standards for School Leaders*. Washington, DC: Council of Chief State School Officers.

Leithwood, K., Jantzi, D. and Steinbach, R. (1999) *Changing Leadership for Changing Times*. Buckingham: Open University Press.

Lipsky, M. (1980) *Street Level Bureaucracy: Dilemmas of the Individual in Public Services*. New York: Russell Sage Foundation.

McNeil, L.M. (2000) *Contradictions of School Reform: Educational Costs of Standardized Testing*. New York: Routledge.

Mintzberg, H. (1983) *Structure in Fives: Designing Effective Organizations*. Englewood Cliffs: Prentice-Hall.

National Council of Teachers of Mathematics (2000) *Principles and Standards for School Mathematics*. Reston, VA: National Council of Teachers of Mathematics.

Newmann, F.M. and Associates (eds) (1996) *Authentic Achievement: Restructuring Schools for Intellectual Quality*. San Francisco: Jossey-Bass.

Newmann, F.M., King, M.B. and Rigdon, M. (1997) Accountability and school performance: Implications from restructuring schools. *Harvard Education Review*, **61**(1), 41–69.

O'Day, J. (2002) Complexity, accountability and school improvement. *Harvard Education Review*, **72**(3), 293–329.

Office for Standards in Education (2003) *Inspecting Schools: Framework for Inspecting Schools*. London: Department for Education and Skills.

Oliver, C. (1991) Strategic responses to institutional processes. *Academy of Management Review*, **16**(1), 145–79.

Ouston, J., Fidler, B. and Earley, P. (1997) What do schools do after OFSTED school inspections – or before? *School Leadership and Management*, **17**(1), 95–104.

Public Agenda (2001) *Trying to Stay Ahead of the Game: Superintendents and Principals Talk about School Leadership*. New York: Public Agenda.

Reynolds, D. and Teddlie, C. (2000) The processes of school effectiveness. In C. Teddlie and D. Reynolds (eds), *The International Handbook of School Effectiveness Research*. London: Falmer Press, pp. 124–59.

Robinson, V., Ward, L. and Timperley, H. (2003) The difficulties of school governance. *Educational Management and Administration*, **31**(3), 263–81.

Rothman, R. (1995) *Measuring up: Standards, Assessment, and School Reform*. San Francisco: Jossey-Bass.

Shipps, D. (2003) Pulling together: civic capacity and urban school reform. *American Educational Research Journal*, **40**(4), 841–78.

Smith, M. and O'Day, J. (1991) Systemic school reform. In S.H. Fuhrman and B. Malen (eds), *The Politics of Curriculum and Testing*. Bristol, PA: Falmer Press, pp. 233–67.

Spillane, J.P. (1998) State policy and the non-monolithic nature of the local school district: organizational and professional considerations. *American Educational Research Journal*, **35**(1), 33–63.

Stein, M.K. and Nelson, B.S. (2003) Leadership content knowledge. *Educational Evaluation and Policy Analysis*, **25**(4), 423–48.

Tyack, D.B. (1974) *The One Best System*. Cambridge, MA: Harvard University Press.

Wallace, M. and Pocklington, K. (2002) *Managing Complex Educational Change: Large-Scale Reorganization of Schools*. London: RoutledgeFalmer.

CHAPTER 12

PROSPECTS FOR UNDERSTANDING AND IMPROVING COMPLEX PUBLIC SERVICE CHANGE

Mike Wallace

In this final chapter, Mike Wallace offers a personal overview of some key themes that have emerged, explicitly or obliquely, across many or all of the contributions in Parts I to III. He concentrates on those that imply either tentative answers to aspects of the questions posed at the beginning of the editorial introduction to the book, or promising avenues for further work in search of answers.

He suggests that the contributions, taken together, provide a useful set of starting points for moving forward public service change management as a field of enquiry and practice. They offer valuable insights for deepening our understanding of the complexity which characterizes contemporary public service change, and of the ways in which policy-makers and managers may both unwittingly help to create complexity and more consciously develop strategies for coping with it. Some of the ideas they offer have clear implications for informing practice in managing particular complex changes and in developing more generic coping capacity. Wallace concludes by pointing to the extensive agenda for further research and theory building that addresses the complexity of public service change and how it is generated and coped with across national and service systems.

Catching up with Complexity

The rationale for the work leading to the contributions in Parts I to III was explained in the introduction to the book. The 'big idea' was to seek greater purchase on the unprecedented degree of complexity that is so widely reflected in public service change across many countries, and on how this complexity is addressed empirically. It was argued that while much is already known about the management of change in the public services, the phenomenon of change itself is changing. Therefore old understandings and old prescriptions for practice are in danger of becoming increasingly outmoded and, ironically, contributing to some of the unmanageability of contemporary change experienced by policy-makers and managers alike. New, relatively inductive research and practically oriented theory building that squared up to this new complexity was held to promise new understandings which might inform new practices.

At the same time, contributors were acutely aware of the significance of contextual factors at the level of detail affecting the nature of this complexity and of related management practice, as expressed most fully by Thomas (Chapter 6). So while the aspiration is to focus generically on complexity, a compromise has had to be struck on the range of public service settings and systems in which the contributions are grounded. To the extent that organizations are central to public service change anywhere, and that there are parallels between different public services and national or regional service systems, it seems likely that the focus on education and health in Anglo-American settings will have some wider applicability. But at what level of abstraction? Readers must be left to assess for themselves how far the concepts and generalizations in each chapter, including this brief overview, do have some wider relevance for deepening understanding or informing policy and practice, with what degree of generality, and with what limitations imposed by contextual contingencies.

What makes public service change increasingly complex to manage?

Taken as a whole, the contributions to this book reflect a shared concern with complexity, a feature of so much change in the public services, which reaches beyond the boundaries of individual service organizations, even if it emerged there. The various chapters address different facets of complex change, from the change process, through antecedent reform policy making, to consequent coherence making in the face of multiple pressures. Yet they all portray something of the extent and limits of human agency, especially in relation to the agency of others, which militate against a lock-step approach to policy making, implementation or fostering emergent innovation.

The first message the chapters convey about why complex change becomes complicated for any group of stakeholders to manage is that such change is fundamentally pluralistic, inherently restricting its manageability. A pluralistic orientation, of course, drove the investigation reported in Chapter 1 that led to the identification of characteristics of complexity expressed in single and programmatic change. Their relevance to other settings was confirmed by several contributors. (In contrast the application of chaos and complexity theory ideas to public service change was judged to be unhelpful by Wallace and Fertig, on the strength of their literature review in Chapter 2. Although the advocates of such ideas share the assumption that complex change is inherently unpredictable, they tend to build prescriptions – with minimal empirical backing – on the contradictory basis that these prescriptions can be predicted to work.)

The power to instigate, govern, lead, follow, resist or mediate change is unequally but very widely distributed. Consequently complex change is bound to be relatively unmanageable, even where formal authority goes unchallenged and is enforced through strong accountability measures. Levin's (Chapter 7) first-hand account of the frequent distractions faced by senior figures in provincial government, where the imperative to make a short-term response often took priority over their longer term change agenda, bears witness to the limitations of formal authority. It is supported by Seashore Louis's literature review (Chapter 5) on policy making, highlighting how pluralistic, informal, behind-the-scenes negotiations may take place between elite and non-elite groups leading to 'pre-decisions' long before a policy is formally adopted. The distribution of authority in service organizations is inherently ambiguous, especially among professionals from different specialisms and service managers, as discussed by Lamothe and Denis (Chapter 3). Even where a formal hierarchy of authority in the workplace remains uncontested, Schneller and Wallace (Chapter 8) showed how a subordinate profession can, on occasion, contest that authority on the national stage and harness sufficient influence to get the upper hand over the dominant profession.

Equally, the change-related beliefs and values to which different groups hold allegiance are likely to be at least partially incompatible, shaping their perceived interests and uses of power to bring about their realization. There is not a single rationality for changing to which change agents or service organization managers can turn, but multiple rationalities. Each makes good sense to its adherents, but they do not necessarily all align. The increasing prevalence of network forms of service governance discussed by Thomas serves to legitimate these divergent rationalities and so further to reduce the capacity of any one group of stakeholders to impose their rationality on the change process. Lamothe and Denis revealed how the hybridization of organizational forms related to the legitimation of practices which were variably related to new values underlying the move to integrated health care, and to older values associated with separate provision. The picture gets even more complicated: the same groups may hold contradictory values, leading to the endemic and ultimately unresolvable dilemmas that Wallace and Hoyle highlighted (Chapter 4). Or they may face contrary pressures posing the kinds of tension that Levin argues to be intrinsic to reform policy making, as where the strength of central direction has to be compromised to create conditions of local autonomy that favour commitment – but also favour emergence of local innovation and so less-than-faithful implementation of central reforms.

A second, related message to be taken from several chapters in Parts I to III is that change exacerbates the level of ambiguity that is endemic to organizational life, so adding to its complexity because of uncertainty and contestation over the meaning and legitimacy of new practices. Hence the likelihood of actions generating unintended consequences that may undermine change agents' good intentions, or may occasionally exceed them. This idea is explicitly developed in the ironic perspective articulated by Wallace and Hoyle. But it is also consistent with, say, Levin's conclusion that unintended consequences are inevitable in major reform efforts, Seashore Louis's suggestion that the greater availability of electronic information may actually contribute to difficulties with making decisions about policy options, and Firestone and Shipps' account of conflicting external pressures for change and accountabilities which together may inhibit the capacity for a coherent response in service organizations.

A third message, mapped in Chapter 1, is that any change is set experientially in the context of other organizational or policy-making activity, not least addressing other changes that may impinge on and compete for attention with the one to hand. Programmatic change associated with reform policies generates a profile of innovations whose implementation in service organizations has to be dealt with as an ensemble, alongside the maintenance of normal service provision. The configuration of changes and the new practices they imply are likely to be unique at any time in the experience of everyone involved, from policy-makers to service providers. Consequently, as Chapter 4 describes, some degree of learning is implied for everyone caught up in complex change, as is an inevitable degree of ambiguity for a time over how to put the profile of changes into practice and what the new practices will mean. Contributors most centrally concerned with the facilitation of learning between groups from different organizations at the local level have highlighted the complexity of the learning experience. Transferring knowledge between organizations was discussed by Hartley and Rashman in Chapter 9, and Casebeer offered an account in Chapter 10 of the nurturing by researchers of collaborative 'learning communities' involving practitioners in healthcare organizations.

How do people involved in the change process cope with this new complexity?

The evidence that most contributors drew on, whether from their own research, professional experience or secondary sources in the literature, suggests quite a strong first message about the way people cope with the complexity of change. It relates back to the pluralistic character of the process discussed in the previous section. Individuals and groups of stakeholders express their agency to realize their perceived interests, linked in turn to their relevant beliefs and values, at whatever stage of the change process they are implicated. Those directly involved in managing complex change may mediate reforms to a greater or less extent through what Wallace and Hoyle called 'principled infidelity', so as to render them workable in their contingent service organization settings. Or their mediation may result in the legitimation of the hybrid organizational forms observed by Lamothe and Denis. In respect of reform policy making, Seashore Louis points to the impact of different interest groups on shaping the agenda for change, while Thomas refers to the 'strategic conversation' between government politicians and their public servants as they work towards the practicalities of implementation. With emergent change, originating with diverse and separate organizational practices, mediation by key stakeholders may include intervention to generate a sense of wholeness, as in the case of the US hospitalist movement explored by Schneller and Wallace. Hartley and Rashman show how the recipients of knowledge transfer engaged in the 'adaption' of ideas, rather than straight adoption, to fit their contingent circumstances. In sum, people cope by mediating the change process at every stage. They iteratively mould the content of the change itself as it shifts back and forth between promoters' ideas and organizational practices.

Associated with mediation was the second message that coping is likely to involve some stakeholders playing a more strategic role than others in progressing complex change. Wallace coined the metaphor of 'orchestration' in Chapter 1 to capture something of the proactive, partly behind-the-scenes contribution of people in formal leadership positions to shaping change and its outcomes according to their different interests. Orchestrators were conceived as forming a loose and widely distributed network across the administrative and service organizations involved in implementation. Schneller and Wallace found that the metaphor could be stretched to cover both the attempt to counter external pressure for acceptance of an undesired change, and to accelerate the dissemination and coalescing of disparate emergent change into a more complex whole. Some other contributors indicated that the metaphor resonated with their own conceptualization of the way change was progressed. But its limited applicability to decentralized change processes was also highlighted. Thomas noted that in relatively unhierarchical partnerships, the notion of governance offers stronger purchase on informal interaction to achieve shared goals. While Casebeer argued that local improvisation was more feasible than orchestration, within a framework of policies facilitating collaborative local experimentation. Both she and Thomas were writing about change in Canadian health care, bringing us back to the view articulated at the beginning of this chapter that contingent contextual factors are bound to impact significantly on the parameters for managing complex change.

How could the management of public service change be rendered more effective?

Some contributors were more directly concerned with developing knowledge-for-action than others, but the key message to emerge across the different chapters is one of modest potential. There are possibilities that stand a reasonable chance of making significant improvement in the manageability of change – but only up to a point. 'Command and control' that will reliably produce faithful implementation and no unintended consequences is ruled out. So also, therefore, is any guarantee of success according to the values of any stakeholder group. Change involves risk, but as Wallace and Hoyle contend, there are good risks worth taking and bad ones worth avoiding. The possibilities identified by contributors imply that conditions creating sufficient autonomy for incremental experimentation are necessary to enable practices that looked promising in one context to be tried out, adapted in other settings, and if they do not work, ultimately rejected. For example, Hartley and Rashman portrayed how recipients of knowledge transfer used their agency to do just this. The argument for coherence developed by Firestone and Shipps rests on the assumption that service organization managers have sufficient agency to decide whether, as well as how, to respond to the multiple external and internal pressures for change.

A second message is that developing the generic capacity to cope as effectively as possible with the complexity of public service change across all system levels is a worthwhile focus for policy making. Capacity building could support local innovation within parameters governing acceptable variations in service provision. One way of freeing up capacity is what Wallace and Hoyle construe as a temperate approach to policy making and change leadership. Temperance fosters emergent change through local innovativeness for incremental improvement that is sensitive to locally contingent circumstances. More proactive means might include facilitating local learning communities whose members can provide mutual support, on the lines suggested by Casebeer, or interventions designed to foster conditions favouring knowledge transfer and adaptation as identified by Hartley and Rashman.

A third message, a corollory of the second, is for policy-makers and organization managers whose degree of agency puts them in a position to regulate the amount of complexity faced by administrators and service providers. Beware of reform policy making that significantly adds further complexity, because the modest potential for enhancing coping capacity is far outstripped by the potential for policy-makers to devise unmanageably complex change programmes.

Where might practically oriented academic enquiry productively go from here?

Individual contributors have offered an extensive menu of ideas in their chapters for taking forward research and theory building relating to their area of interest. The key overarching message here is that there is plenty of scope for engaging with complexity and using different approaches to do so. These approaches could span investing in social science-based research to develop knowledge-for-understanding to expand the range of ideas that might inform policy and practice (Wallace, Chapter 1), through to the collaborative development of knowledge-for-action that directly engages with and impacts on participants' practice (Casebeer, Chapter 10). It was noted above how the empirical base for the ideas developed by the various contributors is confined to education and health services in a few countries. Much could be done to assess whether and, if so, how far these ideas apply to other services and other national settings. Conversely, such studies could generate new ideas which may have implications for the services and national settings covered in this book.

It will be important to avoid unhelpful reification of organizations and the inter-organizational change process that is often a feature of knowledge-for-action enquiry. If government and public service organizations are treated as if capable of corporate action independent of the people who constitute their parts, attention becomes deflected from conflicting interests, differential access to power and different interpretations among members of these organizations. Berger and Luckmann (1967:

106) define reification as the 'apprehension of the products of human activity *as if* they were something other than human products – such as facts of nature'. As noted in Chapter 2, collective nouns such as government, healthcare system, school, are inescapable. But reification of organizations reduces the potential for exploring the dynamics of complexity and of coping strategies that work in settings where people's actions and interpretations may be ambiguous, diverse, incompatible and contested. To this end, a way forward could be to opt for the main unit of analysis for studies of the change process to be cross-administrative level. The collection of data could then span the experiences of people based in organizations at each of the different levels being investigated. It could focus on interaction as stakeholders attempt to influence practice at other organizational levels, both the hierarchical flow from central government to service organization level, and the contra-flow from service organization to central government level.

Whatever the theoretical orientation adopted, it seems equally important to keep the focus sufficiently broad to gain a deep sense of interaction in its context. The complexity of managing change dictates that that those involved – from politicians to frontline service providers – have to engage in multi-tasking to cope with whatever change is at hand alongside other changes and the remainder of their ongoing work. A profitable line of enquiry would be to explore how stakeholders within and between all system levels variably set, shape and cope with the evolving profile of changes that they face (including any reforms, emergent innovations, unplanned environmental changes requiring a response), all in the context of their other work. This focus could generate knowledge-for-understanding about the coping strategies that keep services running while simultaneously instigating and mediating change connected with service provision and its management. International comparative studies would help determine which strategies translate between national and service contexts, and at how abstract a level.

The terrain is self-evidently huge. But individual small-scale or larger studies could be designed to tackle a defined area. It would even seem plausible in principle to plan complementary investigations that tackle different areas or replicate the same areas in different service or national contexts. Their combined results could contribute towards a more robust understanding of the complexity of public service change and strategies for coping with it. The outcomes of such a research base could inform the development of realistic and context-sensitive policy and practice to improve the management of public service change. Depending on the political will to encourage emergent innovation to deal with local problems, to invest in capacity building for coping, to avoid adding avoidable complexity to public service change, and to sponsor practically oriented research, there are grounds for cautious optimism that we could collectively get better at managing the relatively unmanageable.

REFERENCE

Berger, P. and Luckmann, T. (1967) *The Social Construction of Reality*. Harmondsworth: Penguin.

INDEX